JOHN HUSTON

also by Axel Madsen

fiction

BORDERLINES

non-fiction

HEARTS AND MINDS
MALRAUX
THE NEW HOLLYWOOD
WILLIAM WYLER
BILLY WILDER

JOHN HUSTON

by Axel Madsen

Doubleday & Company, Inc.
Garden City, New York
1978

CONTENTS

PART I

PART II

v

Pray madam, who were the company?
Why, there was all the world and his wife.

Jonathan Swift

PART I

PART I

I

JOHN HUSTON

John Huston is a tall, vigorous man whose voice has the quality of melted caramel. The red-brown eyes, set in the face of an ancient tortoise, glow like sapphires above enormous puffy bags. As he sits on a rock in the Beverly Hills palm garden, his hands dangle from the steep angle of his bony knees.

Huston is a movie director who has always dressed the part, always flown to remote locations with hundreds of kilos of excess wardrobe baggage. At the Beverly Hills Hotel, which is linked to various episodes of his life, he is in a ginger suit and tweedy deerstalker. Unusual clouds race across the California sky. Huston has had a wonderful time making a lot of wonderful movies and the circumstances of their making are often more memorable than the movies themselves.

He is living slightly more cautiously since aneurism of the aorta had him at death's door in 1977 while he was preparing *Love and Bullets, Charlie.* That film—like *Saud*, which he started less than six months after he left the hospital was a modern production, "packaged" in a way that was inconceivable ten or fifteen years earlier. Huston has stayed relevant in the new math of moviemaking. In a world of stars obeying their own arithmetic, of deal memos, arbitrations, amendments and of financiers who in addition to box office certainty need tax shelters, he is very much in command, even if his director's chair is a self-effacing distance from his actors' emoting. John has always been good at keeping the risk-reward adrenalin flowing.

He gets up from his stone and gives the sky a long, wrinkled squint. He carries himself in a stiff slouch as he crosses the cramped lawn toward the main building and heads for the deep shadow of the Polo Lounge. The springy lope has slowed to a graceful gait, but in his seventies he looks ten years younger than he is, with his close-cropped white hair and beard framing the corrugated mosaic of his handsome, lived-in face. His voice and his way of leaning in and wrapping velvet resonances around you add a rustle of promise and mood to his expressions of enthusiasm, surprise, and ennui. His vocabulary ranges from words of eight syllables to four letters, but there are no showbiz italics. His body English is round and rich and conveys literacy and dignity. Some years ago he was, after his friend Orson Welles, the most sought-after narrator. In *The Bible*, the voice of God was, appropriately, his.

Some have said he is out of touch with real human emotions, that he is a laughing sadist who will jab at your soul with an icepick. Others have said he is a shy, tender idealist, still others that he is really a very forlorn, lonely man whose public style is an impenetrable bluff of rude theatrical charm. When interviewed too closely, he is glib and puckish, parrying questions rather than answering them. His ready laugh can give way to a non-verbal No—a stabbing stare. "*The Life and Times of Judge Roy Bean* was an extravagant concoction—not in money but in ideas." Stare. End of discussion. As another phrase crosses his mind he smiles. "Perhaps my greatest contribution has been that of keeping certain films from being out-and-out disgraces, of turning them into mediocrities instead. Take *The Mackintosh Man*. We all needed money, Paul Newman, John Foreman, and I. I'm not rich. I've spent it as I've gone along. I have to work. But I've had a helluva good time."

In the Polo Lounge, he finds an unobtrusive table and orders a discreet drink. Since the illness he is supposed to watch his health but he hasn't been able to cut out the smoking. As for alcohol, he says he didn't ask the doctors and they didn't men-

4

tion it. "So, I still enjoy a drink." His last feature shot entirely in the United States was *Fat City*, another of his works to have found vindication in history rather than the box office. *The Treasure of the Sierra Madre* was only a modest moneymaker in its first release. *The Asphalt Jungle* never earned its cost back, nor did *Beat the Devil*. "And people very often say to me that *The Misfits* is their favorite among my works. Well, it is to me too. But it got mixed reviews at the time and was not a success, to my disappointment and also to my surprise."

At other times *Moby Dick* is his favorite. Puffing cautiously on a Don Diego, he will frown and say critics never recognized the *idea* of *Moby Dick*. "And that is that the whole thing is a blasphemy. Melville hated God! I never saw Ahab as a ranting madman and Peck furnished a kind of nobility, a heroic stature, O'Neillesque. But the role didn't coincide with their ideas about Ahab."

His father died in the Beverly Hills Hotel. John's chance, his *big* chance, he says when the Jack Daniel's and water arrives, was being the son of Walter Huston and of Rhea Gore, a newspaperwoman. It was his father who kept him from skidding totally out of control in his youth. After John tried out as an itinerant prize-fighter and between stabs at being a short-story writer, a journalist on his mother's paper, and a sidewalk artist in Paris, Walter Huston had him hired as a writer on the pictures he starred in. Walter and John had a rare, loving father-son relationship that John didn't manage to give his own children. Anjelica remembers a childhood between a young mother whose talents were not acknowledged and a father who wasn't there much. To get his daughter's forgiveness, John gave her *A Walk with Love and Death* as a seventeenth-birthday gift. It didn't occur to him to ask her first if she wanted to be a movie star.

Darryl Zanuck has said he doesn't envy John his talent or his success but his friends. Huston collects people—bums, moochers, philosophical drunks, talkative tarts; and his various homes have always been half full of people in need of getting back on their feet. But he easily gets bored and needs new people to feed on. "When you are with him you have his un-

5

divided attention—until he feels the need to move on," Lauren Bacall says, "then there you are with egg on your face." Humphrey Bogart loved him like a brother and affectionately called him The Monster and Double Ugly. John was Bogey's kind of snake charmer, a natural-born antiauthoritarian, a guy with panache and style. Bogey thought John had more color than 90 per cent of Hollywood's actors. When John called and said, "Hey, kid, let's make this picture," Bogey knew he was being conned but he also knew he would have a great time. John has always called grown men, "Kid," and men say he is "all guy," a man's man.

Women think differently. Marilyn Monroe said she couldn't see how a woman could be around John without falling in love with him. His secretaries always do, because of the caramel voice and because they become victims of his torture. He made one of them his fifth wife. Olivia de Havilland, who almost became the third Mrs. Huston, says he is capable of "tremendous love of a very tense order." Evelyn Keyes, who did become No. 3, says that when married he continues to conduct himself as a bachelor, meaning that at parties he takes ladyfriends into the next room and closes the door on wife and guests. She remembers tender togetherness and moments when she thought the marriage might actually work, even if now and then he was still flying apart. When he divorced her, in a hurry in Mexico, he had nineteen-year-old Enrica Soma seven months pregnant. Ricki was the wife who lasted the longest.

No matter what experience people have gone through with him, he leaves them a little dazed. He is unpredictable to work with, inconsistent and volatile and, like a prosecuting attorney, he has a way of taking people apart. He can't write by himself but must have someone with him. "When I put pencil to paper, I find myself sketching," he says. "I can't write alone—I get too lonely." In his moments of inspiration, his script collaborators have stood in awe. At other times they have found the experience degrading and needed months to find themselves again. Jean-Paul Sartre wrote an unfilmable eight-hundred-page *Freud* script without realizing John didn't understand Freud; by the time Ray Bradbury was through with *Moby Dick*, he had written twelve hundred pages of outlines and screenplay; Leonard Gardner cried each time John added anything to *Fat City*; John Milius' revenge for the way the *Judge Roy Bean* script finally looked on the screen was to *cast* Huston in one of his own pictures. The humiliations of writing the final version of *The African Queen* drove Peter Viertel to publish a novel starring a thinly disguised Huston as a macho director who becomes a crazed big-game hunter and wrecks the preparations for a picture in Africa.

Not that John cannot stand in awe of others, "Let me tell you about Tennessee Williams on *The Night of the Iguana*. Tony Veiller and I had a pretty good scene written where Burton is alone in his room in a fever and in a drunk, and all these things are going on inside him. Sue Lyon comes in and tries to seduce him and he is doing everything in his power to keep away from the girl. Well, we gave the scene to Tennessee to see what he'd think of it. The only change he wrote was the thing that made the scene. When the girl opens the door suddenly, a glass falls onto the floor leaving broken bits of glass scattered around the room. When the scene is played both of them are barefoot. Burton walks on it and doesn't even feel his feet being shredded. The girl sees this and joins him walking barefoot across the glass. That was the difference between a pedestrian scene and an extraordinary one."

Huston has a gift for taking notoriously high-strung individuals on tense, emotional rollercoaster trips, to con and cajole, to flatter and to overpower actors and other collaborators to come along on his investigations of forlorn hopes, criminal conspiracies, tensions of betrayals, and the inner geometries of modern sensibilities. "I wouldn't mind if he would only sweat once in a while," Richard Burton has said. "At least it would show he is human."

Film crews like him because of his habit of referring all technical questions to them and of agreeing to whatever they ask. Producers have felt he spends too much time amusing them with practical jokes and catering to their whims, but the crews love him and will work themselves half to death whenever he asks them to do so. Literally. *The African Queen* was finished

7

in Uganda with Katharine Hepburn desperately sick with dysentery and crew members carrying equipment around while shaking with malaria. One man died of malaria in Chad on *The Roots of Heaven*, where the company doctor logged nearly one thousand sick calls. Eddie Albert became delirious, and Errol Flynn shortened his last months with booze and drugs. Clark Gable's response to John's goading on *The Misfits* contributed to the heart attack that killed him two weeks after the wrap.

John himself is immune to the dangers. Excepting his wartime moviemaking, which saw him fly camera runs against Japanese positions in the Arctic and run ahead of his cameramen toward German lines in Italy, his closest call came on *Moby Dick* when a dummy whale he was on broke its towline in mid-Atlantic.

He is a very good shot, a superb horseman, and an inveterate gambler. He is still working partly because he has lost fortunes since as a twenty-one-year-old he blew his first publisher's advance in casinos at Saratoga. The eight hundred-plus acre ranch he owned in Encino in the 1940s and 1950s would, in the inflated Southern California real estate market of today, make him a multimillionaire, but it went the way of the $5,000-a-week salaries he had studios pay him in cash on Friday and never seemed to hang onto beyond Saturday. Making a killing on the thoroughbreds he bought or on the crap tables he couldn't resist has never been enough for him. Wives, friends, associates, and bookmakers have pleaded with him, but he has never listened. Viertel's novel has a chapter where the fictionalized Huston says how a thoroughbred he pushed too hard made him realize his own limits—the worst realization anyone can make. The horse was a nice two-year-old filly, but cleaning up at six-furlong races was not enough for him and he entered her in a mile race against really good colts. "Well, for six furlongs she beat them all and then at the three-quarter post she stopped as if someone had shot her through the chest with a six-inch gun and the field went by her and she lost. It broke her heart and she never won again and I went home and lay down on my bed and saw my life absolutely clearly, for what it was worth. I was that filly, Pete. A seven-thousand-dollar claiming race, that's what you can win, I told myself, and my career stopped dead for two years after that race." The Irish citizenship in 1964 was one way of escaping the income attachments of the Internal Revenue Service.

Because of his desperate need for money, his career includes assignments accepted without hope, and he has jumped, fallen, or been pushed from a number of other deadbeat projects. Of late, he has prospered as a craggy character actor in films less distinguished than most of his own. When these pictures are filmed in the United States his parts are scheduled down to the last day. For complicated reasons that have to do with the IRS he, like his friend Orson Welles, can only work a limited number of days in his native country.

He has been accused of becoming bored and leaving the final stages of his films in other people's hands, where they have been changed, sometimes ruined. His answer is a benign smile and a "that's show business" shrug. He has directed most of the legendary screen idols, often with a sporting irreverence for their projected images. His actual setside directing relies on a certain studied passivity and on carrying the film in the making in his own head. Actors accustomed to overdirection are uneasy the first time they work with him. When Claire Trevor asked for a few pointers at the start of *Key Largo*, he told her, "You're the kind of drunken dame whose elbows are always a little too big, your voice a little too loud. You're very sad, very resigned. Like this." He leaned against the bar with a peculiarly heavy sadness. It was the leaning she caught onto and, without further instruction, developed into an Oscar-winning performance. David Niven says John likes to keep the actor's first tentative approach and, through rehearsals, build it up, then have the cameraman watch a run-through and, while technicians light the scene, retire to his canvas chair with a box of panatelas and a good book.

His open secret is spending more time on casting than telling actors to move from camera-left to camera-right. "When I cast a picture, I do most of my directing right there in finding the right person. I use actors with strong personalities, ones who

9

are like the characters they play and then I try to guide them through the picture as discreetly as possible. Acting is part intuitive and part technique. The English train their actors to be superb technicians, to take on any shape, and it's marvelous. Americans tend to rely on charisma and they are better at expressing conflict in nonverbal ways. Some actors like to talk about what they're going to do and I've discovered over the years it's not really to get information, or your opinion, but just to talk their way into it. Others do almost no talking. On *Reflections in a Golden Eye* I suppose I addressed myself to Brando no more than a dozen times during the making of the picture. Just stood back and watched this phenomenon."

A prodigious reader, he regrets that he can only get through three or four books in a week. In the words of Henry Blanke, the Warner Brothers house producer who gave him his first chance to direct, Huston has "an amazing capacity for falling for, and losing himself in, relatively mediocre fiction," but John considers himself fortunate to have worked on a number of stories by W. R. Burnett and Dashiell Hammett, authors he thinks vastly underrated. His acknowledged influences are Rudyard Kipling, James Joyce, Ernest Hemingway, and Eugene O'Neill. He pored over Kipling as a boy and found adventure, high honor, and distant, shimmering horizons. Walter's breakthrough on Broadway came in *Desire Under the Elms* and it was as an eighteen-year-old that John sat watching his father go through rehearsals with the playwright. "I think I learned more about films from O'Neill than anyone—what a scene consists of, and so forth." Joyce was language and a filmization of *Portrait of the Artist as a Young Man* was an advanced project at one time. Hemingway was a feel for the times, grace under pressure. Huston wrote the script for *The Killers*, the only screen adaptation of any of his work that Hemingway liked. With Evelyn, John visited Papa and Mary at La Finca in Havana and still doesn't despair of making a film out of *Across the River and into the Trees*.

He has been a California expatriate for half his adult life and lives mostly in Mexico now. Like Hemingway, he has made

Europe his movable feast. Between pictures in Rome and in Vienna, he bivouacks at The Dorchester and the George V and goes gallery crawling in South Kensington and St. Germain des Prés. There was no conscious withdrawal from America in the beginning. He was just a little ahead of the pack in the 1950s and '60s when Hollywood went multinational.

He is a good drinker and used to say he got a little cockeyed before dinner but always went to bed sober. Now, he drinks less and talks about his battered body with awe. At his Mexican hideaway, built on rented Indian land at the edge of the jungle, he likes the sound of long drinks swishing in glasses to the accompaniment of the waves almost lapping his porch. He also likes to have people and animals around, and friends and cronies find their way to the small bay south of Puerto Vallarta to talk and drink, or just to sit silently with him and watch the sun sink into the Pacific. He loves art more than anything and likes to think his movies include moments of reserve when things aren't so much spelled out as artfully suggested.

The mature Hemingway, he feels, had this capacity for moving you by what he left out. Bogart had it too, a capacity for expressing not so much lack of feeling as why feelings aren't there. Great paintings, Huston says, can give the void a meaning. In a secular world, great art bestows if not immortality, at least timelessness and, perhaps, a sense of meaning. He loves pre-Columbian and Etruscan art because, like good modern art, it is direct—angles, form, and space rather than rendition of flesh tones, lacy trees, and sugary clouds. It is silly to confuse art with its objects.

He has enjoyed neither cult following nor track-record box office superstardom. His detractors—and they are many—say he is coasting on a reputation of a wronged individualist, with an excuse for every bad movie. His defenders say he is one of the few filmmakers who knows that poetry needs to be tough-minded. They call his charm the charm of American movies at their best—directness, generosity and a belief that things can be improved—and they applaud him for not playing it safe, even on big, expensive pictures and even if his daring hasn't always paid off. He claims he is not conscious of themes, yet a Hustonian hero does exist, most of the time someone who looks life in the teeth and then has the drive to go on kidding himself.

"After *The Treasure of the Sierra Madre*, the Europeans said my message was that the end didn't matter, that it was the means, the undertaking rather than the achievement that mattered. Well, that sounds pretty good." When pressed he *will* go a little further and say that although he doesn't set out to tell one story, his choice of stories is not accidental but something so deep in him he doesn't think about it.

When asked to sum himself up, he had this to say: "My greatest defect is misplaced faith in certain horses. I suppose my greatest virtue is that, in filming a scene, I refuse to compromise with anything but the best or, at least, the best as I see it.

"What defeats most men in life? Probably the fact that they make false gods for themselves and strive to attain things that don't have an enduring value for them. I've never had any goal except the immediate one, whatever that might be."

The movies have always lived as if there were no tomorrow, and no yesterday and Huston's wish is that the cinema remains in the mainstream, a mirror of popular demands for insights and ecstasy. To be all things to all men films must not confine themselves to expressions of distress, anguish, and anger but must be able to be elevating, cheerful and romantic. Authorship has given directors dignity, but it has also led to private works, obscurantism, pretentiousness, and unwieldy experimentalism. He likes packed moviehouses and feels grandiose, superlative advertising is insulting in deserted cinemas. The essence of movies is packed, entranced audiences, a multitude of livid, expectant faces hanging on the screen.

His most memorable films have celebrated singular men shaking their fists at destiny and going after dreams that often exceed their grasp. In the Hustonian world social success is an exercise, not an end to itself. Adventure, including amorous adventure, is there so we can refine ourselves and learn not so much to conquer each other as to master our own lives. Alienation doesn't lead us out of society but deeper into its maze, forcing us to learn about the evil we want to escape. As innocent bystanders, as moviegoers, we are changed by what we perceive.

2

YOUTH

The beginning was the stuff legends are made of.

John Marcellus Huston was born in Nevada, a town in western Missouri that his grandfather, an engineer and professional gambler, had, by the most ambitious version of the family legend, acquired in a poker game. John's father, Walter, was born in Toronto, the son of a Scottish mother, Elizabeth McGibbon, and the gambler Robert Houghston, whose father had come to America from Ireland in 1840. John's mother, Rhea (née Gore), descended from a Richardson family in Ohio. Her grandfather was a Colonel William P. Richardson who on April 23, 1863, received a silver-sheathed sword for his valor in fighting the Civil War in the 25th Regiment, Ohio Voluntary Infantry. The sword was still in the family.

Walter was to have taken up engineering but had become stage-struck in school. He liked to say that a hellfire and brimstone preacher turned him to acting. At eighteen he ran away from home and joined a traveling stock company. When a Canadian sheriff closed it down, he set out to take Broadway by storm. It was an expedition that was underfinanced, to put it mildly. Walter arrived in Manhattan clinging to the rods of a freight train. Semistarvation was broken, however, when he obtained a three-line part in a Richard Mansfield play. It was his "big chance," but stage fright gripped him. He fumbled his lines and Mansfield personally escorted Walter to the stage door, with the stern admonition to stay away from the theater, except as a paying member of the audience.

He refused to heed the advice, tramped from agent to producer to agent and landed in a play called *Convict's Stripes*, written by Hal Reid. When the show closed, hunger forced Huston to join a road company presenting *The Sign of the Cross*. By 1905, Walter reached the decision that the stage was not for him and, to earn a living he beat his way back to engineering. The retreat coincided with his meeting Rhea Gore, a St. Louis girl with two passions—travel and horses. When he proposed, she said yes—if he would stay away from the theater. Walter was twenty-one and easily exchanged the stage for marital bliss. The newlyweds moved to Nevada, Missouri, ostensibly owned by grandfather Houghston. Soon Walter was gainfully employed at the local water and power company, learning civil engineering via a correspondence course. John was born August 5, 1906.

One night a year later, the town caught fire and the firemen kept telling engineer Huston to give them more water pressure. He obliged and overstrained the system. At daybreak, the young couple found it prudent to put a certain distance between themselves and the citizens of Nevada and, with their baby, they hopped on a train to Weatherford, Texas, another of grandfather Houghston's jackpots.

In 1950, when *Life* ran a twelve-page profile on "the most inventive director of his generation," Ken Postlethwaite, editor of the Nevada *Daily Mail*, sent the magazine a wire saying he could find no local record of Huston's birth but that he was certain the town had not been won by grandfather Houghston in a poker game. The telegram continued, LOCAL FILES SHOW TWO FIRES IN YEAR AFTER HUSTON BORN. WATER PRESSURE GOOD AT BOTH CONFLAGRATIONS. NO RECORD OF RUINED MACHINERY AT WATER PLANT. TOWN DIDN'T BURN DOWN. NO RECORD OF HUSTONS FLEEING COMMUNITY. When *Life* asked John to comment, he wrote "That is as it was told to me by my father, mother and grandmother and it is absolutely true. Perhaps Mr. Postlethwaite is confused."

Recorded evidence exists that Walter next worked for the Union Electric Light and Power Company in St. Louis, that he won an engineer's license and worked up to managership at the Charles Street plant. Walter, Rhea, and their baby boy lived three years in St. Louis. Rhea took up journalism and Walter earned the respect of his boss, who told him to keep it up. There was a great future in electrical engineering. "Everybody thought I'd be a good engineer," Walter would say later. "I even looked like one." John was an only child, curly-haired and with big ears. He was precocious and had a way of knitting his brow that made Walter think he could be an actor and that father and son could form a smart vaudeville act. Rhea would hear nothing of it.

Walter didn't see much of his family. His two sisters were taking opposite roads. The elder, Nan, was as much a bore as the younger, Margaret, was fascinating. Margaret was an opera singer. She had married W. T. Carrington, one of the founders of U. S. Steel, a man much older than she. An avid horseman, Carrington had fallen off a horse in New York's Central Park and left his young widow a millionaire. She kept the townhouse on Park Avenue but instead of returning to the lyrical theater, she became a patron of the arts, a speech therapist who gave private elocution lessons to actors she found worthy of her attention. Nan had remained a spinster.

When John was three, his parents split up, Walter to return to the theater, Rhea continuing her newspapering, first in St. Louis and later in Los Angeles. For most of his childhood, John shuttled between the gambling, horse-loving Rhea, who taught him that all horses in a race but one are losers, and the three-shows-a-day-and-catch-the-sleeper-to-Cleveland vaudeville life of Walter, growing up in many parts of the United States but actually spending most of his adolescence with his mother in Los Angeles.

"I traveled a great deal with each of my parents," he recalls. "From overnight fleabags with Dad to spacious hotels with Mother. She hated France but loved Turkey. She was crazy about playing the ponies and I remember she was broke once, down to ten dollars. We were out at the track and she put the money on a hundred-to-one longshot that came in. She taught me that money is for spending."

Rhea was brutally realistic. She had no patience for fairy tales and burst her son's Easter morning fantasy when he was five, telling him, "Listen I dyed those lousy eggs and hid them myself. There *is* no Easter Bunny."

Peter Viertel's 1953 novel *White Hunter Black Heart* contains a passage where the fictitious Huston remembers himself as a fifteen-year-old living with his widowed mother. "She's a woman in her late thirties, still kind of beautiful, with a great manner. Their life is drab, colorless. They have only one thing to make them happy and that's their love for horses. They save on food all week long, just to be able to go to the livery stable on Sunday and hire a couple of hacks and go riding for an hour. Every Sunday they do that. They each have their favorite horse. That's what they live for, this one hour of happiness a week, when they can ride out into the country together. Well, a guy comes into their life, a kind of flashy guy, who's passing through the town, a salesman. He's there on a business deal that will keep him in town for a couple of months and so he goes on the make for the widow. Of course she has to work all week long and she doesn't get a chance to go out with the guy on any day except Sunday. At first she fights it, and goes riding with the boy anyway. But she's been lonely too many years. Nobody has made love to her. And so finally she gives in and makes a date with this guy who's been after her. And the kid goes out alone. Well, it happens once and then the next week again, and then their whole life together collapses. The kid doesn't complain. He's too proud to. He just goes out by himself every Sunday morning on his horse, and when he gets way out in the country he gets off, and sits down and cries. The horse stands there and waits for him to finish, and then he gets on again."

When John was fifteen, Rhea married a vice-president of the Northern Pacific Railway. John was stuck in one school or another now and then, but mostly he was on the road with his father and his father's vaudeville partner and mistress.

Her name was Bayonne Whipple. For twelve years, the

vaudeville act of Whipple and Huston was a headliner, and in 1915, Walter made Bayonne his second wife.

There was one skit Walter did for his son alone. "I was six when I first saw Dad do this act," John would say in his special tone of wonderment. "Dad played a house painter, come to paint this lady's house. There was a picture of her husband inside the front door. The husband's face would begin to make faces, and then this big head would shove through the door with electric lights for eyes. And I'd roar. And Dad would sing, 'I Haven't Got the Do-Re-Mi.'"

Walter called the skit "Spooks." By the 1920s, Whipple and Huston were a headliner act on the Keith and Orpheum circuits. Deciding they weren't really getting anywhere, Huston started building a new act, investing $5,000 in equipment and a cast. The Keith people liked the act but weren't willing to pay more than $1,250 a week for it. Walter held out for another $1,500 and the Schuberts, launching an abortive foray into vaudeville, offered $1,750 a week.

When John was twelve, he was pronounced mortally ill with a heart murmur and put in a sanatorium where every bite he ate and every breath he drew could be professionally analyzed. As a result, he became virtually paralyzed with timidity and fear. "I haven't the slightest doubt that if things had gone on like that I'd have died inside a few months," he told James Agee when the author-critic interviewed him for the *Life* profile. His only weapon was a blind desperation of instinct. Late at night when the medical sages were asleep, he sneaked out and slid down a nearby rocky moss-covered waterfall to frolic in icy water. "The first few times, it scared the hell out of me, but I realized—instinctively anyhow, it was exactly fear that I had to overcome."

When they caught him at this primordial self-therapy, the doctors were aghast. On second thought, they decided he might live.

Sent to a boarding school in Los Angeles in 1918, John was growing up to be a six-foot-two beanstalk carrying himself in a perpetual gangling, graceful slouch. School didn't interest him but he had a vast appetite for knowledge and a prodding mind.

18

By his late teens, he was opinionated and streetwise. He spent 1923–24 at Los Angeles' Lincoln High School. There was a high school right around the corner from his house but he preferred Lincoln High because Fidel La Barba and Jackie Fields, two future boxing champions, went to Lincoln.

"After school we boxed," he remembers, "at the Los Angeles Athletic Club and the Hollywood Athletic Club. We were amateurs but there was a kind of secret payoff. The winner would get a watch which he would hand back to its owner for ten or fifteen dollars' kitty we all kicked in to. We had to make some money. Not I, my family was all right, but there were guys who needed money to survive."

What appealed to John was that as a boxer he wouldn't have to stay in one place but could travel up and down California. He ended his amateur status with a broken nose and the Amateur Lightweight Championship of California, then became a pro. As he would say in 1972 when he made *Fat City* about small-time boxing in California, "I wasn't bad, I wasn't bad at all."

"It was little towns like Monrovia, Bakersfield, Stockton. They paid you fifteen or twenty dollars. And there was the Springfree Athletic Club in L.A., a marvelous place which belonged to black fighters, a kind of huge shed derisively called Madison Square Garden West. Sure. They set up bouts with names and weights they invented. You went there and they nodded in your direction and said, 'You, you fight with this guy.' I fought twice, under two different names. The whole thing was a joke. I was seventeen and passed welterweight."

Walter was rather proud of his fighter son—or so he told him, but to enlarge the boy's horizon he invited him to New York for the summer of his eighteenth birthday.

At forty, Walter was making his breakthrough—*sans* Bayonne, although he stayed married to her for another seven years. And the theater world he and his sister Margaret evolved in was exciting enough to impress an impressionable young man.

After fifteen years of song-and-dance routines and road stock company acting, Walter had appeared on Broadway in the title role of Zona Gale's *Mr. Pitt,* a sentimental play about small-town America. He had been so convincing as Pitt—a meek, pathetic figure—and in a similar part in *The Easy Mark,* that he was almost typecast.

But in October 1924, his new brother-in-law, Robert Edmond Jones, suggested him to Eugene O'Neill for *Desire Under the Elms.* Jones—Bobby to everybody—was a striking-looking New Englander whose long pale face and large gray eyes were set off by a beard and unruly shocks of reddish-brown hair. Born and brought up in New Hampshire, he was, as Brooks Atkinson would write, "of the Emersonian faith and a believer in the oversoul." Like O'Neill he was haunted by an unhappy rural childhood and the gothic images of his family background would help O'Neill's thinking when he wrote *Mourning Becomes Electra.*

Bobby was younger than Margaret, who continued to call herself Mrs. Carrington. Since he was a homosexual, she sent him to Vienna to see Sigmund Freud and later claimed the father of psychoanalysis had cured her husband. They were a strange couple—she with her millions, her speech coaching, Park Avenue townhouse, and, on the West Coast, a baronial home in Santa Barbara; he as a director and scenic designer who imparted an exaltation to every production he was associated with. Bobby and Mrs. Carrington were to remain devoted to each other to the end of their lives. When they were old and cancer-stricken, they would always get up to sit and watch dawn together.

As man and wife, their first theatrical triumph had come in 1920. Together with his new wife, Blanche, John Barrymore had spent some time at White Sulphur Springs, West Virginia, where he had recited *Richard III* in the woods as a child. Soon he knew the whole play by heart again, but he found his voice had a high nasal tone which bothered him. He wanted to stage *Richard III* and Blanche knew Mrs. Carrington as the person who knew more about voice training than anyone else. For three months, Barrymore studied with Margaret, six hours a day, while Bobby went to England to assemble costumes and to study scenery. The opening night of *Richard III* was Barrymore's greatest triumph, with the final curtain going down at one thirty in the morning. In 1921, Mrs. Carrington coached him for his no less memorable *Hamlet*.

As John came to New York to spend the summer with his father, Bobby was both the director and the stage designer of *Desire Under the Elms*. When he suggested his brother-in-law to O'Neill, the playwright was skeptical. In *Mr. Pitt* and *The Easy Mark*, Huston had projected characters who were the exact opposite of the harsh, tough old farmer. O'Neill agreed to let Walter read for the part and was immediately impressed.

John was captivated by all this. He attended every rehearsal, met O'Neill, already a bitter alcoholic, and thought he would rather be a writer than a boxer. Walter was perfect in *Desire Under the Elms*. "There have only been three actors in my plays who managed to realize the characters as I originally saw them," O'Neill would say toward the end of his life, naming Charles Gilpin in *The Emperor Jones*, Louis Wolheim in *The Hairy Ape* and Walter Huston in *Desire Under the Elms*.

Walter, who loved his only son and showed his affection with pride and confidence, did better than introducing John to famous theater people. He got him a part in the Greenwich Village dramatization of Sherwood Anderson's *The Triumph of the Egg*. The comedy was double-billed with O'Neill's *Diff'rent* at the Provincetown Playhouse. The New York *Times* reviewed the plays and gave John a glowing paragraph: "John Huston, son of the Walter Huston who is playing in O'Neill's 'Desire Under the Elms,' made his first Provincetown appearance as Father in the Anderson play. His work was gorgeous. Young Mr. Huston, beyond a doubt, is an actor who should be kept on display in New York theaters."

It was a great summer. John didn't live with his father and stepmother but had his own small apartment on Macdougal Street, above one occupied by an aspiring actor named Sam Jaffe. Walter was there for the eighteenth birthday party. Jaffe had asked John what he wanted as a present and he had said a horse. "Well," Huston says, "Sam, the kindest, most retiring guy in the world, had gone out and bought the oldest, saddest,

21

most worn-out gray mare. It was all wonderful. The best birthday I ever had."

In October, John was back in Los Angeles for an unhappy year with his mother and railroading stepfather. The following summer, he was in New York again and the next year, he was in Los Angeles—and married.

Not much is known about Dorothy Jeanne Harvey, who in the subsequent divorce proceedings was described as an actress. Agee would pass off the union as "a high-school marriage [which] lasted only briefly," but John was twenty when he married Dorothy and when he sued for divorce in 1933, they had been married over six years. There is a poignant paragraph in *White Hunter Black Heart* where the middle-aged director remembers his first wife: "I knew I had lost the best dame I was ever likely to meet, and I'd lost her because I'd acted like a horse's ass. And it turned out that way. I'd done something wrong and I had to pay for it, and so every time I fell in love again after that, I knew the disenchantment would ultimately turn up. And it did. Never failed. Because you get one chance at everything in life, and that's all." Walter would make a revealing comment on his son's first marriage to Evelyn Keyes when *her* marriage to John was in ruins in 1950. "I'm sorry," Walter told Evelyn when she tried to explain. "And I understand. John has always been a bit of a free soul. I'll tell you something, for what it's worth. When he married the first time, he was twenty and broke, and I gave him five hundred dollars to set up housekeeping. That was a lot of money then. He spent the entire amount on a chandelier." After a pause, Walter added, "I haven't worried about him too much since then."

A free soul. Without Dorothy, John took off for Mexico. The year was 1927 and, he would say, "I was looking for adventure."

Mexico would become a lifelong love. "It was an extraordinary country and I had friends who were just as extraordinary —generals, politicos, and pistoleros!" he would fondly remember late in life. "They were all driving in Pierce-Arrows. They never let their chauffeurs drive. The chauffeur sat in the back seat, breaking out the champagne and handing the bottles forward. They drove like crazy!"

John's meeting with the first general—a cavalry officer married to a German lady who owned a riding school—was tame enough. Always trying to improve his riding skills, John decided to take lessons from Hattie Weldon. One day, the general asked if John really had enough money to continue the riding lessons. "Because if you don't we can give you an honorary rank and you can ride in competitions."

John said, Si, señor,—and for the next six months he rode in cavalry shows. He became a top jumping rider and performed with the Mexican Army horse show at Madison Square Garden.

But the real fun was not visiting the States. It was in small Mexican towns with his fellow officers. "We'd make the rounds, starting with a poker game in some big hacienda in the morning. We'd take the game to a brothel, then finally to somebody's hotel room where we'd play a kind of Mexican roulette. When some guy won a big pot we'd turn out the lights, cock a loaded pistol, and throw it into the air. The pistol would go off when it hit the ceiling. Then we'd turn the lights back on to see who was dead. If the winner survived he could keep the dough. If not, we all split even."

After the Madison Square Garden horse show, John resigned his commission. But he was barely back in California before he longed for Mexico again. When Walter sent him some money, he booked passage on a coastal steamer and sailed down the Pacific Coast to Acapulco. The boat stopped at several sleepy fishing villages, including Puerto Vallarta which, nearly forty years later, he would put on the tourist map with *The Night of the Iguana*.

"There was no road from Acapulco to Mexico City in those days," he remembers. "You had to do it on the back of a mule. It took seventeen days."

In the spring of 1928 he was back in California. Author Patrick Mahony was a sixteen-year-old schoolboy and aspiring actor who was to remember John that year at Mrs. Carrington's Villa Aposa in Santa Barbara. "John was a very slim, nice-look-

23

ing and pompous twenty-one-year-old. He was an awful nice hanger-on. He put on terrific airs and his aunt called him a conceited ass. Of course he didn't pay much attention to me or to my mother who had met Mrs. Carrington on an Atlantic crossing. Mrs. Carrington didn't really trust her nephew but she knew he was smarter and more ruthless than anyone in the family. She was no longer young and to see her in a bathing suit was awkward, but she was someone who had an odd charm, even for a sixteen-year-old. Something always happened when she was around."

John *was* a conceited ass, Mahony would tell Huston when he visited him in Ireland in 1963.

When John had enough of cadging from his aunt, he went to New York to visit with his father—and his mother, who was now a reporter on the New York *Graphic*. In Mexico he had written a book of sorts, a retelling of the many "Frankie and Johnny" ballads of his St. Louis childhood. He called his adaptation "a kind of musical play for puppets," and showed it to his father, who gave it to the Albert and Charles Boni publishers who, to everybody's astonishment, paid the young author a five-hundred-dollar advance. That decided it for John. Why, he was going to be a writer.

3

HANGING OUT

The five hundred dollars went fast enough. With the Boni advance in his pocket, the twenty-one-year-old neophyte author took the train to Saratoga Springs and headed directly for the casino crap tables. By the most ambitious version of the disposal of the money, he ran it up to $11,000 in one evening before losing it all. It is a matter of faith in early Hustoniana whether one believes he actually reached that figure,* but he did lose it all and to recoup, took a friendly interest in writing.

Frankie and Johnny is an astonishingly mature work, a funny, hard satire in the Brechtian vein on the 1899 shooting by Frankie Baker of Allen Britt which had inspired a number of "Frankie and Johnny" and "Frankie" ballads about the cakewalker and her lover "who done her wrong." Dedicated to Dorothy, Huston's *Frankie and Johnny* has Frankie on the scaffold with the noose around her neck when the curtain opens. "Has the condemned anything to say afore we take in the slack?" the sheriff asks with his hands on the hangman's rope. Before she is hanged, Frankie tells her story, "How I loved an' done wrong" working for Johnny Halcomb in his mother's cathouse, how she saved money in her stocking, how

---

* In 1967 "constant dollars" $22,000 and, in inflated 1978 money, $41,800.

he discovered her roll of bills, refused to believe it was all for him, how he went up to Nelly and how Frankie shot him for his faithlessness, and now the sheriff can pull the cord since she will join her man in the grave. Boni published the slim volume with lovely cubist illustrations by Miguel Covarrubias, a Mexican caricaturist famous for his *Vogue* drawings of the Revue Nègre. The volume included twenty versions of the "Frankie and Johnny" songs and the St. Louis *Dispatch* news story of the actual 1899 shooting.

John didn't really like the solitary métier of writing, even if it paid hard cash. He needed to bounce off things, needed fresh ideas coming to him, instead of formulating them in solitude. When he faced the white page, he had a tendency to doodle and sketch. He wrote a short story, however, which his father showed to his friend Ring Lardner, who showed it to his friend H. L. Mencken, who published it in the March 1929 issue of *American Mercury*. "Fools" was a first-person vignette of a pair of school chums who become small-time boxers hanging around arenas in Los Angeles suburbs. Harry, the narrator, is a tall, gangling kid who can win because of his long arms; his buddy is a compact Italian knot of nerves and muscles called Victor. One night when another boxer doesn't show, they are matched. They agree to fake it, but in the ring Harry can't help hitting Victor although he knows Victor can knock him cold anytime. Victor lets Harry bloody his nose and win the decision although the black fans boo the fight they clearly see is rigged. On the way home in a streetcar, Victor says, "Listen, I believe that Christ and Judas were in cahoots. I believe it was all laid out between."

Next, John sent Mencken another short story called "Figures of Fighting Men"; it was also bought and published.

Rhea had no high opinion of her son. Never had, apparently. During the making of *The Red Badge of Courage* when she had been dead for twelve years, John said, "Nothing I ever did pleased my mother," but in 1929 she got him a job on the *Graphic*. The journalistic experience was a disaster. "I was the world's lousiest reporter," John would admit. "I'm sure that I was fired more times than any reporter in the paper's history.

The city editor on nights hated my guts and he'd sack me at regular intervals, but the managing editor on days, a real nice fellow named Plummer, kept hiring me back."

The night editor got his revenge one night when John was out on assignment and a singer's pearl necklace had disappeared. Gallantly, reporter Huston offered to play private detective. "I figured I could get a great story out of it. When I went to meet the gal at her club the cops were there, and I had to admit I was a reporter for the *Graphic*. But they didn't believe me. So I told them to call the city editor. Well, this was the guy who kept firing me. They asked him if a reporter named Huston worked for the paper. 'Nope,' he said, 'I never heard of the sonofabitch.'" John's facts-be-damned approach to journalism caught up with him when he was sent over to New Jersey to cover a trial and he switched the names of the victim and the accused. This time his discharge was permanent.

Walter was making his first picture and John headed West. *Gentlemen of the Press* was a Paramount picture directed by Millard Webb, a fast newspaper melodrama with Walter as a boozy, big-time reporter. Walter didn't like Hollywood and would go back to New York on every possible occasion. "I was on the stage twenty-five years before I went to Hollywood and made all that money," he would say in 1935. "If it hadn't been for Broadway, the pictures never would have wanted me. I owe it to Broadway—and to myself, to come back."

All that money. The movies had learned to talk, and although the United States was headed into the Great Depression, Hollywood was embarking on its dizziest decade. Its combination of unlimited capital and professional expertise set it out on a prodigal, wasteful, and ruthless pursuit of excellence that made movies the world's most popular entertainment and the thirties the classic age of American cinema.

A ruinously expensive but finally profitable policy of buying the best talent, no matter where it came from, made Hollywood a company town. The moguls made the movies. They chose the story ideas, hired the talent, and bartered for stars on "loanout" from other studios and anointed favorite house directors. Everybody was under contract. Walter, too, to First

27

National. He was in demand and constantly loaned out—to D. W. Griffith and United Artists to play the title-role in *Abraham Lincoln,* to Metro-Goldwyn-Mayer to star opposite new bombshell Jean Harlow in the gangster drama *Beast of the City,* and to Universal Pictures for a pseudo-*Desire Under the Elms* called *A House Divided.* At forty-seven Walter was becoming a star.

He was also getting a new wife, divorcing Bayonne in Reno where people in a hurry could be granted a divorce in six weeks flat. John's new stepmother was Nanette Eugenia Sunderland, the actress daughter of the former mayor of Fresno, California. Nan had made her Broadway debut in 1927 in George M. Cohan's *The Baby Cyclone* and Walter had met her while they were both in *Elmer the Great.* There was no question of Nan's abandoning her career. She was under contract to Radio-Keith Orpheum (RKO) and during her first year of marriage was in *Trigger,* with Katharine Hepburn, Joel McCrea, and George Brent.

John didn't live with his father and stepmother, but had his own apartment. He was still married to Dorothy, but he went out with a married woman of striking beauty. Zita Johann was an actress of distant Hungarian origins with glowing dark eyes and a statuesque body. She had made her breakthrough opposite an equally unknown Clark Gable in Broadway's crusade against yellow journalism, *Machinal,* which had been costumed and designed by Bobby Jones. Irving Thalberg had brought her to Hollywood, put her under a Metro contract but not in any films. She had returned to New York, married would-be playwright-director John Houseman, and starred in *The Struggle,* D. W. Griffith's last picture. With an RKO contract but without Houseman, she had returned to Hollywood. Huston and Zita were an attractively odd couple, he a wobbly youth beginning to put on weight, she, in Houseman's phrase, "a beautiful and exciting and vulnerable" girl who had illuminated *Machinal* with a deep, tragic tenderness of her own. John and Zita were invited everywhere. He was always wonderful company; she was pretty.

Walter and Nan lived in a rented home on Camden Drive

in Beverly Hills and John had an apartment in Wilton Place off Hollywood Boulevard, but father and son were the best of friends. To keep his son from flying completely apart, Walter steered him toward work. A *House Divided* represented a first such chance. John was a writer, Walter told his young director, couldn't he perhaps work on the script?

John's contribution to the script of A *House Divided* was limited, but his friendship with the director and another young man who was down as assistant producer was immediate and lasting. William Wyler and Paul Kohner were a pair of Europeans brought to Hollywood by Universal's impish, impulsive, unpredictable, and cheerful founder, Carl Laemmle. On his mother's side, Wyler was the second cousin of Uncle Carl, who had a habit of collecting people. Each year on a visit to the spas of his native Germany he found ambitious young people whom he brought back to America and put to work at Universal. He had picked up Erich von Stroheim at the studio gate, Irving Thalberg on Long Island, Kohner at the spa in Carlsbad. On their way up Hollywood's greasy pole, half of filmdom's great names spent time at "Uncle Carl's film farm," as Universal Studio was less than affectionately nicknamed. Laemmle didn't know how to hang onto talent—he let Thalberg go to his rival, Louis B. Mayer, over a petty question of a raise—and in the hierarchy of studios, Universal was near the bottom. Its production was formula fare.

After a year as office boys in New York, Wyler and Kohner had managed to get themselves transferred to Universal City, and here their careers had diverged. Willy had become a director, first of two-reel Westerns, later of five-reelers. Paul's ascent had been more checkered. After a stint as assistant casting director and supervisor he had become someone generally considered to be Uncle Carl's nephew—a mistake Kohner rarely tried to dispel—and by 1929, the boss's roving ambassador.

Not counting twenty-six two- and five-reel Westerns, A *House Divided* was Wyler's sixth full-length film and his third talkie. John was impressed. Willy was only four years older than he.

A *House Divided* was a grim, Calvinistic plot scripted by

John Clymer and Dale Van Every from Olive Eden's magazine story. It told the story of Seth Law, a fisherman who likes his liquor straight, his women strong, and his somewhat delicate son not at all. Walter Huston was Seth Law, Ruth Evans a girl he gets from a matrimonial agency, and Kent Douglass the cowed son who falls in love with his stepmother. When Seth is ready to kill his own kin, son and stepmother decide to leave, but the night of their prepared departure a storm blows up, providing a big finish in the raging surf, with the girl adrift in the fishing boat, the elder Law tying himself to a smaller boat and rushing to her rescue and the son, to prove he is no weakling, swimming out to save her while the old man drowns.

The writing credits on A House Divided read: Screenplay John B. Clymer and Dale Van Every. Dialogue John Huston, but John would remember himself as being "no great shakes there, what I wrote didn't really go down." What impressed him was Wyler's directing on the sound stage. Lights, camera! And there was Willy taking Walter, Ruth Evans, and Kent Douglass through the paces. The raging sea was shot in the studio tank with process-screen photography, and the opening graveside scene where Seth Law buries his first wife in the back lot. Willy wanted to be creative with sound in the opening scene and put microphones inside the coffin so it scraped down the side, and he had the mourners throw pebbles instead of earth on the lid so it would *sound* dramatic.

Although by his own hindsight John had been "no great shakes" on A House Divided, his name showed up on two other 1932 Universal movies—Law and Order, starring his father under the direction of Edward Cahn (another of Uncle Carl's European discoveries) and Murders in the Rue Morgue, directed by Robert Florey, who, with James Whale, was Universal's horror "ace." The Frenchman had come to America all by himself and when Whale had been given Frankenstein, Florey was handed the Edgar Allan Poe classic. But John preferred the company of his own generation and if Willy and he became friends it was because the admiration was not one-sided. Wyler had come to America as an eighteen-year-old from his native Alsace and had always worked for Uncle Carl. The young Huston had bummed around and knew a lot about life out there beyond the studio gates. Besides crap games and dates with would-be actresses and starlets, bachelor Wyler could only think of getting a picture with a bigger budget, bigger stars, and perhaps a more significant story. He knew a lot about movies but not much about anything else.

Together with Wyler and Kohner, John attended the Glendale neighborhood preview of *A House Divided*. Women walked out in droves during the stark graveside opening which, as a result, was eliminated. Willy and John talked a lot about doing something contemporary and meaningful. Seventeen million Americans were out of work. President Hoover still insisted the nation's economy was basically sound although Franklin D. Roosevelt had just won the Democratic nomination in Chicago and, to unseat Hoover, asked for "bold, persistent experimentation." John had traveled the lower rungs of society, including poorest Mexico. He read widely and through his father, Bobby, and O'Neill was up on the latest trends and thrusts in the theater. The new thing, he said, was to use symbolism in the service of naturalism.

Aware directors wanted to make socially significant movies and several of Willy's older colleagues were actually getting away with it. Right here at Universal, the elegant John Stahl had made *Back Street* and at Warner's Mervyn LeRoy made *I Am a Fugitive from the Chain Gang*. King Vidor had made *Street Scene* and was rumored to be preparing a real proletarian statement, *Our Daily Bread*. To get themselves into the proper framework, Willy and John spent twenty-four hours on skid row. As Wyler remembers it, they dressed in old clothes, brought ten cents each, and headed downtown: "We got a lousy free dinner in a mission after we had listened to a spiel and signed statements to the effect that we had come to Christ. Then we spent the night in the flophouse. Ten cents it cost."

Almost by mistake, Universal had bought the rights to Oliver LaFarge's 1929 Pulitzer Prize winner, *Laughing Boy*. The novel was a piercing look at Indians and whites rubbing together in dehumanizing squalor and the theme was enough to make any studio nervous—miscegenation, with Slim Girl, Laughing Boy's wife, playing a white lover against her husband.

Willy said he would like to take a crack at *Laughing Boy*. He had John hired for a first draft and together they took off for Navajo country to write and scout locations. In Flagstaff, Arizona, they met LaFarge and spent days conferring with him, and in Monument Valley they lived two weeks with the Navajos. "We visualized it like another *Nanook of the North*, another Robert Flaherty semidocumentary," Wyler remembers. "But we couldn't cast it. For Slim Girl, we made tests with Zita Johann . . . We worked at it for months but we couldn't get it off the ground."

Undaunted, they threw themselves on another Universal property, Daniel Ahearn's story, *The Wild Boys of the Road*. This was the Depression at its rawest, the tale of small-town boys leaving home to avoid being a burden to harassed families and, on a freight car, meeting a young girl beating her way to an aunt in Chicago.

While John was looking for significance, his father created two of his most memorable roles. On a loanout to Columbia, he starred in Frank Capra's Depression satire *American Madness*, a "gee whiz" film about business shenanigans that created bitter contention in financial circles. Under Lewis Milestone's direction, Walter created the terrifying preacher opposite Joan Crawford's Sadie Thompson in *Rain*, the film version of Somerset Maugham's immortal shady lady short story, "Miss Thompson." In real life, Walter was battling evangelist Aimee Semple McPherson on the Prohibition repeal issue. On March 28, 1932, they had it out at a rally chaired by Upton Sinclair, with Walter characterizing the Eighteenth Amendment as "an appalling and disastrous failure" and the evangelist claiming the twelve-year noble experiment hadn't been given a real chance.

On February 24, 1933, John smashed up Zita's face in a car accident. He was booked for drunken driving and later given a thirty-dollar fine. Zita suffered facial lacerations, but when Houseman saw BEAUTY MARRED under her photo in the New York *Daily News* and called her at the hospital, she said it was nothing. Six months later, John filed for divorce against Dorothy. Since California divorce laws demanded a motive, his petition accused her of being extravagant and of keeping him continually in debt, but promised to pay fifty dollars a week alimony for three years. Five weeks later, a car driven by him struck and killed a Brazilian girl as she was crossing Sunset Boulevard at Gardner Street. The girl was Tosca Roulien, a dancer and recent wife of Raoul Roulien, "the Rudolph Valentino of South America." Police took John into custody and had him come with them to the city morgue. In reporting how the twenty-year-old girl had been hurled thirty-six feet through the air in the late night accident, the press dug up the February accident and drunk driving conviction. Huston was cleared of all charges, however, as eyewitnesses testified she had dashed onto the boulevard without warning.

This and the fact that Willy and he were getting nowhere with *The Wild Boys of the Road* put John on the move again. Ironically, both *Laughing Boy* and *The Wild Boys of the Road* were made, but not by Universal. Carl Laemmle, Jr., Uncle Carl's son and heir-apparent, sold *Laughing Boy* to MGM, which was looking for a story for Ramon Novarro. Directed by the prolific W. S. Van Dyke and costarring Gary Cooper's girl friend Lupe Velez as Slim Girl, the film was a disaster. Novarro was laughed off the screen for trying an Indian accent but the story was still so hot the New York Board of Censors scissored gaping holes in the plot. *The Wild Boys of the Road* was to play a curious role at the dawn of the anti-Communist hysteria. Footage from the First National picture, directed by William Wellman, was used in a fake newsreel, manufactured at MGM by staunch Republican Thalberg to help defeat ex-Socialist Upton Sinclair, who was running for governor of California on a Democratic ticket that promised heavier taxes on the rich and a special tax on movie studios. The bogus newsreel, using one of the sequences pulled from *The Wild Boys of the Road*, had extras dressed as anarchist riffraff from Mexico crossing the border to assume control of Hollywood. Sinclair was defeated.

4

PARIS AND WARNER'S

Like so many Americans of his generation, John went to Paris because he rejected the predictable and the coherent, gloried in the eccentric and the breezy, and because, as they said, Americans were freer there than anywhere else. John's Paris was not so much a Parisians' Paris as the international Bohemian ghetto. He got there in 1933, the year the United States went off the gold standard, and the one-dollar-to-twelve franc exchange that buoyed the Lost Generation went by the wayside.

He had started in London, with a vague writing assignment at Gaumont-British that hadn't lasted long. After rolling drunks and homosexuals in Hyde Park, he crossed the Channel. The Americans of the thirties weren't the Gerald and Sara Murphys, the Cole Porters, and the Scott Fitzgeralds. The Montparnasse Americans who crowded the Dôme, Le Select and La Coupole cafés were mostly bad artists, unpublished writers, daydreamers, the kooks, the addled, and the haggard, who mingled with more desperate Russians, Spanish and German artists, writers, and plain refugees. The women—models, minor actresses, pretty girls—were, all of them, kept by somebody. Few had money.

Huston wanted to study painting. He had always doodled and sketched and thought of himself as not hopeless with oils and canvas. When his money ran out, he began cadging like everybody else, happily taking drinks, food, books, and a good shirt in exchange for his gab and his drawings. So many Americans and near-Americans lived on Montparnasse, making art and talking first novels and little magazines that sponging meals and drinks from Greenwich Village tourists, the last of the Babbitts, was a specialty for such longtimers as Henry Miller. John had charm and he could draw. With his Cheshire Cat grin, he would ease his long frame down at American sidewalk tables, hunch forward, and wrap his melted caramel voice around his prey. Usually, the tourist fell under his spell.

He could have written home for money, but he was too proud. If Aunt Margaret didn't like him and might only send a one-way steamship ticket to New York, his father was rolling in money, and, as the wife of a railway vice-president, his mother wasn't exactly without means either. Walter had signed a long-term contract with Metro and he didn't blow his five thousand a week at crap tables or the Hollywood Park race track but plowed it into real estate. He and Nan liked to get out of Los Angeles whenever possible, and they bought a ski lodge in the Big Bear Lake area high in the San Bernardino Mountains in the pine forests of Running Springs. The mountain retreat was without a telephone, but it was only eight miles from Los Angeles. A little later, the Hustons bought an eight-thousand-acre cattle ranch in Porterville, near Nan's home town of Fresno and the Sequoia National Park.

John didn't speak French. When he was desperate, he tried Spanish and called people *amigo*, but he stayed for the better part of one year. Parisians were fighting rising prices; John repeated the old saw that the artist was a bum in America, but someone who could have pride and dignity in Paris. He knew a lot of people and no one in particular except George Antheil, the *enfant terrible* of the expatriate musicians who carried a pistol in a holster in his evening clothes and often took it out and placed it on the piano when performing in public. George was from Trenton and was involved with a Hungarian girl named Boske.

The French period was more serious than John would like to

admit. He studied painting with passion and in art found a clarity and order wholly missing from his own life. The year and a half of fringe existence, of drawing tourists at sidewalk cafes and selling the sketches to them for croissants and wine, gave him a lasting affection and love for art. He would always go on gallery crawls, always buy and collect art with authority, always mingle with painters and designers. In any city, he would love nothing more than to stroll the streets and wander into art shows and museums. At chic table settings, he would always have the conversation to match.

Legend has it that a beautiful streetwalker provided his fare back to an America still in the depth of the Depression. In reality, it was Aunt Margaret who paid. For a while, he edited New York's *Midweek Pictorial*, and watched his relatives and friends become famous. At the Schubert, Walter and Nan were rehearsing *Dodsworth*; at the Radio City Music Hall, Willy's latest picture, *Counsellor-At-Law*, starring John Barrymore, was running.

Maybe his true calling was acting. By summer, John was in Chicago playing the title role in a Federal Theater production of *Abe Lincoln in Illinois*. No one would have thought that acting could be a profession covered by the Roosevelt administration's revolutionary idea of work relief. But the Federal Theater was part of the Works Projects Administration (WPA) scheme of things and more than fifteen thousand men and women were on its payroll at an average wage of twenty dollars, all eager and idealistic people. Adding to the satisfaction of accomplishing a social task in a time of national crisis was the feeling that the theater was suddenly part of the mainstream of things. *Abe Lincoln in Illinois* was a dramatization by Howard Koch, a spindly, hollowed-eyed Chicagoan, who was thinking of abandoning his law practice to become a writer. John and Howard became friends, but John's real interest was a pretty English teen-ager visiting with her American cousins. To occupy the long summer, Leslie Black was part of the Federal Theater experience. Within fifteen minutes of meeting the willowy girl, John asked her to marry him.

Leslie was only eighteen and didn't know what to make of

36

such imperiousness and said she would have to think about it. They saw a lot of each other during the run of the play and John fell desperately in love and told himself he knew why she wasn't instantly swept off her feet. He was a twenty-eight-year-old bum.

His father and stepmother spent the summer in England, Walter starring in a Gaumont-British picture variously called *Rhodes of Africa, Rhodes,* and *Cecil Rhodes.* Peggy Ashcroft was a preposterous woman novelist and Oscar Homolka Boer leader Kruger in this piece of British Empire propaganda. The director was Berthold Viertel, an Austrian emigré and former manager of the Reinhardt Theater in Berlin, who had been brought to Hollywood by W. F. Murnau to make *Sunrise* and who subsequently directed a trio of Fox pictures. His wife was the screenwriter Salka Steuermann Viertel, coauthor of *Queen Christina* and *Anna Karenina* for Greta Garbo.

When Leslie went back to England, John hotfooted it to Hollywood to show her he could be somebody. Leslie might be back in Chicago the next year and, John told her, by that time he would be a gainfully employed writer.

The people opening the doors were, again, his father and Willy. Wyler was now Samuel Goldwyn's star director. He had left Universal shortly before Uncle Carl's panicky sellout and was happy to work for the mercurial Goldwyn, who financed his pictures with his own money, produced films others shied away from, and wanted the end-result to be more than box office hits. Goldwyn and Wyler had been in New York and seen *Dodsworth* after Wyler had directed *These Three,* Goldwyn's toned-down screen version of Lillian Hellman's *The Children's Hour* and Sam had clunked down twenty thousand dollars for the screen rights to the Sinclair Lewis book and the Sydney Howard dramatization.

For the screen version, Walter had been chosen as a matter of course, supported by a cast of Goldwyn contractees—Ruth Chatterton as Fran Dodsworth, Mary Astor as the "other woman," and Goldwyn's newest acquisition, David Niven, as a smart young man flirting with Fran. Willy and John spent Christmas 1935 at Running Springs with Walter and Nan.

Since his teens, Willy had been a skier and he now introduced John to the sport. They all rang in 1936 with a couple bottles of 1908 vintage Moët & Chandon, and when the filming started at the Samuel Goldwyn studios on Formosa Avenue, John was on the set almost every day.

Sam was one studio boss who had more than a measure of respect for writers, but he had little time to discover Walter Huston's son. During most of the filming of *Dodsworth*, Goldwyn was hospitalized for a combined gall bladder and appendix operation, and it was at Warners over in Burbank that John got himself a writing job.

The brothers Warner had no high regard for writers and studio boss Jack seemed almost to pride himself on being relatively illiterate. He was demanding and despotic, quarreling not only with his yes-men but also with stars and members of his own family (Mervyn LeRoy had married his daughter, Doris).

The man who gave John his chance was one of the yes-men. The son of a well-known Berlin painter, Henry (Heinrich) Blanke was a diminutive man who had gone to work for Ernst Lubitsch when he was nineteen and had come to Hollywood with the director when Mary Pickford had imported the suave Berliner in 1922 to direct her. Blanke had returned to Germany to be production manager on Fritz Lang's *Metropolis* and had been chief of foreign productions at Warner Brothers before settling in at the studio as a house producer of some of the studio's prestige pictures.

John's desk was far away from Jack Warner's central power command, far from Blanke's suite of offices, and even from the offices of the lot's top directors—Mervyn LeRoy, Jack's son-in-law and the director of the studio's most polished and ambitious pictures, and a pair of imports from Berlin, Michael Curtiz, the master of elegance and sly wit, and William Dieterle, the technician of distinction. John's desk was in what was euphemistically called the writers' building. Scripts weren't so much written as they were talked into existence in "buzz sessions" in conference rooms which at Warners were called "echo chambers." Under scenario editor Richard Schayer, John was assigned to the second floor and introduced to his fellow writers, Allen Rivkin, Tom Buckinghan, Tom Reed, J. P. (Pinky) Wolfson, and John Balderston. They were two to a cubicle and a secretary. The hours were nine to six, Monday through Saturday.

Rivkin remembers John as his officemate on the second floor. "Huston would pound up the steps, his legs wobbly, his arms shooting off in all directions, his head bobbing like it was on a wild concentric. I guess that was why he had won an amateur lightweight boxing championship somewhere along the way—his opponent never knew where to look for a blow." Rivkin was three years older than Huston, but John called him "kid"—as he did everyone.

Rivkin recalls Christmas Eve 1936 with everybody amiably sozzled. Wolfson, who was a gun aficionado, had brought a vest-pocket .25 revolver to work that day. He was demonstrating it and his knowledge of firearms to the secretaries when John, in jodhpurs, rode down the staircase railing, talking to his imaginary horse and pounding a can on the edge of the risers.

"He was having a helluva time, depicting the entire race for those of us watching from the upper landing," Rivkin remembers. "For some reason, Pinky didn't realize that John was reining his brilliant mare over the jumps and shot at the large white bowl around the electric light over the stairwell. The glass showered down on everything, including the steps. That didn't stop John. It was just another obstacle he had to overcome in already difficult terrain. When he reached the top of the steps, seemingly no worse for the sharp bits of glass, we saw blood oozing out from his jodhpurs. Turning him around, we discovered the whole seat of his pants, including his shorts had been ripped loose. We started looking for a doctor or, at least, a first-aid kit. When we found some iodine and bandages, we couldn't find John. But soon we discovered him, leaning over Pinky's desk, drunkenly explaining to him the fine expertise needed for discharging lethal weapons."

Huston was to remember the early years at the writers' building for what he, Rivkin and the others tried to go up against. "There were certain advantages to having a kind of police state," he would say in 1972. "It gave you something to buck. We were writers in revolt, fighting to write well. With rare exception they believed only in the cliché and making pictures to formula. Of course, the fact that you were on a salary gave you a luxury that is unknown today. Writing is a form of madness anyway. One time I was with Hemingway on his boat and he was talking about the joys of writing, when the words took wing and so forth. I listened to this and thought, 'Yeah, sure.' About a month later we were together again and were talking about dancing. Papa was saying he loathed dancing, getting up and walking around a crowded floor with some broad. He said, 'Jesus, I hate it so much, I'd rather write.'"

In 1937, John married Leslie Black. His father, stepmother, Willy, and Blanke attended the ceremony. In 1950, when James Agee interviewed Blanke, the producer said he remembered John before and after Leslie. Before, said Blanke, John was "just a drunken boy; hopelessly immature. You'd see him at every party, wearing bangs, with a monkey on his shoulder. Charming. Very talented but without an ounce of discipline in his makeup." Leslie, Blanke was convinced, was the best thing that ever happened to Walter's son. She set standards and incentives which brought his abilities into focus.

5

TAKING OFF

Huston and Bogart were a happy accident for each other.

The Bogart John met when both were assigned as second bananas on *The Amazing Dr. Clitterhouse* was, like himself, someone coming into his own after a long and not particularly energetic climb. Like himself, Bogart was newly married and enjoying the first whiffs of success. It was less than two years before that Leslie Howard had persuaded Jack Warner to use Bogart opposite Bette Davis in Archie Mayo's filmization of *The Petrified Forest,* the Robert Sherwood play that Howard and Bogart had done together on Broadway. The studio hadn't missed a chance on capitalizing on Bogart's sudden appeal. *Dr. Clitterhouse,* in which he would costar with Edward G. Robinson, was the fifth picture since *The Petrified Forest.*

Bogart was seven years older than Huston and had twelve years of Broadway conditioning behind him. He was just beginning to catch on to the persona of leading thug in residence—after James Cagney—that the studio publicity department was creating with press release about phony bar brawls. Bogart was a handsome little actor with a beautiful mouth that was scarred by a tiny scallop on the upper lip. Over the years he learned to exploit this deformity, which women found irresistible, and he used for his full range of snarls, lisps, and slurs to accompany his painful wince, his leer, and his fiendish grin. Supremely confident of his own attractiveness to women, he scorned all demonstrativeness and had had devoted wives at each corner of his climb. When he began on Broadway in 1925 and had so much to learn, he had married Helen Menken, the star of *Seventh Heaven*, whose thin, white face, Louise Brooks would say, "was always ecstatically lifted up to her version of the Drama." They had divorced when Helen had become a sensation in *The Captive* and his career had gone nowhere. Mary Philips was his second wife, an actress he had shared the stage with in several unsuccessful plays and with whom he had a first trip to Hollywood in 1930. His failure that year was as predictable as Cagney's success. Cagney played to perfection the wisecracking little hood he had made famous on stage and he was exactly right for the new all-talkie talkies. Mary had been there during those years when Bogart required comfort more than inspiration.

Mayo Methot was Bogart's new wife, a girl who had set him on fire. They had carried on a stormy affair, slipping out of back doors at Beverly Hills parties when either of their spouses rang the front doorbell. They were passionately in love and, said friends, Mayo had brought to a boil those emotions of envy, hatred, and violence which had been simmering beneath his failure. Less auspiciously, she was also a heavy drinker.

Besides his wives, Bogart owed most to Leslie Howard. It was while they had starred in Robert Sherwood's play that Leslie had helped him overcome the "striking attitudes" technique in favor of a quiet, more interiorized kind of acting. Bogart's miserable training would leave him permanently afraid of words. He would always be best playing with inarticulate energy and he would always remain extremely sensitive to his directors.

Warner Brothers kept its new contract writer as busy as its new contract player. For *The Amazing Dr. Clitterhouse*, the story of a psychiatrist turning jewel thief in order to test criminal behavior, Huston was paired with John Wexley, a radical leftist vegetating in the writers' building and calling Hollywood a warm Siberia. Universal had brought Wexley west when it bought his off-Broadway success, *The Last Mile*. It was for the filming of this plea for prison reform that Willy Wyler had surreptitiously tested the actor playing the convicted murderer in the road company version—Clark Gable. Writer and director had fought over whether Gable was better than the other unknown who had played the lead on Broadway, Spencer Tracy, but their tug-of-war had remained academic, as Universal had decided *The Last Mile* was too grim and resold the screenrights. Since *The Last Mile*, Wexley had written *They Shall Not Die*, an impressive dramatization of the Scottsboro trial.

The director assigned to *Clitterhouse* was Anatole Litvak—Tola to everybody—a distinguished-looking Russian four years older than Wexley and Huston. Litvak had directed pictures in Berlin and Paris, including *Mayerling* with Danielle Darrieux and Charles Boyer, and was currently Olivia de Havilland's beau. A few years later, John and Tola were to be great friends.

While Litvak shot *The Amazing Dr. Clitterhouse,* Huston joined Wyler on *Jezebel*. Willy was on loanout from Samuel Goldwyn and easily convinced associate producer Blanke that he needed Huston for a rewrite of the new Bette Davis starrer. Already adapted by Clements Ripley and Abem Finkel from Owen Davis' 1931 play, *Jezebel* was the story of Julie Marsden, a spoiled and imperious southern belle who destroys her chances for happiness by flouting conventions. The setting was the New Orleans yellow fever epidemic of 1853, which left eight thousand dead and—as southern writers would have it—"steeled the spirits of men and women to endure when still greater devastation was loosed on them in the Civil War" eight years later. Costarring Henry Fonda, George Brent, Margaret Lindsay, and Fay Bainter, *Jezebel* was the first important screenplay John worked on. Willy—and Bette Davis—wanted Julie Marsden to be a complex individual.

Huston managed to pop in almost daily on the filming which started in October 1937 as the *Gone With the Wind* craze over the casting of Scarlett O'Hara reached its highest pitch. Wyler, who had been in and out of a short marriage to his *The Good Fairy* star Margaret Sullavan, had evolved a lot since *A House Divided*. He had more authority and directed with a controlled, compelling thrust and wasn't afraid of going

43

through scores of takes to get what he wanted. Bette Davis adored it and called him the first real director of her career.

John's mother died in 1938 shortly after *Jezebel* finished shooting. Neither John nor his father attended the funeral in Seattle. Walter felt no need to delve into a past that had been buried for thirty years and for years John's relations with her had been tenuous at best. Also, both father and son were happily married—and busy. Walter was at Paramount, starring, with Ronald Coleman and Ida Lupino, in William Wellman's adaptation of Rudyard Kipling's war-correspondent-back-from-the wars theme, *The Light That Failed*. And Willy had taken John with him back to Goldwyn for a little script doctoring on the Ben Hecht–Charles MacArthur adaptation of *Wuthering Heights*.

On October 23, they were all together, marrying Willy to David Selznick starlet Margaret Tallichet at Running Springs. Walter and Nan supplied the champagne, Willy's mother the tears, John and Leslie the wedding cake, and Lupita and Paul Kohner the flowers. After the debacle of the Laemmles at Universal, Paul, at first in desperation, had become an agent. Willy was Paul's first director client, Walter one of his first movie stars. When it was time for John to have an agent, he too went with Kohner.

The doctoring of the Hecht-MacArthur script was, if nothing else, vocal. The changes were worked out in the "echo chamber" fashion with Sam himself joining Willy and John. So much screaming went on at these story conferences that John suggested a financial penalty for whoever started the shouting. "Let's make a wager," Huston said. "Each one of us puts up fifty dollars and the first one who starts yelling loses."

"Fine. I'm with you," Willy agreed.

"I'm good for it," Sam nodded. He was too rich to carry money.

The trio had the quietest story conference in memory and when they got up, Goldwyn reached for the one hundred dollars on the table.

"Well, I win," he said, scooping up the money.

"What do you mean, you win?" Wyler asked.

44

"Well, I didn't yell."

It took Willy and John a long time to explain what the bet had been about.

While Willy went to England to cast *Wuthering Heights,* John went back to Warners to work on a couple of historical prestige pictures. Aeneas Mackenzie had already worked two years under Henry Blanke, turning Franz Werfel's play *Juarez and Maximilian* into a screenplay simply called *Juarez.* When Paul Muni was cast as the Mexican President, Bette Davis as the ill-fated Empress Carlotta, Brian Aherne as the refined and absurd Maximilian von Hapsburg, and John Garfield as Porfirio Diaz, the direction was assigned to William Dieterle, an ex-actor and former student of Max Reinhardt in Berlin. To no one's surprise, John was soon "paired" on the script with one of Reinhardt's sons.

Wolfgang Reinhardt was a meticulous man of John's own age, with thinning dark hair, who, together with his brother Gottfried and his father, tried to make it in the film industry. Actually, it was only Gottfried who, as a Metro-Goldwyn-Mayer producer, could claim any measure of success. The elder Reinhardt had come to Hollywood in 1934 to direct *A Midsummer Night's Dream* at the Hollywood Bowl. The production had been a sensation because an unknown nineteen-year-old, Olivia de Havilland, had replaced the star as Puck, and Jack Warner had signed Reinhardt to direct a screen version. The filmic *Midsummer Night's Dream* had not been a success and Max Reinhardt was now running an acting school while trying to get another directorial job.

During the summer of 1939, John taught a class in screenwriting at Max Reinhardt's Workshop, but lost interest when he was assigned to *Dr. Ehrlich's Magic Bullet,* an account of the career of the pioneer in the application of chemistry to medical science. The studio had bought the story idea from a writer named Norman Burnside and together with Heinz Herald and Burnside, John went through letters, clippings, and notes preserved by the Nobel Prize winner's widow. Three doctors helped them. With Edward G. Robinson play-

45

ing Ehrlich and Dieterle directing, the film was another highly serious, somewhat stately addition to the genre.

During the fall of 1939, Huston dropped everything when his father offered him a chance to direct him on Broadway. With Leslie and his stepmother, John followed his father to New York and the Ethel Barrymore Theatre.

A Passenger to Bali was written by Ellis St. Joseph. Most of the action takes place aboard a freighter crossing the South China Sea and concerns the evil machinations of a phony clergyman. Walter Huston starred as the Reverend Mr. Walkes who incites the crew to mutiny and drives the captain (Colin Keith-Johnston) to the brink of murder, only to be left to go down with the sinking ship during a typhoon. With a suggestion or two from Herman Shumlin, John managed to conjure up an effective third-act storm and to elicit a swaggering performance from his father. The reviewers panned the play, liked Walter's performance, and gave the director a nod for keeping the action simple and believable. The play closed March 16, 1940, after four performances.

John had wanted to be a director for a long time now and despite the less than overwhelming triumph of *A Passenger to Bali*, he returned to Hollywood more determined than ever to force Jack Warner, Hal Wallis, and Henry Blanke to give him a chance.

To his astonishment, Warner said yes. One more and then.

The one more script was *High Sierra*. It would star Humphrey Bogart (George Raft had turned it down because he didn't want to die in the end). The story of a hunted criminal fleeing on foot into the Sierra Madre mountains toting a machine gun in a violin case was an original by W(illiam) R(iley) Burnett, a novelist seven years older than John, who had made a fortune selling gangster bestsellers to the movies. Burnett had published his most famous one, *Little Caesar*, when he was thirty, and also wrote historical novels. For the final draft of *High Sierra*, John got to work with Burnett.

Raoul Walsh, Warner Brothers' veteran Western director, shot most of *High Sierra* at the 11,000-foot level of Mount

Whitmore. Bogart was backed up by Ida Lupino, Arthur Kennedy, Joan Leslie, Cornel Wilde, and a dog named Pard. The one-eyed Walsh and Huston had horses in common and after the filming the two of them flew to Kentucky to have a look at the yearling sale at Lexington.

John now had Jack Warner's tentative okay to direct if and when he found the right property. In the meantime, it was back to writers' row, where he was assigned to the office he had shared with Allen Rivkin in 1932.

"What's happening?" asked Rivkin.

Huston had a sinking feeling nothing would ever happen. Here he was, nine years later, in the same goddamn cubicle with the same goddamn Rivkin. He nevertheless told Rivkin about Warner's promise. As Rivkin remembers it, John tossed *The Maltese Falcon* on his desk, took a stance, pointed a finger at the book, and said, "Kid, Warner said if I can get a good screenplay out of this Dash Hammett thing, he'll let me direct it."

Rivkin thought it was dumb, since *The Maltese Falcon* had already been filmed twice before by Warner Brothers, once by William Dieterle and once by Roy Del Ruth. John screened both pictures. Del Ruth's 1931 version was a polished and intriguing exposition of Hammett's complex plot with Ricardo Cortez as Sam Spade and Bebe Daniels as the hard luck dame Brigid. Dieterle's 1936 remake was a nonsensical spoof finally titled *Satan Met a Lady*. To accommodate Bette Davis' star status, the emphasis was shifted from Warren Williams' Sam to Brigid, and the result had been a box office bomb.

Rereading Hammett's original, John decided on a radical approach—to *follow* the book rather than depart from it. Rivkin grunted and said he would help, and together they began breaking the story down into shots, scenes, and dialogue.

"I knew that if I could get a solid screenplay out of the book," John reminisces, "they'd let me direct it."

But he didn't get very far. One Monday morning, he was told to report on *Sergeant York*, a prowar propaganda piece which was suddenly given top priority. Before he left his cubicle, however, he gave Hammett's book to his secretary and told her to recopy the printed text in shots, scenes, and dialogue as he and Rivkin had started to do.

On *Sergeant York*, John joined his *Jezebel* teammate Abem Finkel, Harry Chandler and—Howard Koch. Since *Abe Lincoln in Illinois*, Howard had been on Orson Welles's radio show (and actually coauthored *The War of the Worlds* radio script). He had indeed abandoned his law practice and, with his wife and two children, gone to New York where John Houseman—no longer married to Zita Johann—had hired him on Welles's CBS radio show. Koch had come to Hollywood a year ago and had just soloed the screen version of W. Somerset Maugham's *The Letter* for Wyler and Bette Davis. John and Leslie had the Koches over for dinner and over after-dinner drinks the two writers were deep into discussing things to do together. Something meaningful that would say something significant about the darkening world situation.

Sergeant York was a join-the-army story set in the closing months of the previous war when the United States had finally joined the Allies. This time, America was again sitting out the war. Franklin D. Roosevelt, in his eighth year in the White House, was heavily preoccupied with the conflict. By mid-summer of 1940 the defeat of England seemed entirely possible and a great debate was going on in the United States between the internationalists, who favored rushing material aid to Britain and the isolationists, who opposed any U.S. involvement in the war. Charlie Chaplin's *The Great Dictator* was the talk of Hollywood in the spring of 1940 when Adolf Hitler's armies invaded Denmark and Norway in order to win bases for an impending assault on Great Britain and, in May, overran Holland and Belgium.

Not everyone was making war movies, but Huston admired the spunk of those who were. Alfred Hitchcock was shooting *Foreign Correspondent* and Tola was making *Confessions of a Nazi Spy*. John had an even greater admiration for filmers of the real thing—the documentarians. There were Joris Ivens, John Ferno, and Robert Capa returning from China with the material for their impressive feature, *The 400 Million*. There was Herbert Kline, who had covered the Czech and Polish crises with his reportages *Crisis* and *Lights Out in Europe*. Like others of European origin, Wyler found it hard to concentrate on colonial Singapore in *The Letter* and begged Goldwyn to let him film *Watch on the Rhine*, Lillian Hellman's new play about complacency over Nazism. Willy's cameraman on *The Letter* was Tony Gaudio, who, between takes, listened on short-wave radio to Benito Mussolini declaring war on England and France. "Son of a beeetch!" Gaudio exploded, with his head halfway inside the radio before translating for the tense set. In June, France fell, and the ragged remnants of the Allied armies stood at Dunkirk while Britain set up a rescue mission to get them across the Channel. In July, the Battle of Britain began.

The script of *Sergeant York* was quickly thrown together to become one of the eighty Hollywood movies dealing in one way or another with the war during the uneasy "lend-lease" and "bundles for Britain" period. As written by Huston, Finkel, Chandler, and Koch and directed by Howard Hawks, Sergeant York was a stirring metaphor of the quiet American finally aroused. It told the story of Alvin York, a good-natured, gangling Tennessee hillbilly who at the height of the Meuse-Argonne battle of 1918 had singlehandedly picked off twenty German machinegunners—enough to persuade the entire salient to surrender. Before surrendering to Hollywood, the now fifty-three-year-old York had made three demands—that Gary Cooper impersonate him; that no oomphy girl play his wife, and that the picture be an honest account. When it was released in late July 1941, *Time* said that *Sergeant York* was "one of the cinema's most memorable screen biographies."

Huston and Koch decided to write a play together about the causes of this war. With the exception of Italy which, under Mussolini, had switched sides, and neutral Russia, the new war was a replay of the 1914–18 conflict, with the same enemies and the same allies. Together Huston and Koch burrowed into America's involvement in the First World War and the failure of President Woodrow Wilson's League of Nations. The monstrous butchery of World War I had produced an ever growing public demand that some method be found to prevent the renewal of the suffering and destruction of modern warfare.

This demand had been so great that within a few weeks of the opening of the Paris peace conference in January 1919, unanimous agreement had been reached on the need for a "never again" League of Nations. What had gone wrong? The two authors decided to concentrate on the crucial month of April 1919, when Woodrow Wilson's peace of reconciliation was wrecked by the national and territorial demands—by France, which had suffered most, and by the host of little new countries carved out of the Reich and the Austro-Hungarian empire—which undermined Wilson's basic idea that precautions should be taken against aggression not against Germany.

John and Howard recreated the whole gallery of April 1919 personages—Wilson's second wife, Edith; French Premier Georges Clemenceau, who wanted the League of Nations to develop into a system of security against Germany; British Prime Minister Lloyd George, who regarded it as a system of conciliation which would include Germany plus Wilson's trusted advisers; Edward House, who in 1915 had visited London, Paris, and Berlin in an attempt at mediation; and Louis Brandeis, whom Wilson had appointed to the Supreme Court in 1916. They also had a villain—reactionary Republican Senate leader Henry Cabot Lodge. Chronologically, they covered the time span from September 1918 when Wilson was thinking of attending the prospective peace conference, to March 4, 1921, when, a broken chief, he left the White House with the ashes of his great idea. To give their play a passably ominous title, they called it *In Time to Come*.

"Then," as Huston recalls it, "the damndest thing happened."

A copy of the outline his secretary had typed up of *The Maltese Falcon* fell into Jack Warner's hand (that was routine, Rivkin told him, a copy of everything the secretaries typed went "upstairs"). What was not so routine was that Jack Warner had thought the breakdown was the final script. The boss called in Henry Blanke and Huston and told them, "I just read it and it's great. You've really captured the flavor of the book. Now go shoot it with my blessing."

Blanke, it was understood, would be the producer and closely

50

supervise the filming. On the way back to Blanke's office, the little producer told John, "Shoot each scene as if it is the most important one in the picture. Make every shot count. Nothing can be overlooked, no detail overlooked."

To dip into Warner Brothers' vast pool of talent and cast *The Maltese Falcon* was a pleasure and only the casting of Sam Spade was up in the air for a few days. As a matter of course, the part was offered to George Raft first. When he refused, Bogart was cast. To play Brigid, Huston and Blanke chose Mary Astor, who projected just the right kind of false innocence. For the role of Casper Gutman, the villain who has a way of saying, "By Gad, sir," producer and director signed up Sydney Greenstreet, a sixty-one-year-old stage actor who had played comedy parts on Broadway for thirty years but never been in a movie. Peter Lorre, Warners' resident pervert with an accent, was cast as Joel Cairo, and Elisha Cook as the trigger-tense killer working for Gutman.

Jack Warner wasn't taking any risks with *The Maltese Falcon*. It was a gangster flick, with a routine shooting schedule of six weeks and a routine budget of $300,000.

The new director prepared himself. He prepared literally hundreds of sketches, showing the precise camera angles to cameraman Arthur Edeson (who had filmed Lewis Milestone's awesome *All Quiet on the Western Front* ten years earlier) and the position of each actor in the shot. "Obviously a horror tale and a pastoral story should not be photographed through the same lenses," Huston recalls. "I tried to transpose Dashiell Hammett's highly individual prose style into camera terms—i.e., sharp photography, geographically exact camera movements, striking, if not shocking, setups.

"As the book is told entirely from the standpoint of Sam Spade so also is the picture. Spade is in every scene save one (the murder of his partner). The audience knows no more and no less than he does. All the other characters in the story are introduced only as they meet Spade, and the attempt is made, upon their appearance, to photograph them through his eyes, as it were. This, too, was something of an innovation at the time."

51

Huston insisted that Mary Astor run around the set several times before appearing before the camera so as to give her a nervous, out-of-breath appeal. In the best Eisenstein tradition, he had Edeson photograph Greenstreet from low angles, to emphasize the bulk of the 285-five pound actor. Hammett was not sentimental about private detectives, and John had Bogart play Sam Spade as a man who is constantly testing himself, a hard-boiled man who is fascinated by the greed of the people twirling around him, especially Brigid, whom he cannot figure out. Money is the concern of everybody and Huston's plot and economic dialogue is designed to bring out the full viciousness of the characters, Spade included. Scene for scene, character for character and often gesture for gesture, Huston sticks to the book. Only toward the end does the screen version allow itself a few cuts. Gutman's daughter disappears, the relation between Cairo and the punk killer is left unmentioned, the political meat of Spade's meeting with the attorney-general is deleted. Having opened with a driving tempo, Huston cannot allow himself to slow down in the last reel.

As a private joke, Huston had his father play an unlisted bit —a sea captain sieved with bullet holes who appears in Spade's office long enough to deliver the falcon, mumble a word or two, and fall dead. One evening after he had played his bit scene, Walter Huston's phone rang, and a woman's voice said she was Hal Wallis' secretary. Mr. Wallis had seen the rushes and felt Walter had "overacted" in taking a lamp down with him in his death scene. Would he mind coming back for a re-take? Huston was white with anger when he answered that he had never been accused of overacting but that he would be in the next morning to redo the scene. Then a man's voice came, "Walter, this is Wallis. Hope you don't mind a retake. You were pretty *bad* you know."

"Goddamnit!" Huston almost dropped the phone. "I said I'd do the scene again, didn't I?" The man on the other end of the line roared with laughter, making Walter realize his son was 'Hal Wallis' and Mary Astor the secretary. For years, John would rib his father about this one.

Filming ended in late July 1941, and in October, *The Mal-*

tese Falcon was released. It was an instant classic and a trend-setter for a franker, tougher, and more sophisticated gangster genre. Since then it has grown to be thought of as the best crime picture ever made in Hollywood. As Dwight Macdonald would write twenty years later, "Huston knows just what he is doing all the time; the mood he established is matter-of-fact and humorous, counterpointed against the melodramatic intrigue. The movement is brisk—how nice to be a little behind the director instead of, as normally, ten minutes ahead of him."

John was in New York when *The Maltese Falcon* opened, not so much to glory in his own fame as to be with Koch for the first rehearsals of their play. *In Time to Come* was going into rehearsals at the Mansfield with the première set for December 28, Richard Gaines was set to play Woodrow Wilson, Nedda Harrigan was Edith, Russell Collins was Colonel House, Bernard Randall was Judge Brandeis, Guy Sorel was Clemenceau and Harold Young, Lloyd-George. The director was an Austrian émigré named Otto Preminger with a hot temper and a bald pate.

Howard had his wife with him; John was without Leslie. The marriage was on the skids, to the chagrin of such friends as Blanke, Willy and Talli Wyler, and the Koches. But John had never stopped behaving as a bachelor. He had never stopped seeing other girls he picked up at huge, star-studded parties where he was always welcome, with or without his pet monkey on his shoulder. There was never a dull moment when John was around. He was famous for his pranks, for the amount of alcohol he could hold, his vast and heteroclitic knowledge and —with the ladies, his milk-and-honey voice, frank concupiscence, and his way of moving his long body forward and to listening attentively to what a woman was saying.

And he was also a man's man, an easy companion at crap tables, sports arenas, and especially race tracks. He loved the saddling paddocks, with jockeys getting on their mounts, sitting there, tucking their crops under their legs while trying the girth. He had ridden, he told people, before he had walked. His mother had once crossed the Mississippi River on horseback on

53

a dare and she had often propped her young son before her in the saddle. If he was to be believed, he got calluses on his behind before his feet. His usual greeting was "For God's sake," called women "honey" or "darling," and, when he wanted to impress them, by their real first name.

Huston and Koch didn't stay for the rehearsals but repaired to Hollywood for *In This Our Life*, which Howard would write and John direct, with Bette Davis, Olivia de Havilland, and George Brent. Young Huston was the talk of Los Angeles and he was giddily impatient all of a sudden. *In This Our Life* would shoot sometime in early 1942. So why sit still until then? Why not go out and get a look at the war? Willy Wyler was starting *Mrs. Miniver* at Metro, but he was ready to join John and Tola on a flying trip to a front somewhere as soon as he was through. One Sunday morning the trio met at Litvak's beach house in Malibu with a travel agent. The only place they could get to was China.

And why not? China had been involved in an undeclared war with Japan since 1937. The Nationalist government under Generalissimo Chiang Kai-shek had steadily lost territory to the Japanese invaders and, after the defeat of France, the Japanese had occupied parts of Indochina and now talked openly of an Asiatic empire embracing an area as great as North and South America. What excited the three directors was American aviation ace Claire Chennault's Flying Tigers, a group of volunteer flyers airlifting supplies to the embattled Chinese army. John also had his own reason for being enthusiastic about China. He and Koch were writing an original screenplay which he wanted to direct with Humphrey Bogart, Sydney Greenstreet, and Mary Astor. It dealt with a mystery woman who picks up two men on the eve of the Chinese New Year and takes them to her apartment, telling them that goddess Kwan Yin will grant the wish of any three strangers who make a joint prayer to her on this particular night. Their wish is granted, and tragedy follows.

It was at noon that Sunday when the radio flash came that the Japanese had attacked Pearl Harbor.

6

WARRING

America's entering the war changed John Huston's life even if it was work as usual at the studio December 8 and the following weeks. All during December and the first months of 1942, the United States tried to recover from the shock of Pearl Harbor. The military situation grew worse as the Japanese swarmed over the Philippines, captured Singapore and Burma, and President Roosevelt's immediate tasks were to hasten the military and economic preparations for all-out war.

In Time to Come opened on Broadway December 28 as scheduled and ran for forty presentations to close February 6, 1942. Quite naturally, Pearl Harbor killed public interest in a play that tried to explain why peace was lost at the end of that other, and suddenly distant, war. But the reviews were glowing. In the New York *Times*, Brooks Atkinson called *In Time to Come* "profoundly sobering and impressive."

"There, by the grace of God, went a chance to prevent the scourge of warfare that is now beating the aching back of the world," he wrote, adding that the authors had not averted their eyes from Woodrow Wilson's sharp temper and high-handed use of men. "They have unfolded a great tragedy of ideals and the hero who stood for them, and they have not cheapened it. When Woodrow Wilson goes down in the last scene, you know that the ancient blackness is setting down over the world again."

As Wyler returned to *Mrs. Miniver* and Litvak started *The Devil and Daniel Webster*, with Walter Huston and Edward Arnold, John began *In This Our Life*, a "woman's picture" that he had eagerly said yes to a few months earlier. But John Ford, Wyler, Litvak, Huston, Koch, and a lot of other Hollywoodites on the right side of forty were uneasy about making tinsel instead of joining the armed forces and handling the facts on the screen. Filmmakers of every description were sought for the various branches of the government's vast information program and it wasn't long before the word was out that the Army Signal Corps and the Navy had been mandated to start making pictures explaining why Americans were in the war. The first to go to Washington were Frank Capra and Darryl Zanuck. President Roosevelt and his chief of staff, General George C. Marshall, felt that the eight million men the country was calling up could be superior to totalitarian soldiers if they were given answers as to why they were in uniform and if the answers they were given were worth fighting—and dying —for. Unlike their European counterparts, many of the enlisted Americans had very little idea what the war was all about.

For Huston, it was back to Burbank and the woman's picture under Hal Wallis' somewhat distant producership. *In This Our Life* was a brand-new novel by Ellen Glasgow, the southern woman writer who, more mordantly than Margaret Mitchell, knew how to write about a disappearing way of life and of women's place in these changes. The aristocratic Virginian had both a highly developed sense of humor and a pessimistic turn of mind, and although her approach to sexual relations was rather dry, her heroines displayed a gritty selfhood and were chosen to conserve true values rather than destroy false ones.

If Glasgow's novel was original, the screen version was frightfully derivative, a shoddy ripoff of *Jezebel* and *The Little Foxes*, with Bette Davis doing her perfidious-bitch number, Olivia de Havilland playing the younger, prettier, and good sister, and Huston directing the whole thing in Wylerian deep focus. The effort was condemned in advance by Koch's improbable and inept script. The plot has Davis elope with her sister's sentimental beau (Dennis Morgan), only to return after his inevitable suicide to try and woo back her first fiancé (George Brent) who, in the interval, has focused his interests on the kid sister. It is only in the last reel, when Davis kills a pedestrian with her car and flees the scene so the accident can be imputed to an ambitious black law student (Ernest Anderson) that the script catches up with the real theme. The main interest is in the implications of a mutating society and in Charles Coburn's intelligent interpretation of the *pater familias* whose indulgence of a stubborn daughter is finally tempered by his refusal to accept responsibility for her actions.

The story was, as Huston later commented, "pretty heavy going."

So was the shooting. John fell in love with Olivia. She responded, and the romance soon had Bette seething. Although she had the lines, John gave Olivia the best camera shots.

The way Jack Warner remembers it, Huston told him in a few hand-picked words to mind his own business and it occurred to the studio chief to have Bette solve the problem. "I took her to the projection room with producer, Huston and de Havilland, and I let her see how Huston's manly pulse, beating for Olivia, had ruined her big scenes," Warner would write in his autobiography. When Bette caught on, she came close to tearing out every seat in the projection room, and the next day Huston reshot many scenes he had taken from her. "Bette later made her peace with Olivia, but after that she wouldn't have Huston around driving a truck."

The twenty-five-year-old Olivia was Hollywood's most eligible bachelor girl, assiduously courted by the likes of Howard Hughes, James Stewart, and Burgess Meredith. John was still married to Leslie, but he took an apartment and saw a lot of Livvy, as intimates called her. When he asked her if, once he was free, she would marry him, she said yes.

But there was also a war to win. In offices borrowed from the Department of Interior, Major Capra and Colonel Zanuck kept Washington Army brass hopping, commissioning people to write the first *Why We Fight* scripts. The work had been parceled out to seven Hollywood civilians and the incoming scripts were a little too left-leaning for Capra and his military superiors. On May 2, he therefore got the power to enlist and commission his own personnel. Immediately, a couple of writers, Anthony Veiller and Sy Bartlett, were enrolled. Bartlett, erstwhile screenwriter of *The Road to Zanzibar*, recommended John Huston, Litvak, and Wyler.

Huston, who at thirty-five was the youngest of the trio, was commissioned as a lieutenant in the Signal Corps, Army Pictorial Service, with Livvy coming with him to Washington. Once in his brand-new uniform, however, he was told to go home and sit tight.

"Jesus, sir! The war is going to be over . . ."

"We'll call you," said Colonel Schlossberg of the Army Pictorial Service. To Wyler, the colonel had put it most succinctly: "You Hollywood big shots are all alike, all a pain in the ass."

While Livvy starred in *Government Girl* for RKO, as the secretary to Sonny Tufts coming to Washington as a dollar-a-year industrialist to boost bomb production, Warner offered John to direct *Across the Pacific* with his *Maltese Falcon* cast, *sans* Peter Lorre. Huston called Schlossberg in Washington to ask if he could do it. He was told that as long as Warner Bros. and he understood that as a commissioned officer the Army could put him on active service with twenty-four hours notice, he could go right ahead.

Across the Pacific was a fast one, the story of Sydney Greenstreet as an urbane spy for the Japanese, who want to blow up the Panama Canal but are prevented from doing so by Bogey. Mary Astor played a mysterious and sophisticated lady who, to the audience's great disappointment, turns out to be totally blameless. With a weak screenplay by Richard Macaulay, based on a *Post* serial by Robert Carson called *Aloha Means Goodbye*, Huston and cameraman Arthur Edeson had fun shooting the beginning. Everything is atmosphere here—a fogged-in harbor front with a departing ship, ropes slackening, rumbling engines and the ship gliding slowly in front of docks, followed by the misty deck and, indoors, the hypnotic ceiling fan, the clinking of ice in a glass and, finally, faces in closeups giving the least blinking of eyelids or quiver of lips a sudden intensity to the building drama.

They all had fun doing *Across the Pacific*, but they missed Peter Lorre. He visited occasionally and one day, without telling anybody, John had him don a waiter's white coat and walk through a scene in which Greenstreet, Bogey, and Astor were being served breakfast aboard ship. "We didn't know John had made the switch with the actor who was playing the waiter," Mary Astor remembers. "He was behind us, so we wouldn't see him, and Peter served us, making tiny mistakes—holding a platter a bit too far away, just touching Sydney's arm as he lifted a cup of coffee. Finally he leaned down and kissed me on the back of the neck and we all broke up." The plot had the tension continue aboard the ship as motives and relationships among the characters are sorted out, but once everybody disembarked in the Panama Canal Zone, things fell apart in an accelerating rush toward an impossible ending.

The ending was its own joke. The *Across the Pacific* company was only a few days from wrapping when Colonel Schlossberg called from Washington and asked why the hell Huston hadn't reported. An official-looking envelope had indeed arrived but John had put it aside without realizing it contained his marching orders.

"I told him that it was a mistake, and that I only needed a few more days to finish my picture, but he wouldn't listen," John remembers. "He gave me twenty-four hours to report."

"I sat down and altered the script and set up a wild scene with Bogey trapped in Panama. Made him a prisoner of the Japanese who were out to bomb the Canal. I fixed it so his hands were tied behind him and packed the room with Japanese soldiers armed with machine guns. Outside, more armed soldiers surrounded the house.

"That night we shot it right up to the part where Bogey is hopelessly trapped. I knew there was no way in God's green world he could logically have escaped. I also knew Warners would never reshoot the whole ending. I had them. So I waved good-by to Bogey and was in Washington the next morning."

Army life was, proverbially, hurry up and wait, and the joke turned out to be on Huston, who was sent back to Hollywood to await his overseas orders.

In the meantime, Vincent Sherman who had just graduated to directing after years as writer, actor, and production manager, was told to finish *Across the Pacific*. He called off shooting for two days while he and a squad of writers tried to get Bogart out of the trap. As it was finally filmed, a Japanese soldier suddenly goes mad and begins to shoot up the room. Bogart comes out of the melee with a gun in his hand, shouting, "I'm not easily trapped." When the scene's logic was questioned, Sherman grunted, "Listen, if you ask me, we were lucky to get the bastard out of there at all."

Jack Warner forgave the immobilized warrior, possibly because *The Maltese Falcon* was suddenly a Best Picture nomination (eventually losing the Oscar to John Ford's *How Green Was My Valley*). While John waited again, Warner set him to work on a couple of scripts.

Of the pals, John was about the only one still cooling his heels in Hollywood. The services played openly for the favors of Hollywood "big shots," and the Navy had lured John Ford while the Air Force had grabbed Wyler, who had nearly gone to Moscow with Lillian Hellman to direct *The North Star*, the first film sympathetic to the new Soviet ally. Litvak was in Washington with Capra, clipping Nazi combat footage, after capping his civilian filmmaking with *This Above All*, a love story set in the London blitz. Six million Americans were lining up each week to see Wyler's *Mrs. Miniver*, a picture whose first fan was President Roosevelt.

The properties the impatient John was handed were a George Raft vehicle and a picture for Warners' new sex queen, Ava Gardner, and its new leading man, Burt Lancaster. *Background to Danger*, which Raoul Walsh got to direct, was a novel by British author Eric Ambler, and Huston's involvement in the writing was limited to attending a series of script conferences. On *The Killers*, however, he wrote the complete adaptation of the Ernest Hemingway short story, although Anthony Veiller was given the screenplay credit. "I was in the Army and felt that a film credit might suggest to my superiors that I was not devoting all my time to the job," John would say after the war. As directed by Robert Siodmak, *The Killers* became the first film from any of his work that Hemingway actually liked.

In August 1942, Huston finally got to go to war.

The assignment was at the remotest spot on the globe, a flake of a volcanic island that was closer to Tokyo than it was to Seattle. Together with a crew of six, John flew to the Aleutian island of Adak, 1,700 miles southwest of Anchorage or 180 miles west of the International Dateline. The enemy held Attu and Kiska islands, 500 and 350 miles farther to the west in the Aleutian chain, meaning that the nearest Japanese were an hour's flying time away.

As the United States was slowly losing the Philippines, Wake, and the Solomon Islands while at the same time inflicting crippling blows to the Japanese Navy, the enemy occupation of Attu and Kiska seemed to threaten an invasion across the Aleutian "bridge," especially after a June 3 bombing of Dutch Harbor, halfway to the Alaska mainland. In midsummer, a U.S. task force was landed on Adak to build bases for Liberator bomber attacks on the Japanese on anywhere in the northernmost Pacific and the Bering Sea. John's assignment was to make a film about this airbase building and the bomber missions against the Japanese positions on Attu and Kiska.

Huston stayed six months on Adak. The climate was oceanic, with heavy rainfall and almost constant fog. No trees grew here, but the ground was covered with a luxuriant growth of grasses, hedges, and flowering plants. The coastline was rocky and the approaches exceedingly dangerous. With his crew, John filmed the wind-whipped bulldozers converting one tidal flat into a runway and, once the missions against Attu and Kiska began, flew along on bombing runs. To get the color footage Huston wanted, he went out fifteen times and narrowly escaped disaster in one crash landing. He had a second brush with death when a 20-mm shell from a diving Zero fighter killed the waist gunner next to him.

Report from the Aleutians was released by the U. S. Signal Corps in August 1943 (shortly before U.S. and Canadian troops landed on Kiska and found the Japanese gone). The forty-seven-minute documentary, "written and directed by Captain John Huston," and narrated by Walter Huston is a sober look at Arctic warfare, where even the weather is the enemy. It is also a near-impressionistic collage of man and machines, of tents on ice floes, of kitchen smoke rising in spirals until flattened by the ever-blowing wind, of bulldozers clawing at wet ice, of Liberator bombers sailing up from flooded runways and enemy flak exploding silently in little black bursts down below.

The major Allied offensive of the closing days of 1942 was in North Africa. Italian troops had invaded Libya in 1940 to secure the Mediterranean, conquer Egypt, and gain control of the Suez Canal. They had done so badly, however, that German units under General Erwin Rommel had gone to their rescue, and since 1941 the British had been fighting both. In November, U.S. troops landed in French Algeria and Morocco to begin a pincer offensive against the Germans and Italians in Tunisia and Libya.

Suddenly, John was ordered to London. "It seems that President Roosevelt had asked to see a film on the North African landing and there wasn't any," he remembers. "It was to be a joint British-American operation, under the supervision of Frank Capra. The English had some swell footage but the only American footage on the fighting had gone down and been lost, so we were forced to fabricate combat film in California and Florida. There were canvas tanks and glorious air battles over Orlando, and the War Department was satisfied. After a while the film was edited and put together, but that was the extent of it. The mess was never released, which is a blessing."

John had spent a lot of time with Livvy and she accompanied him as far as New York.

Blacked-out London was an exciting place in the summer of 1943. Every other street had bombed-out ruins, but the Londoners behaved like soldiers at the front. "They were kind to each other, and brave," John remembers, "when everything was going to hell all around them. Willy was there, finishing his on-the-spot documentary about air-force raids over Germany. When he wasn't on missions over Wilhelmshaven, Willy was quartered in Old Audley Street behind the Dorchester Hotel. The action for Hollywoodites in uniform was the Dorchester, where Willy introduced John to such media VIPs as *Collier's* correspondent Hemingway and *Life* photographer Bob Capa, who shared a penthouse in Belgravia Square with an attractive girl. Half of Willy's former stars were there too, it seemed. Laurence Olivier wanted Willy to direct him in *Henry V* and offered to have Churchill pull the necessary strings to have Wyler out of the U. S. Air Force long enough, but Willy was only interested in the ongoing war.

John pulled strings to get Eric Ambler transferred from British ranks to his own unit. Ambler, whose *Background to Danger* John had been involved in, was a writer fascinated by foreign cities, the mechanics of travel, and obscure plots to overthrow governments. He was with the Army Kinematography service of the War Office and was more popular with Hollywood studios than with his British army superiors. Warners had *Background to Danger* before the cameras and at RKO Norman Foster was directing his *Journey into Fear*, after a screenplay by Orson Welles and Joseph Cotten.

The U.S. and British forces had linked up in Tunisia and, in July, had landed in Sicily in preparation for the assault against Italy. The Sicilian campaign had been relatively quick and easy and so were the first landings in Italy. Then things got difficult. As summer turned to fall and fall to winter, the fighting became bitter and brutal. Twenty German divisions fought stubbornly, and when the Allies were unable to dislodge the enemy, they tried a landing behind the German lines near the port of Anzio. At first, the maneuver seemed successful, but Field Marshal Albert Kesselring launched a furious counterattack against the Anzio beachhead and the Allies were forced to renew their pressure against the main German positions—including the almost impregnable stronghold near Monte Cassino. The decision in February 1944 to bomb Monte Cassino and the fourteen-hundred-year-old Benedictine monastery on its summit was one of the most controversial of the war. The monastery was reduced to rubble by B-17s, but the Allied Fifth Army advanced only mile by mile. Huston and his crew threw themselves into the battle ten miles above Monte Cassino.

"Our unit followed a Texas infantry regiment, the 143rd of the 36th Division, all the way through the fighting," John remembers. "The courage of these men was fantastic. I've never seen anything to match it."

The slowly retreating Germans had dug in at San Pietro, a small hillside village at a fork on the inland Naples-to-Rome road. The eastern splitoff led to Avezzano through the Liri Valley, the western fork led to Rome, and the Germans controlled both from the hills.

A false army-intelligence report nearly wiped out Huston, Ambler, and Lieutenant Jules Buck, in charge of the camera crew. "We were informed that the Germans had pulled back out of San Pietro and that it was okay to advance. Jules and Eric and I cut across the fields toward the village. We were well ahead of the troops and wanted to get some street footage. I was limping—had sprained an ankle and this slowed us down. Saved our lives, in fact, because when we reached the wall at the base of the hill leading up to the village, the Germans lobbed in a couple of mortar shells. In the dust these raised we got out okay, but I was annoyed as hell over the mistake."

Irritation with superior officers once made John race up five flights of headquarters stairs to sock an officer. Arriving at the top, he was so pooped he could hardly stand. Time to catch his breath was time enough to cool off and he just wobbled downstairs again.

The siege lasted for weeks. "It was the time for tilling. There were mines everywhere. The peasants knew that but continued their plowing and every day one or two got killed. It was the time for tilling and nothing could stop them. The respect that was born in me then for the Italian people can never disappear."

Huston and his crew got it all on film, the GIs freezing in their foxholes, the Stukas diving to bomb them, and the series of brutal attacks against the ruins of the village through a murderous wall of fire that resulted in eleven hundred American deaths. "We finally got into the village after the Germans had withdrawn," says Huston. "And the villagers themselves came slowly out of hiding, from caves and basements, mostly old people and kids. That's when we got the stuff with the kids."

This closing sequence of the film shows the numbed faces of the children of San Pietro while Huston's softly spoken narration says that in a few years, "they'll have forgotten there ever was a war."

In the early spring of 1944, Huston, Buck, and crew flew to Washington where their footage had been processed without their ever seeing any "rushes." In May, Livvy made the planned marriage public, telling Louella Parsons she was in love with John and that they would marry as soon as he was free.

"I had a curious experience," Olivia told the syndicated columnist. "When John was in Italy I was visiting a friend and I said, 'I have to go home—there's a cable for me.' Two hours later a cable came from John, the first in many weeks. Another time I was sitting for still pictures in the Warner gallery and I said, 'There's a telephone call for me.' When I went home a friend of John's was trying to call me from New York to say he had a message for me from England." When Parsons asked her if she was a psychic, she said, "I don't know about that. Maybe it's just a woman's intuition."

During the summer when the tide was turning for the Allied forces everywhere, Huston and Buck cut the film which they simply call *San Pietro* (and the U. S. Army Pictorial Service sometimes called *The Battle of San Pietro*) and John was promoted to the rank of major and awarded the Legion of Merit. The first roughcut was stark and elemental. Scenes of survivors grimly gathering the dead were juxtaposed with shots of wounded and dying GIs and entire patrols cut down by shellfire. The print was cut by a third to soften it for home consumption, and the War Department asked that General Mark Clark of the U. S. Fifth Army be asked to preface the film.

"So I wrote a kind of model, explaining the purpose of the

65

Italian campaign and so on, figuring that Clark would naturally have it redone by his staff at the Pentagon," Huston remembers. "But he memorized the whole damn speech. Now, here was this four-star general repeating word for word, the strategy of the campaign as I saw . . . and me just a dogface in it! I guess he didn't know any more about what was going on than I did."

Major Huston flew to Hollywood, in pursuit of Olivia and a quick divorce from Leslie. Livvy was still the girl with those big, soft brown eyes, but she was nervous and distraught, locked in an ugly battle with Jack Warner. Bette Davis had struck the first blow for a measure of self-determination for performers. The star system had always been based on contractual employment. Following a few poor decisions by a few stars, producers had become frightened and proclaimed that no artist, no matter how big, had the right to decide what films he or she wanted to work in. The penalty for disobedience was, as always, suspension, which meant the particular artist was declared persona non grata on his or her home lot, was forbidden employment elsewhere, had pay checks stopped and the weeks or months of the suspension tagged onto the end of the running contract. Olivia had taken Warner Brothers to court to challenge this "tagging-on" of suspended time. She called Warners "a model prison" and suspension "doing solitary." Among them, she, Bette, Cagney, and Bogart had twenty suspensions.

There was still a third army assignment in the offing for John, but in the meantime the footloose major hung out with friends and acquaintances and even popped up at the set of *Three Strangers*, which Howard Koch and he had written in '42. His old *Juarez* coscripter, Wolfgang Reinhardt, had become the picture's producer, and a nervous Romanian, Jean Negulesco, its director. *Three Strangers* didn't star Bogey, Greenstreet, and Mary Astor, but Geraldine Fitzgerald, Sydney Greenstreet, and Peter Lorre. It was wholly in the *Maltese Falcon* vein. In the climax, Greenstreet uses a Chinese statuette to club Fitzgerald to death, then turns himself in to police while Lorre stands holding a thirty thousand-pound winning lottery ticket he cannot redeem without involving himself in the murder.

John obtained a divorce from Leslie in Las Vegas as *San Pietro* was released. Livvy won her suit. On appeal, the California Superior Court said in a landmark decision that time lost by a player on suspension could not be added to a term contract after its expiration, but she and John were drifting apart. She began dating a Major Joseph McKoen, and John was hanging out with the boozing crowd. A fight between him and Errol Flynn at one of David Selznick's celebrated Sunday parties made gossip headlines. The fight was also to be remembered in a number of Hollywood memoirs. William F. Nolan reported in *John Huston, King Rebel,* that a sullen Huston was too quick to take offense to a casual remark by the actor. Within a minute the pair were squaring off in the garden, with Flynn knocking down Huston ten times, then asking that they stop, and John quoted as saying, "That's when I knew I had him." In *Selznick,* Bob Thomas says that Flynn made a disparaging remark about a lady friend of Huston's, and the two of them, both attired in tuxedos, retired to the garden to begin "a slugging match more brutal than any in Flynn's film adventures." Selznick wanted to join and, when he was restrained, the producer shouted to Flynn, "Put up your fists, you sonofabitch, and fight like a man!" According to David Niven in *Bring on the Empty Horses,* the slugfest came about because Huston and Flynn were bored with the Selznick party and both combatants ended up in the Cedars of Lebanon Hospital "for emergency repairs."

At the "Battling Bogarts'," Huston was a more innocent bystander if not infrequent witness. Jealousy of Bogey's current leading ladies, mixed with booze, sparked the incidents that after a while usually featured Bogey goading the drunken Mayo until she started hurling bottles at him or, on one occasion, going after him with a carving knife. The success of *The Maltese Falcon* had led to *Casablanca* and true stardom, but as Bogart's popularity soared, Mayo became a confirmed alcoholic. Her looks and figure collapsed and she made an increasing number of hideous scenes in public. Bogey's consolation, it seemed, was *Santana,* a sixty-five-foot ketch he bought from Dick Powell and aboard which he increasingly cruised the Catalina Island channels with his pals.

More dangerous to John's own fortunes was his falling in with the high rollers—Jack Warner and Selznick on occasion—and a jockey named Bill Pearson, but now that the Army took care of all expenses, he managed to make one sound investment with the money from his various bootleg scripts. With his father's help, he bought a 480-acre ranch on the modest slope of the Beverly Hills ridge of the Santa Monica Mountains. The place was out beyond Encino, all the way up past Edgar Rice Burroughs' estate, Tarzana, in the western end of San Fernando Valley. The spread had trees and shrubs, native sycamores, live oaks, copa de oros and trumpet vines. The house, built on two knolls and spread across them, was of Wisconsin pinewood with a wisteria vine running the entire length of the beamed front terrace. The patio was under the house, with the swimming pool on the side. The diving board was on the upstairs porch. The living room was designed by builder Rachelle Lewis, and one day shortly after John bought it Frank Lloyd Wright paid a visit.

"From time to time he would pause before some architectural feature and remark, 'Oh, that's very F.L.W.'" Huston remembers the following dialogue taking place:

FLW: Your ceilings are very high—too high, I think. I like low ceilings that give me a sense of shelter.

JH (*respectfully*): Isn't that because you are a small man, Mr. Wright—five feet eight, I should judge. You haven't gone through life bumping your head on chandeliers and the tops of doorways. Now, I'm six feet two."

FLW: Anyone over five ten is a weed.

JH (*after a pause*): Perhaps you'd rather see the garden.

John could have stayed at his ranch forever, fixing up the place in his own style, but in January 1945 the Army called him back for a new assignment.

Huston's third and final army film was never seen by the public. Started during the closing months of the war, the documentary was already a demobilization project. The War Department was concerned with what would happen in civilian life to those who had been mentally crippled in the war, those tens of thousands crowding the psychiatric wards of Veterans Administration hospitals.

Huston's orders were brief and to the point. "They told me they wanted a film to show to industry, to prove that nervous and emotional veterans were not lunatics," he remembers. "At that time these men just weren't getting jobs: Our purpose was to help them."

With a six-man crew, Huston moved to the Mason General Hospital on Long Island, New York. No script was possible, he decided. The men would have to tell their own story. When they couldn't he'd record their emotional disturbances with hidden cameras.

He filmed veterans discussing their problems under hypnosis and under the influence of drugs and at night treated himself to a crash course in Sigmund Freud and elementary psychoanalysis. It wasn't easy. Moments when things happened couldn't be foretold and Huston often had his hidden cameras relay each other in grinding out endless therapy sessions. Sometimes it paid off. One day they got on film the moment when a young soldier regained his power of speech. Because of shellshock, the youth had developed a terrible stutter, but suddenly he cried out, "I can talk! Listen, I can talk! Oh God, listen! I can talk!"

Huston was caught up in the staff's exultation when light triumphed over darkness. "This was the most joyous, hopeful thing I ever had a hand in," he would say years later. "We traced the slow rising of the spirit. A wounded psyche is hard to watch, almost too personal. Making that film was like having a religious experience."

The title he chose was biblical. *Let There Be Light,* he felt, was a happy film. "What happened there in front of us was a wonder and a miracle," he said about the sequence of the youth regaining the power of clear speech.

Seventeen years later, when Huston was filming *Freud* in Vienna, he would tell interviewers that it was at the Mason General Hospital that he discovered the deeper recesses of man's mind. "During the filming I saw things that disturbed me profoundly. I didn't know much about psychoanalysis, at least I wasn't especially interested. But there I discovered unconsciousness. I have experimented with hypnosis and already then I knew that I would one day do a picture on Sigmund Freud."

The footage was edited in New York and during the month in the cutting room Huston managed to play an elaborate joke on David Niven, who was returning to his Hollywood career with Goldwyn after five years in the British armed forces. John ran into David at Jack and Charlie's, where after stories and drinks, more stories and more drinks, Huston asked if the returning warrior would like to join him at the greatest whorehouse in New York. Niven, who was married to the former Primula Rolla and was the happy father of two small sons, declined, but John insisted. "Oh come on. You don't have to do anything . . . Just come and case the joint, then we'll take the madam out for dinner—she's a lot of laughs."

Hungry, Niven agreed, and after Huston had made a phone call, they set off. The house on Park Avenue looked impressive, and when John rang the bell, a saucy-looking maid opened the door, took their coats and offered them drinks while they waited. Sipping their scotches, John explained away a Monet on the wall as the madam's own specialty—screwing some old guy out of an occasional impressionist painting. "She has a dandy Braque right over her bed," he added. "It leaves marks on the wall as it swings."

When the petite, beautifully dressed madam appeared, John kissed her hand and introduced the actor. She was most civilized, saying John had told her so much about Niven and that she was happy he could join them.

"Well," said David, "I don't really want any action tonight, I just came to take a look at the place. Where are the girls . . . all upstairs banging their brains out?"

The madam looked mystified and, Niven would write in his memoirs, "Huston, like a canary-swallowing act, smugly broke the news to me that she was in fact Nin Ryan, the most elegant hostess in New York City." John was an old friend of

Mrs. John Barry Ryan, of her sister Maud, who as Lady Marriott, was one of the last really luxurious expatriates in Paris. Lady Marriott was a friend of John's Aunt Margaret and Nin Ryan a friend of his current girl friend, Marietta Tree.

Some years later, Niven would try to get even with John. When they and the Bogarts were at a chic London restaurant, Niven introduced them to John Albert William Spencer-Churchill, tenth duke of Marlborough, but John demolished the January pheasant hunt invitation Sir John extended to Niven with the remark that in January the pheasant season was over and only a few bad shots, the local butcher and people like that, were invited.

In less happy circumstances, Willy Wyler also came through New York. While filming the last matching shots of his second air force documentary over Rome, he had lost his hearing. Too depressed to write Talli, too deaf to phone her, he lingered at veterans hospitals in the East. Slowly hearing began to return in the left ear, but the diagnosis was the same everywhere—the nerve had been damaged and there was no cure for nerve deafness.

Huston wrote a narration for *Let There Be Light* and had his father record it for the soundtrack. When New York *Post*'s Archer Winsten saw the film, he called it a noble and fiercely moving picture. "It's so great, so inspiring medically and humanly, so tremendously graphic . . . a visible ascent from Hell."

The War Department didn't feel the public needed graphic descriptions of ascents from those regions and banned the picture. When the demobilized Major Huston heard the picture had been restricted, he was outraged. "I never dreamed they'd ban it," he said. "I guess they didn't want the public to see what war can do to a man's emotions and nerves—so they claimed that it would be an invasion of privacy to let the film be shown. Yet we had obtained signed releases from each of the patients."

Let There Be Light remained restricted "to the medical profession and allied scientific groups." In 1953, Dr. Adolf Nichtenhawser reviewed it for the Health Education Council and called the narrator's comments during the treatment scenes "pertinent and concise" and the story planning and directing "excellent." Noting that the film never touched therapeutic failure, only on the positive, Nichtenhauser recommended it for parents and relatives of psychoneurotic soldiers, professional groups, physicians and psychiatric hospital personnel, social workers and civic groups.

7

HAPPY DAYS

Evelyn Keyes was a pert, hazel-eyed blonde from a tough neighborhood of Atlanta, who had been under contract to Cecil B. DeMille when David Selznick had cast her to play Scarlett O'Hara's younger sister. Evelyn knew how to look after herself. When Selznick had tried to pull her to the casting couch in his office, she had run around his big mahogany desk. The smoldering producer had run after her until he was out of breath. Then she had made her getaway, running weeping and disheveled into the arms of a surprised production assistant. She got the part anyway and on the *Gone With the Wind* credits appeared after Clark Gable, Leslie Howard, Olivia de Havilland, and Vivien Leigh in fifteenth place.

It was at one of Selznick's Sunday parties that John met Evelyn, now a Columbia contractee, and it was David's current mistress, Jennifer Jones, who seated Evelyn between Errol Flynn and John Huston, who this time didn't start any fights.

Unwittingly perhaps, Walter had been the matchmaker. He and the southern starlet had been on a Liberty Bond selling tour together during the war. Shortly after D-Day, Walter and Evelyn had shared a Re-elect Roosevelt platform in Seattle with Harry Truman. "Walter was so proud of his boy," Evelyn said. "He kept dragging out pictures and talking about him.

73

My curiosity was aroused. We eventually met at a party, leaving early arm in arm. John was the most direct, vital man I'd ever encountered."

The first night he took her to Tarzana but instead of trying to seduce her, kissed her good night on the forehead and had her sleep in the guest room. After a week's coy courtship they became lovers. "His lovemaking was sure, with authority, and cool as always," she would write in *Scarlett O'Hara's Younger Sister*, her autobiography. "And it was fun. Isn't this an amusing thing we're doing! was the tone of the action."

They were both working, he writing *The Treasure of the Sierra Madre*; she costarring with Dick Powell in *Johnny O'Clock*, Robert Rossen's second directorial job, but on weekends they were together at his place. When Selznick invited her to come along on a yachting trip for the long Fourth of July weekend, she said yes, if her new boy friend could come along. By all means, said David. It was a memorable weekend. Besides David and Jennifer, Burgess Meredith and his wife, Paulette Goddard, were along as was William Paley, president of CBS, who apparently had been intended as Evelyn's date. Anchoring in Avalon Bay on Catalina Island, they partied, bathed, and received the visits of Alexander Korda, Orson Welles, and Howard Hughes. On shore, they went bowling and tennis playing. Evelyn thought she won. "At least I always felt that I won everything," she would write in her autobiography. "John, long arms and legs thin as shafts of wheat, getting all tangled up with the racket when he served. David, a shock of tousled hair already going gray, his eyes bright when you could find them behind the thick lenses, pitching in with all his energy into whatever was going on, bringing enthusiasm and excitement to all the games." Evelyn's mother made her first visit from Atlanta and John took both mother and daughter to a preview of *The Killers*. The following Sunday, Evelyn was doing retakes, but when she called John to say she would be through early and perhaps make it to his place after all and he said Ava Gardner was there, she thought he was trying to make her jealous. They didn't see each other for two days. When he called, they made a date for dinner at Romanoff's. Nothing was mentioned of Ava Gardner and the previous Sunday. Evelyn was happy to be with John again, "content to watch him smile, notice his tiny mannerisms, the way he tapped the ash into the ashtray or narrowed his eyes to form a thought with just the right amount of dramatic pause, content to listen to his quiet talk, ranging from painter and painting to horses and racetracks, to movies and books." They said they had missed each other. When in a dramatic way he said he never wanted to be without her again, she heard herself say, "Then why don't we get married?"

John didn't move. "He remained hunched over the table. He looked at me sideways, brows slightly raised, no smile, no flicker of—anything. He just looked at me for the longest time, eyes slowly blinking. And then he said—and I don't know what possessed *him*—'Why not?'"

The rest of the night was a whirlwind out of a forties movie. The diminutive Mike Romanoff got someone to fish a wedding ring out of his swimming pool and phoned stunt pilot Paul Mantz to fly them to Las Vegas. At 3:30 A.M., John and Evelyn were pounding on the door of a justice of the peace on the Strip and, with the pilot and the cabdriver as witnesses, they were married and headed for a casino. At dawn, they flew back to Los Angeles. At the airport, John said, "Good-bye, dear. Have a nice day," and headed for Warners while she went to work at Columbia.

Bogey had also remarried—his nineteen-year-old leading lady in *To Have and Have Not*, after painfully shedding Mayo. Lauren Bacall—everybody called her by her real first name, Betty—was the best thing that could have happened to him, friends agreed. The pals didn't say the same thing about John's new marriage. Crazy John, he's done it again, was the general reaction. Bogey laughed, as did all of John's Warner Brothers pals, and Anatole Litvak, Willy, and Talli Wyler. Evelyn was to remember that her new father-in-law laughed the loudest at his son's latest caprice.

John wanted Bogey for *The Treasure of the Sierra Madre*. Bogart was Warners' biggest male star. *Casablanca*, coauthored by Howard Koch, had really put him over the top. *Sierra*

Madre was a property John had been itching to do for years and Henry Blanke had managed to save for him.

"Shoot, kid," Bogey said when John brought up the project.

The Treasure of the Sierra Madre, John explained, was written by a mysterious German under the pseudonym B. Traven. It was a helluva yarn about a guy named Fred C. Dobbs and two other American bums in Mexico who strike gold. It was a story about greed and the instinct of self-preservation with a tragic, ironic ending.

Bogart listened. Since *To Have and Have Not*, he and Bacall had been in *The Big Sleep*, directed by Howard Hawks, and he was getting tired of the private eye stereotype. They were about to start another one, *Dark Passage*, for Jack Warner's new pet director, Delmer Daves, and Bogey was certainly ready for a change of pace. There wasn't a part for Betty in *The Treasure of the Sierra Madre*, but Bogey said that was okay. She'd come along to Mexico, where John insisted they'd have to shoot the picture.

"She makes great scrambled eggs," Bogey grinned.

Dark Passage had to go first, Warner decreed, which was fine with Huston because he had an offer to try his hand again at directing a Broadway production. Before he and Evelyn left for New York, he got Traven's literary agent to give him the writer's post office box address in Mexico City. On Warner Brothers' stationery, Huston wrote Traven announcing the upcoming production start of *Sierra Madre*. He added that he and Blanke were doing everything in their power to convince the powers that be at Warners to let them film it in its natural habitat in interior Mexico.

The play Huston was to direct at the Biltmore Theater was *No Exit* by Jean-Paul Sartre, the "pope" of the new French philosophy, existentialism. John liked stories which arbitrarily threw together people for some purpose—idealistic, cynical, or downright criminal—and characters who, when they question their beliefs, come to realize how ambivalent things really are. If *Sierra Madre* was about the collusion of greed and self-preservation, *No Exit* was about diabolically thrown-together people and, *ad absurdum*, the importance of free will. Called

Huis clos (literally "behind closed doors") in the original, Sartre's play takes place in a drawing-room in hell. Besides a bellboy who introduces the personages to each other, the characters are a diabolic trio, all guilty of bad faith and locked up together in hell. The three are the coward, Garcin; the lesbian, Inez, and Estelle, who has killed her baby. To while away eternity, Garcin loves Inez who loves Estelle who loves Garcin . . . until that most famous line of Sartre's, "Hell is other people."

Huston's actors in the Herman Levin–Oliver Smith production were two French expatriates and Ruth Ford. Claude Dauphin was Garcin (in the London version Alec Guinness played him) and Annabella was Inez.

John's New York crowd was different, Evelyn realized to her mortification. That her husband was a popular man, she knew, but she was not quite prepared for open-ended affairs with Park Avenue society women. Shortly after their marriage, she had overheard visiting Walter ask his son, And what about Marietta? She had never heard John's reply, but in New York she found out the girl was Marietta Tree. And there was also Pauline Potter, head designer at Hattie Carnegie, who was to become Madame Philippe de Rothschild. These and other ladies managed to make Evelyn feel inferior at various chic dinner parties. The blowup came on the opening night of *No Exit*, when Pauline chose to interpret Evelyn's relaying a message from John as a declaration of war.

When John and Evelyn got back to Hollywood there was a letter from Traven. Over twenty pages the author made suggestions about the filming, lighting, and set construction. When *The Treasure of the Sierra Madre* was definitely set for production start in early 1947, John wrote Traven and asked for a personal interview. "I can guarantee nothing," Traven wrote back, "but if you will come to the Hotel Reforma in Mexico City, early in January, I will try to meet you there. I make no promises."

Who *was* this Traven? Blanke tried to find out and was told by German émigrés in New York that Traven came from a misread signature. Traven was really Traum (dream) which was the anagram of Marut, or Maurhut, a revolutionary of the

77

breakaway Republic of Bavaria of 1918. Kurt Eisner, a pacific socialist, had proclaimed the republic three nights before the end of World War I but had become embroiled with Bavarian rightists over German war guilt and was murdered two months later by a young nobleman. Workers' and soldiers' councils set up in Munich, had been ruthlessly crushed by the Reich army and Maurhut was one of the few barricade leaders to escape. Traven certainly had lived in Mexico for many years and worked in every job from gold prospector to midwife. His fiction told his adventures with a compelling flair for a plot and a deep sympathy for all victims of oppression and inhumanity. *Der Schatz der Sierra Madre* was his third novel, published in 1927.

Huston decided to take a chance and flew down to Mexico City for the date Traven had specified. He waited patiently at the Reforma, but no one showed up. He was ready to fly back to Los Angeles when a thin little man with gray hair handed him his business card: H. Croves. Translator. Acapulco.

Introducing himself, the man showed Huston a typed note from Traven saying "This man knows my work better than I do." He added that the author was sorry he couldn't make it, but that he, Croves, was authorized to answer any and all questions the director might wish to discuss. Huston hired Croves as a technical adviser for a hundred fifty dollars a week and told him to report for the shooting start in April.

Leaving art director John Hughes in Mexico, John flew back for the casting of the picture. Blanke, who was simultaneously producing Litvak's *Blues in the Night,* wanted John Garfield as Curtain, the blunt and honest young man, but when he was unavailable, Blanke and Huston settled on Orson Welles's *Magnificent Ambersons* title-role actor, Tim Holt. For Old Howard, the shrewd veteran prospector with whom Fred C. Dobbs and Curtain go gold-digging, John got his father. Bruce Bennett and Barton MacLane rounded out the American cast and outdoor camera specialist Ted McCord headed a hand-picked crew. With Evelyn and Betty, they all flew to Mexico City in a chartered DC-4 on April 6—Walter's sixty-third birthday.

After matinee idol Alfonso Bedoya had been cast as a primitive bandit and Croves picked up, filming began in Tampico streets with Huston and Bogart changing roles. John played the bit of a rich American tourist who becomes a victim of Fred C. Dobbs's cadging, and Bogey directed the closeups. "I really gave Johnny the works," Bogey was quoted as saying. "Made him do his scene over and over and over. Got him mad as hell!" Huston got back at Bogey later on. In a scene which required the actor to stick his hand into a hole between some rocks, John warned him to be careful of a gila monster they had seen dart about. When Bogart felt tight jaws close over one of his fingers, he let out a yelp. The "claw" that Huston and crew had carefully rigged in the hole was a camera clamp.

The biggest fun, according to Evelyn, was when John asked his father to discard his false teeth for the Old Howard role. "You should have heard Walter yell," she says. "It took four people to hold him down while those dentures were being removed! After he saw some rushes of himself without the teeth he became reconciled—but he actually sulked for weeks over having to give them up."

John applied hypnosis he had seen practiced at Mason General Hospital on Bedoya. The actor approached his role in a state of near-panic, but Huston talked to him in a soothing voice and with his eyes locked with the Mexican's gaze. After a while, Bedoya believed he could successfully handle the role.

Croves was there every day, watching, translating, and, at the San Juan de Purua mountain location, advising on techniques of gold panning. Huston watched the gray-haired little man who always refused to have his picture taken and never commented when Huston complained that Traven never answered any of his letters. Huston was sure Croves was the elusive author, who couldn't bring himself to give up his privacy, yet couldn't stay away from the filming of his novel.

The mountain location was tough, with burning sun, tropical downpours, steep hills, assorted insects and reptiles, and bad meals. Betty made regular trips to the catering kitchen to make ham and eggs for Bogey. Bogart exploded a couple of times at John's affection for authenticity.

"John wanted everything perfect," Bogart said later. "If he saw a nearby mountain that could serve for photographic purposes, that mountain was no good—too easy to reach. If we could get to a location site without fording a couple of streams and walking through snake-infested areas in the scorching sun, then it wasn't quite right."

Walter agreed. "John ran me up too darn many mountainsides!" he said when it was all over.

Unforeseen difficulties and the director's demand for authenticity drove production costs up and Blanke was forced to fly back to Los Angeles to soothe Jack Warner. One particular sequence in which Bogart searches for water had been four days in production. Warner sat through all four days' rushes in his executive screening room with Blanke. When it was all over, the studio boss turned to Blanke, and said, "If that sonofabitch doesn't find water soon I'll go broke!" Warner didn't want Bogart to die at the end and it was with utmost difficulty that Blanke and Huston managed to cling on to their version, in which Dobbs is savagely murdered at a waterhole by Bedoya and his bandits and, in the fadeout, Old Howard laughs as the gold dust is blown to the wind.

For John and Evelyn, Mexico meant adopting a thirteen-year-old boy and discovering pre-Columbian art. The orphan was Pablo Albarran, an Indian youth who had attached himself to the company. An attractive boy with an alive, smiling face, mournful black eyes, and olive skin, he had made himself useful, fetching soft drinks or chairs when needed, cleverly anticipating needs. When it was learned he was an orphan, sleeping in doorways, surviving as best he could, he became a sort of mascot. John put him on the payroll; he in turned hired other kids to work for him. Pablo was most resourceful and John was quite taken with him. "Up to the time we got him, he'd been clawing to stay alive," John says. "When we took him home it was great watching that kid grow backwards—from a young old man to a little boy."

The educating was left to Evelyn and his first English word was "mo-ther," as he followed her as a docile puppy and they eventually found a school in Ojai, north of Los Angeles, that was able to cope with his language difficulty and illiteracy. In retrospect, Evelyn would wonder if they ever did Pablo any good: "You find a kid at the tender age of thirteen scuffling to keep life and limb together, no home to go to. You take him in hand, you feed and clothe him, fix his teeth, give him an education. Sounds really okay. Except everything has been mentioned but love."

After two months, the company said good-by to Croves and flew to California for backlot filming of a bandits' raid on the prospectors' camp. John found an old photo of Traven, showed it to Bogart and asked him if he recognized the man. "Sure, that's Croves," said Bogey. To Huston's satisfaction, the Traven enigma had been solved. To the world, even Traven's death in 1969 was not to be the end. In 1977, the BBC was the latest to try to unravel the Traven mystery in an hour-long documentary that investigated the possibility that Traven was the son of Kaiser Wilhelm, Bavarian socialist Ret Marut, or expatriate American writer Traven Torsvan.

On the Warner back lot, a mountainside had been recreated with sixty tons of earth and a miniature forest of transplanted trees for the bandits' raid sequence. Bedoya was brought along from Mexico. He was now a relaxed and confident actor and therefore an obvious target of one of John's more elaborate practical jokes. In his closeups, Bedoya rode a plaster horse with an electrically stimulated gallop. After a morning in the mechanical saddle, Huston asked Bedoya for one last take before lunch. Wearily Alfonso climbed back into the saddle. The mechanical horse was set in motion and Huston called lunch and walked off the set. When Bedoya realized what was going on and tried to hop off, he couldn't. Huston had had someone smear triple-strength glue on the saddle.

The lengthening schedule made Bogart mad because it caused him to miss the San Francisco-to-Honolulu yacht race with *Santana*. "We had a terrible row and were sore as hell at each other for days," says Huston. "Then we had a few drinks of an ancient tequila laced with scotch, and anger melted into understanding and then sympathy."

The Treasure of the Sierra Madre was released in December

1947 to glowing reviews and, a month later, received four Oscar nominations—Best Supporting Actor, for Walter Huston's toothless Old Howard, for Best Direction, Best Screenplay and Best Picture. But *Sierra Madre* was not an overwhelming box office success—audiences apparently resented Bogart's departure from the immensely popular *Casablanca* stereotype— and its vindication as John Huston's best film was only to come gradually.

On Oscar night, the Hustons—father and son—got Academy Awards, although Laurence Olivier's *Hamlet* copped Best Picture. Holding up his two Oscars—for Best Directing and Best Screenplay, John hollered, "If these were hollow and had a drink in them I'd toast Henry Blanke!" And Walter, standing proudly next to his son, put a hand on his shoulder and said, "A long time ago I brought up a boy. When he became a writer I told him one thing—'Some day you write a good part for your old man.' Well, by golly, he did!"

At the post-Oscar celebrations at John and Evelyn's in Tarzana, the host sported a pet monkey on his shoulder and, later, engaged in a football game with agent Collier Young and writer Charles Grayson. The game was played in the mud with a genuine Ming vase as a ball and with Blanke and Betty as referees. The players wore tuxedos and the spirit of the competition got so keen that two of Young's ribs were fractured, which brought his wife, Ida Lupino, to join the melee. Bogart just watched, impeccable, with a drink.

"So what do we do for an encore, kid," Bogey asked the pooped director after Ida Lupino had sprained her back.

John grinned.

Key Largo became the encore—with Bogey and Betty starring, together with Edward G. Robinson, Lionel Barrymore, and Claire Trevor.

8

HORIZON AND
WITCH HUNT

Huston's instinct—and need for money—told him to forge
ahead while he was hot. *Key Largo* was no problem, just a lot
of nice hard work and laughs with Bogey. It was when he
needed fifty thousand dollars—"to clear the decks," he explained to Jack Warner—and the studio boss turned him down
that he blew his top. Hadn't he worked at the goddamn studio
for ten years and on a dozen pictures? Hadn't they implicitly
trusted him by investing nearly three million in *Sierra Madre*
and letting him shoot it in Mexico? Jack granted all that, but a
personal loan was out of the question. No arguments.

Holding onto money was a problem, had always been a problem. "You get this colored paper and you give it to someone
and he gives it to someone else and that someone else gives it
to someone else," was the way he described money. He was
earning five thousand a week at Warners now and managed to
blow it nearly every week somehow. There were shouting and
ugly words at Tarzana, with Evelyn calling him and his atti-
tude toward money infantile—and Pablo listening.

The way John's jockey friend Bill Pearson told it, Huston

had the studio pay him his weekly salary in cash. "I remember one week he was broke, as usual, and they handed him an envelope with five grand inside," Pearson recalls. "'You riding today, kid?' he asked me. 'Yeah,' I told him. I was aboard a real loser that afternoon and when I went by John's box I gave a kind of shrug, to let him know I didn't have a prayer. Well, he got it wrong—figured I was giving him an inside tip—and he laid every cent of that five grand on the nose of my sixty-to-one filly. After the race as I was coming back past the stands, I saw smoke curling up. And there was Johnny, sadly feeding packages of tickets into a bonfire he'd started."

Huston not only played the horses, he bought them, sometimes against Pearson's advice. One week, John bought a rogue filly named Bargain Lass. He desperately wanted the horse to win a race and Pearson rode her and was almost thrown from the saddle the first time at the gate.

Evelyn was to remember being sent to the track to bet a thousand dollars borrowed from Tola Litvak on a filly John half owned. Her instructions were to check with their trainer if the horse had a chance and, if not, only to make a token bet of a hundred dollars. Tony the trainer shook his head and Evelyn bet a hundred dollars, but on twenty-to-one odds, the horse won. When she phoned John on the set, he had already heard the thrilling news on the radio and multiplied the one thousand dollars by twenty. When she reminded him of his instructions and told him she had only bet a hundred, she was talking to a dead phone. "That night he didn't come home at all," she would write in her memoirs. "Lesson for the day: If you want to win brownie points with gamblers, better to lose big than to win a chickenshit bet."

If gambling and other women had not been a problem, Evelyn could probably have taken the animal menagerie John assembled at Tarzana. Dogs, parakeets, goats, pigs, horses, and a burro named Socrates roamed everywhere. John's attachment to animals was deep and atavistic and something Evelyn and most other people couldn't quite understand. The staff at Tarzana now included Charley, the stable man, Zeke, the caretaker, and his wife-cook, Belle, plus Nancy who kept the house.

One reason why Jack Warner might not have been willing to be too liberal with private loans was that business was bad. The writing on the wall was the nosediving movie attendance —down from eighty to sixty million a week between 1946 and 1948—and the studios were making their first layoffs since the mid-1930s. Louis B. Mayer started the axing, cutting his MGM staff by 20 per cent. Harry Cohn followed suit at Columbia. No one was spared. Jack tried to make life so miserable for Henry Blanke that he would quit. With *The Story of Louis Pasteur, The Life of Emile Zola, The Adventures of Robin Hood, Jezebel, The Maltese Falcon,* and *The Treasure of the Sierra Madre* behind him, the little Berliner had been signed to an "unprecedented" fifteen-year contract that Warner now tried to weasel out of by the time-honored tactic of assigning inferior properties to the producer. Blanke was to hang tough, however, until his contract had run its course in 1959, although the joke around Burbank was that he was afraid of eating in the executive dining room for fear of being poisoned.

Key Largo was formal prewar drama. Maxwell Anderson's 1939 play had come four years after *Winterset,* his most famous play, and was not among his conspicuous successes. It dealt with a Spanish Civil War deserter who tries to justify himself for his failure to perform a duty that might have cost him his life.

Like most Americans, John had been impressed by *The Best Years of Our Lives,* Wyler's picture about the collisions of postwar realities and the tensions and expectations of men and women trying to find each other again. In *Key Largo* John wanted to match *The Best Years* in theme, to say that a man cannot dispel his problems by avoiding them and that a stand must be taken at home too if personal freedom is to be retained. His collaborator on the script was a writer who wanted to become a director. Six years younger than John, Richard Brooks was a pipe-smoking Philadelphian who already had six scripts behind him, including the screen version of his own wartime novel, *Crossfire.*

To get themselves in the mood, John and Richard and their

wives flew to hot and sticky Key Largo and got the owner of the only hotel to come from Key West and open the resort for these off-season Hollywoodites. A cook and a waitress were brought in and the owner discovered John was a gambler by losing a hundred-dollar bet on an unlikely ecclesiastic question. The next day, the owner had craps, roulette, blackjack, and chemin de fer tables installed. Work on the script stopped as John gambled all night and slept all day. Richard, who was not a gambler, got into the act out of sheer boredom and Evelyn and Harriet Brooks took a plane to Nassau without their mates' really knowing. When they came back after a week of Caribbean sightseeing, Evelyn brought John a baby capuchin monkey. John had lost ten thousand dollars, Brooks eight thousand, and the foursome flew back to Los Angeles with the pet monkey which they named Dodie.

The finished Huston-Brooks screenplay changed Anderson's Spanish Civil War deserter into a disillusioned GI veteran who has difficulties adjusting to postwar life. Bogart was completely at home in the reluctant hero persona and played the veteran with a mixture of defensive inwardness and moody resilience. As a brutal gang lord who, with his hoods, takes over a resort hotel in the Florida Keys, Edward G. Robinson was back to his Al Capone routine. The first shot of him, sitting in a tub of water mouthing a cigar, is as famous as John's remark, "I wanted to get a look at the animal with its shell off."

Since most of the action takes place within the confines of the resort, Huston shot 90 per cent of the picture at Warners' stages. He did get to go to Florida for some moody location photography and managed to stay away from the gambling. His cameraman was the legendary Karl Freund, who, besides giving *Key Largo* its compact, moody sheen showed its director some very naughty pornographic home movies.

Huston directed with new assurance, setting the mood of heat, suspense, and threatened violence and sustaining it with movement of characters that emphasized glances and gestures to hypnotic effect. He often concentrated the action in long, depth-of-focus shots that allowed savant groupings and heightened the *No Exit* claustrophobia of involuntary togetherness.

"*Key Largo* was a big job for me," he recalls. "There are a lot of things I don't like about the picture. What I do like is the way it unfolds. It's a very *adroit* picture."

He still needed a fifty-thousand-dollar loan, and at a cocktail party after the completion of *Key Largo* ran into Sam Spiegel, who, after hearing Jack Warner wouldn't advance "a measly fifty grand" on an extra picture commitment, offered to get the money.

"You do that and I'll be your pal for life," John answered.

"How about being my partner instead. If I get you the money will you go with *me* on a picture commitment?"

If Jack didn't appreciate him why not go with this little promoter who claimed they had met before the war in London?

Like Goldwyn, Spiegel was a native of the Warsaw ghetto, a stout, hawk-nosed man with sad, moist eyes, an expression of harried innocence and a habit of running his tongue swiftly over his upper lip. His professional name was S. P. Eagle, and the activities of his confusing career included stock promotion, swamp draining and, after three years in the United States in the late 1920s, assignments for Carl Laemmle in Berlin. He had returned to Hollywood stone broke in 1939 after obscure years in London, living in attics but refusing jobs. He would be a producer, he said, nothing else. He had finally sold Darryl Zanuck on permitting him to produce the very successful *Tales of Manhattan*. That had been in 1942. How he had managed during the intervening years was never discussed.

Now, Sam was relatively affluent and married to a starlet, Lynne Baggett, a tall, statuesque girl with fluffy blond curls piled on top of her head. In forty-eight hours, Sam promoted $50,000 from Bank of America, turned the money over to a stunned Huston, snapped half of it from him again, saying $25,000 made John his partner in Horizon Pictures. Next, he flew to New York and, on the strength of Horizon Pictures and his director-partner's track record, promoted $900,000. Finally, he got a release deal for their upcoming and as-yet undecided first independent production.

John had to admit he was impressed, but he had seen

enough con men at the race track not to be completely bowled over and he never let Spiegel forget on whose reputation money was raised. John was enjoying the heady pleasure of being involved in the best game in town—letting the studios fight over you. Going with Spiegel was the wrong move and therefore, by some screwy Hollywood logic, the right thing to do. Jules Buck, John's wartime buddy and *San Pietro* production chief, became the secretary-treasurer of the fledgling company.

Evelyn was to remember one early executive meeting cum dinner at Tarzana. She and John, Joyce and Jules Buck were waiting for Spiegel, who was late. They were having cocktails and munching nuts while Nancy, the maid, worried about the dinner getting burned. Dodie was out of her cage and playing about on the coffee table when Sam arrived. The slamming of his car door startled Dodie, and she peed in the bowl of nuts on the table before leaping over to nestle on John's arm.

"God, I'm famished," Sam said, sitting down and popping a fistful of nuts into his mouth before anyone could say anything. When Nancy announced that dinner was served, Sam watched twelve-inch Dodie and asked if the monkey was ever allowed in the kitchen.

"Oh sure, Mr. Spiegel," Nancy answered, "she's there all the time."

"In that case," said Sam, "I think I'll just stick to these nuts."

Horizon Pictures—known affectionately between John and Sam as Shit Creek Productions—was neither a strikingly bold move nor a particularly innovative idea in 1948. Wyler, Capra, and George Stevens had started the postwar "independents" phenomenon with Liberty Films, releasing through RKO. Mervyn LeRoy had formed Arrowhead Productions, Alfred Hitchcock and Cary Grant had incorporated together, and now Bogart was setting up Santana Productions. Bogey's partners were Robert Lord, his lawyer, and Mark Hellinger, who had produced *The Killers*, and was therefore the only intelligent producer in the world according to Hemingway. Unfortunately

John Huston today. (Allied Artists)

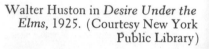
Walter Huston in *Desire Under the Elms*, 1925. (Courtesy New York Public Library)

Baby Uncle Sam, John age three, in his vaudeville debut for Walter.

The Hustons, father and son.

Hamming it up with William Wyler.

John in 1934.

Juarez script writers (left to right) John Huston, Aeneas MacKenzie, and Wolfgang Reinhardt. (Warner Brothers)

The Maltese Falcon
Elisha Cook, Jr., Sydney Greenstreet, Humphrey Bogart, and Mary Astor.
(Collection Cahiers du Cinéma)

In This Our Life
Charles Coburn and Bette Davis. (Collection Cahiers du Cinéma)

Across the Pacific
Humphrey Bogart, Mary Astor, and Sydney Greenstreet.
(Collection Cahiers du Cinéma)

Newlyweds John and Evelyn.

The Treasure of Sierra Madre
John as American tourist. (Collection Cahiers du Cinéma)

We Were Strangers
John Garfield and Jennifer Jones. (Collection Cahiers du Cinéma)

John, Evelyn, and Pablo. (Collection Cahiers du Cinéma)

as soon as Santana Productions got really going, the ever-worrying Hellinger died of a heart attack.

Liberty Films tried to tilt the business toward director authority, but, like the other independents, it was basically an attempt at keeping careers going. "Independence" was a figure of speech insofar as banks demanded such guarantees of distribution as to have the stars back eating out of the studios' hands again. Stars often picked properties for themselves with disastrous results, but even if their choices were judicious and they put up their own money, they needed the majors to bring their finished films to market. The initiative shifted somewhat but Hollywood remained a company town and, most galling perhaps, the independent films that were made weren't even the best pictures. *The Snake Pit*, Tola and Livvy's triumph, was a Twentieth Century Fox picture, Billy Wilder's *A Foreign Affair* was a Paramount picture and the Spencer Tracy-Katharine Hepburn smash *Adam's Rib* was a Metro picture directed by in-house contractee George Cukor.

In take-home pay, Horizon Pictures was something of a comedown for John, but, he hoped, only a temporary one. The company paid its director-partner (and only asset) three thousand dollars a week out of the Bankers Trust kitty—the same as Capra, Wyler, and Stevens paid themselves with RKO's money. Quite naturally Spiegel was anxious to get going before too much capital was eaten up and the two partners quickly settled on *Rough Sketch*, a short story about revolution in Cuba by Robert Sylvester. As distributor, Columbia immediately exercised its *droit de seigneur* and changed the title to *We Were Strangers*.

Huston needed someone to write with and Sam got him Peter Viertel, who since his Marine Corps stint had become a novelist and, like his mother, a screenwriter. Salka Viertel, whose wartime salon had accommodated the Huxleys, Bertrand Russell, and Igor Stravinsky, was past her scripting prime (her latest was *Two-Faced Woman* for George Cukor in 1941) but she was still Louis B. Mayer's trusted script reader. She was very much at home with her son's generation and her long-time lover was Peter's contemporary (and MGM house producer)

Gottfried Reinhardt, with whose brother, Wolfgang, John had been "paired" on the *Juarez* script in 1939. Like John, Peter Viertel was an outdoors type who between writing assignments for Selznick, Litvak, and Hitchcock lived with his wife, Virginia, in Klosters, Switzerland. Viertel was not the only writer John had banging out Latin-American intrigue. Aldous Huxley and Christopher Isherwood were drumming up something they called *Below the Equator* with tried and true ingredients—a dictator of sorts, an American pilot, some revolutionaries—but unlike *We Were Strangers*, their script was farcical. *Below the Equator*, like the previous Huxley-Isherwood attempt, never got off the ground.

To write *We Were Strangers*, John, Evelyn, Peter, and Virginia flew to Cuba and immediately fell in love with the place. An added attraction was that Peter knew Cuba's most famous *norteamericano*, Ernest Hemingway. In due course, the two couples were invited to visit Mary and Papa at La Finca, their home outside Havana complete with swimming pool and yacht moored in the bay. Hemingway was happy to meet the man who had written *The Killers* into a top-notch movie and the visit turned into a May Day weekend, complete with yachting and fishing. When they pulled into a cove on the second day, John shot an iguana sunning itself on an onshore rock only to see the blood-splattered animal disappear. To true Hemingway fashion, Papa said the wounded animal had to be found and, with John and Peter following like chastised schoolboys, the big man picked up a rifle and slipped overboard and waded to shore. Huston and Viertel soon gave up, but Hemingway stayed in the sizzling midday sun searching for the animal until, two hours later, he found it in a crevice, quite dead.

Hemingway was finishing *Across the River and into the Trees*. The title, he explained, was from Stonewall Jackson's dying words, and the story was simply the stoic last days of a veteran of two wars who, in a wintry contemporary Venice, holds death off until he can have one more fling at sport and love. Papa talked about death, saying he was fascinated by the grislier aspects of dying and quoting from *A Natural History of the Dead* about changing colors of unburied cadavers. He also talked about the "child-woman" he was putting into the novel, actually Adriana Ivacich, a nineteen-year-old Venetian girl he had met the year before, and whose brother was staying with the Hemingways.

Besides *Across the River and into the Trees*, which John said he would like to make into a movie, they discussed the picture at hand. Demonstrations of a violent nature could easily take place here, Hemingway warned, and attempts to overthrow the dictatorship of Fulgencio Batista was a constant possibility. If John and Peter wanted to write a movie about revolution, they had come to the right place.

Huston and Viertel wrote a rousing opening for *We Were Strangers*: A revolutionary hands out pamphlets. He is tracked He seeks refuge with his student sister and, feeling safe at the university campus, is gunned down. The sister at the graveside swearing revenge. Meanwhile, the Assembly "votes" emergency measures forbidding all public gatherings of more than four persons. The deputies cast their ayes by standing up. They watch each other as they get up, one by one, until unanimity. Nothing is said.

Parliamentary cowardice was not only a wholly outlandish metaphor. It was in Washington and it panicked Hollywood into giving the House Un-American Activities Committee (HUAC) what it needed most—publicity and an all-star cast for its hearings. There was Adolphe Menjou telling committee member Richard Nixon that anyone who listened to Paul Robeson "singing his communist songs" ought to be ashamed. There was Gary Cooper declaring that Hollywood commies had dared tell him "America will be better off without Congress," Ronald Reagan speechifying against Communist infiltration of the talent guilds and Robert Taylor defending his appearance in *Song of Russia* by declaring that "Roosevelt aides" had instructed him to play in that 1943 MGM picture. More memorable was the testimony of Ginger Rogers' mother who testified *Tender Comrade* was subversive because her daughter had been compelled to say, "Share and share alike— that's democracy." The "unfriendly" witnesses never got a hearing because their testimony was barred, although Dalton

Trumbo managed to yell into network microphones that this was the beginning of concentration camps in America. Within days the studio heads—Mayer, Goldwyn, Warner, Harry and Jack Cohen, Dore Schary and Spyros Skouras—met at the Waldorf Astoria in New York and agreed on a blacklist which eventually grew to about two hundred and fifty names. Self-criticism was the order of the day at the Directors Guild where Cecil B. DeMille was the rightwing rallying point.

Huston was only political in an emotional sense, but he joined Wyler and Philip Dunne in the less than heroic counterforce. They formed the Committee for the First Amendment—an organization soon listed by the California Un-American Activities Committee as "a communist front"—not so much to defend the Hollywood Ten as to plead for sanity. Their credo was, "Any investigation into the political beliefs of the individual is contrary to the basic principles of our democracy. Any attempt to curb the freedom of expression and to set arbitrary standards of Americanism is in itself disloyal to both the spirit and the letter of the Constitution." Some five hundred people joined their committee, including the Bogarts, Gene Kelly, Katharine Hepburn, Burt Lancaster, Eddie Robinson, Ira Gershwin, Gregory Peck, Kirk Douglas, Paulette Goddard and Burgess Meredith, Myrna Loy, and Billy Wilder. Evelyn was to remember their naïveté in chartering a plane and flying to Washington to complain to their congressmen in person about the HUAC hearings: "We faced a hostile, sophisticated, worldly press who made us look like stupid children interfering with grownup problems. When we entered the House hearing room, which was like a movie set with its cameras, bright lights and star performers, the chairman J. Parnell Thomas switched the scheduled witness and brought on Hollywood writer John Howard Lawson, whom the committee claimed was a bona fide, card-carrying member of the Communist Party. The purpose was to make us appear as Party members too, since we were clearly sympathetic toward Mr. Lawson."

John had one close call. Jack Warner testified he had never seen a communist and wouldn't know one if he saw one, but in secret testimony he said communists injected "ninety-five percent of their propaganda into films through the medium of writers." When the committee wanted to know which writers he had in mind, Jack said the obvious cases were Howard Koch because of *In Our Time,* and Ring Lardner, Jr. Warner never mentioned that John Huston was the coauthor of the Woodrow Wilson play and the committee apparently never found out. Howard, however, was branded.

We Were Strangers was made in an atmosphere that wasn't exactly the height of creative serenity. The leading lady, Jennifer Jones, whom Selznick loaned to Horizon for two thousand a week, was in the middle of a breakup with her erratic actor-husband Robert Walker. Then the leading man, John Garfield, was called a friend of all the subversive leftists at the HUAC hearings.

John was glad to get out of town. With cameraman Russell Metty and cast, he flew to Havana for exteriors. The script had American revolutionary Tony Fenner (Garfield) dig a tunnel into a cemetery with the help of Jennifer Jones and Gilbert Roland to assassinate a high-ranking member of a fictitious 1930s Cuban regime. But this was the Cuba of strongman Batista who had ruled behind various straw men since 1935, and the movie company was soon advised that filming in a cemetery was sacrilegious. Constructing matching sets at Columbia stages on Gower Street added to the cost—and Spiegel's ulcers, but Metty cleverly matched shots taken in Havana with the studio interiors.

As *Sierra Madre* and *Key Largo, We Were Strangers* is existentialist and introduces the moral paradox of violence justifying nonviolent ends. The film touches base on all problems confronting the individual in a collective struggle. There is the person who refuses to spill blood, the person who is against injustice and there is the intellectual whose family is close to the dictator. And—maybe independent production had some merit —*We Were Strangers* isn't smeared with incessant Muzak. It had a simple guitar score by George Antheil, John's friend from his Montparnasse days. The fierce gun battle which ends the picture has the dying Garfield holding a smoking machine gun while a calypso tune wells up on the soundtrack and Gilbert Roland sings, "Tony Fenner died for me—and now I have my liberty."

Harry Cohn hated *We Were Strangers*, especially after the *Hollywood Reporter* trade review called it "a shameful handbook of Marxian dialectics . . . and the heaviest dish of red theory ever served to an audience outside the Soviet [Union]." *Time* called the film "murky . . . but above average," and Columbia took it out of circulation shortly after its release.

With author-critic James Agee and Gilbert Roland, Evelyn came along on a Huston deer hunt in Idaho, a trip John would call the best part of their life together. A month later, Evelyn had moved out of Tarzana and into an apartment house above the Sunset Strip where Paulette and Burgess Meredith lived. Announcing the separation to the ever-snooping gossip columnists, Evelyn blamed John's menagerie in Tarzana for the breakup: "I'm allergic to fur—and he's got a regular zoo out there. Each day I had to share my husband with monkeys, horses, dogs, cats, parakeets, goats, pigs, and a burro named Socrates. When he brought home a chimp, that was the beginning of the end."

Huston's first biographer, William F. Nolan, would write that John merely remarked, "I taught that girl to play a sweet game of billiards." Evelyn liked to relate the final scene differently. To her, the final shot was the new pet chimpanzee:

EVEYLN: John, darling, I'm sorry. One of us has got to go . . . It's the monkey or me.

JOHN (after a long pause): Honey . . . it's you.

The truth was less flippant. John had made nineteen-year-old Enrica Soma pregnant and the final confrontation—unmentioned in Evelyn's memoirs—was in the presence of her lawyer, Leon M. Cooper. All John had to do was to sign. He did, agreeing to pay her $42,000 in 524 installments of $81.10 each; $7,500 payable in quarterly installments of $250 each beginning April 1, 1950, and $10,000 for each six months during which her own income didn't reach that amount. She got half the pre-Columbian art collection—the best half, John thought—but he kept the ranch in Tarzana.

9

METRO-GOLDWYN-MAYER

John obtained a divorce decree in Juarez, Mexico, February 10, 1950, and the next day, in La Paz, married the seven-months pregnant daughter of Mr. and Mrs. Anthony Soma, the owner of the Tony's Wife restaurant on East Fifty-fifth Street and Tony's on West Fifty-second Street in New York. The new couple kept the marriage a secret, but Louella Parsons got wind of it and in her syndicated column talked about elopement and hinted strongly that the new Mrs. Huston might have some difficulty convincing a California court it was all legal.

John had been introduced to Ricki by Jennifer Jones at a party she and David Selznick—themselves barely a legalized couple—had given after their honeymoon in Italy. Actually John had seen Ricki at her father's restaurants in New York when she was nine and a budding ballerina. He had been charmed by the lovely, round-faced nineteen-year-old at the Selznicks', a girl who had danced with George Balanchine and attracted movie attention when her photograph appeared on the cover of *Life* magazine. She had been signed by MGM to a dancing and acting contract but wasn't doing anything.

When the evening ended at the Selznicks', John asked if he could take her home. Instead, they went to Tarzana—"eloped?" in Parsons' period phrase. In Evelyn's 1977 memoirs, the question was posed a bit more bluntly: "Is there something appealing about a girl-child growing up to a fuckable age under your nose? Probably. Particularly when the girl-child has no hesitancy in using her newfound wiles. And the wife has cleared the way." When the Somas heard about the seduction of their daughter by a forty-three-year-old married movie director, they exploded. Soma threatened to sue and called John a reckless libertine without respect for women. "He uses them," the restaurateur told the press, "and then he ignores them. He is a mystery to himself, and he doesn't want to be analyzed." Grandfatherhood eventually mellowed Soma.

Divorce and a new stepmother didn't ruffle the existence of Pablo too much. Now a handsome but tiny five-foot sixteen-year-old, Pablo stayed on at the ranch and, between intermittent schooling, was involved in each Huston movie, sometimes as a wrangler, sometimes as a still photographer.

What John needed—again—was money. As a recent double Oscar winner, he wasn't the most difficult director to sell to the studios, and before any negative word-of-mouth could adversely affect his track record, Paul Kohner had him signed up for three thousand a week at Metro-Goldwyn-Mayer.

The fiasco of *We Were Strangers* put independence and Horizon Pictures on the back burner. This was about par for the course in 1949. Liberty Films was also a noble failure, largely because Frank Capra hadn't been able to hit his prewar stride with *State of the Union*, and he, William Wyler, and George Stevens were now employees of Paramount Pictures. With Liberty Films throwing in the towel, others followed suit. Mervyn LeRoy's Arrowhead Productions, the Cary Grant–Alfred Hitchcock combine, James Cagney Productions, and others dropped from the "active list" of the independents.

At Metro, Huston was to make *The Asphalt Jungle* and *The Red Badge of Courage* (and, almost, *Quo Vadis*). The filmization of the Stephen Crane classic was to be an ugly war but a lot of the controversy it stirred tends to fall into place when it is remembered that it was made during MGM's painful decline and Louis B. Mayer's personal fadeout. The biggest, most glittering film factory was still in the hands of tired old men—

Nicholas Schenck at the presidency of Loew's in New York and Mayer in Culver City. In the face of corporate losses and the apparent inability of Schenck and Mayer to revitalize the companies—now nominally "divorced" but still clinging together—they had appointed Dore Schary as head of production, with Mayer acting in a supervisory capacity. Schary, who had been head of RKO until Howard Hughes had fired him for insisting on doing *Battleground*, began paring the studio roster, cutting loose "more stars than are in heaven," as Metro's press releases had said for so long. But he too often made movies that were out of touch and he was let go in 1956, when MGM's annual losses were approaching five million dollars.

John was hired to coscript and direct a new screen version of *Quo Vadis*, a project being pushed personally by Schary. Gregory Peck and Elizabeth Taylor would star with Walter Huston, and the picture would shoot in Rome starting in July 1949. The producer was Arthur Hornblow, Jr., a former Goldwyn and Paramount house producer, who had been Myrna Loy's husband before marrying tobacco heiress Lenora Schinasi Morris. John set to work writing the new script of Henryk Sienkiewicz's 1896 recreation of Nero's Rome, trying to retain some of the Polish author's relish for imperial paganism and to diminish some of his saccharine Christian loftiness. In May, however, while John was in Rome to oversee the construction of the first sets Peck suffered an eye infection and Schary was forced to postpone the shooting start.

To keep Hornblow and Huston busy while Peck convalesced, Schary assigned a completely different property to them—*The Asphalt Jungle*, a new novel by W. R. Burnett, with whom John had worked on *High Sierra* in 1940. John was more than happy to drop *Quo Vadis* for a big-city crime thriller, and together with Ben Maddow, the skillful adapter of William Faulkner's *Intruder in the Dust*, he wrote a fast and clinical screenplay. *The Asphalt Jungle* was passably Hustonian, an inside story of crime in which the interplay of the characters, with all their weaknesses and petty treachery, becomes the nemesis.

The film was cast from MGM's diminished albeit still ample

pool of talent. For the role of Doc, the master criminal and planner of a million-dollar jewel robbery, Hornblow and Huston chose John's old friend from Macdougal Street, Sam Jaffe. For the crooked lawyer who says crime is perhaps nothing more than a malformation of human genius, they got Louis Calhern. Jean Hagen, an unknown stage actress, was cast as the feminine lead. John wanted Sterling Hayden for the role of Dix Handley, a hood hounded by drink and bad luck. Schary didn't. Hayden was fighting his own alcoholic problem and was under psychiatric care. Huston won.

Hayden remembers how it was to meet Huston for the first time: "When you're greeted by John Huston, you know what it's like to be met. You step into his office, and it is full of people and smoke. The moment Huston sees you he swings to his feet, his eyes on you alone. You suddenly sense that simply by coming here today you have relieved this rangy man of some immense burden. You are the one person he wants to see at 2 P.M. sharp . . . He clears the room, then says, 'I've admired you for a long time, Sterling. They just don't know what to make of a guy like you in this business.' "

Still to be cast was the part of the lawyer's mistress, a character only in two scenes. Lucille Ryman of the studio talent department suggested Huston try out Marilyn Monroe, a bit actress under contract to Fox who had not yet had a speaking role. He agreed to let the girl read for the part.

Monroe arrived in John's couchless office having memorized the first of the two scenes, a scene which had her stretch out on a couch.

"I'd like—to—read the first scene on the floor," she said.

"Sure, dear, anyway it feels right to you."

Kicking off her shoes, she got down on the carpet and acted out the scene. Then, before he could say anything, she asked if she could do the scene again. He nodded. After the second runthrough she got up and nervously awaited his reaction.

"You didn't have to do it twice, honey," he smiled. "You had the part on the first reading."

Monroe would always feel her two best performances had been the last scene with Calhern in *The Asphalt Jungle* and the scene of her cracking up in *Don't Bother to Knock*. All that had come afterward—*Seven Year Itch, Bus Stop, The Prince and the Showgirl, Some Like It Hot*—she would consider inferior.

Benny Burt was cast as the stool pigeon, a scrawny little man with large, melancholy eyes. Burt was one of John's race-track friends who had waited for his acting opportunity since he had come to Hollywood in 1933. John also put him in *The Red Badge of Courage* and during the shooting of that picture Burt was to tell his story: "If it wasn't for horses, though, I never would have met *him*," he would say with a gesture toward Huston. "I was at the race track. I'm at the track, and I'm with three hoodlums from Chicago. I'm at the hundred-dollar window betting thirty-five hundred for those guys. He is behind me and he says to me, 'I always see you here.' So I tell him to bet this horse. He did and the horse won. So he says, 'Here's a hundred dollar ticket for you.' I say, 'You owe me nutting.' So he says, 'Then come have a drink with me.' So we had a couple of drinks. Then he says, 'What you doin' for dinner?' He wants me to have dinner with him. From then on I'm with him morning, noon, and night. I was with him the night his dad died. I told him, 'John, don't worry, I'll take care of you.' All my life, nobody ever gave me nutting, but from then on we were like brothers. I did everything for him. I drove him here, there. I let him hypnotize me. I took care of his clothes. His suits cost three hundred dollars apiece. He has fifty pairs of shoes at fifty-five dollars a pair. It burned me up when Cholly Knickerbocker called him one of the worst-dressed men. I was with him on Thanksgiving and I was with him on Christmas. I was his family."

The Asphalt Jungle was Huston's most complex film to date. Its characters are full of odd dimensions; ambiguity is the red thread running through their habitual occupation—crime. If Dix Handley (Hayden) is a criminal it is in order to get money to bet on horses. But should he win, he will use the money to return to his native Kentucky. His vivid sense of honor is illustrated by his stubborn insistence on paying a bookmaker what he owes him. While they all have a profound contempt for life and death, they are deeply conscious of individual dignity; they all despise cowards. One of them loves cats, someone else can't stand messy rooms. They are all after money, but only Cobby (Marc Lawrence) loves money for its own sake; the others want money to fulfill dreams, to satisfy passions and affirm themselves. The difference makes Cobby pitiable, a parvenu among aristocrats. A detective is taking part in the jewel heist not so much for the loot as to be part of something spectacular. When Doc (Jaffe) learns that if the jewels are returned the insurance company will pay half the gems' value, he behaves as if a major obstacle has been overcome. They expect failure, and when they succeed, Doc warns of probable disillusions ahead. When they talk, they are all on the defensive, each trying to detect hidden meanings in the words of the others. The most dramatically "gratuitous" scenes are the moments most heavily charged with significance.

With cameraman Harold Rosson, John shot nearly the whole picture in close shots, scrutinizing faces, movements of lips, and gazes. Dialogued scenes were often filmed with three characters. Sometimes the speaker is not even in the frame and the camera records not only the others' reaction but various connivances and complicities that freeze certain others out of new tenuous alliances. Nearly the whole picture takes place at night, allowing sources of light to play a psychological role. The lawyer's table lamp is the point where glances bisect. Sometimes it dissimulates faces, sometimes its glare dominates them.

The Asphalt Jungle was a success. "Rarely do crime melodramas come through as nearly perfect in writing, direction and performances as this beautifully constructed film version of W. R. Burnett's novel of underworld crime and connivery," said *Cue*, while *The Hollywood Reporter* called it "almost a classic of its type." Marilyn Monroe's boss was also enchanted. Said Darryl F. Zanuck, "John Huston gave her a helluva good role. Jesus, she was good in it. I thought it must have been the magic of Huston because I didn't think she had all that in her. But then I put her in *All About Eve* and she was an overnight sensation."

The Asphalt Jungle won Huston Academy Awards nominations for Best Direction and, with Maddow, Best Screenplay, but Joseph Mankiewicz took both Oscars with *A Letter to Three Wives*. Louis B. Mayer hated *The Asphalt Jungle*. Like Goldwyn, he loved movies where people sang and danced, and he hated stories set in squalor and pictures where people died in the end. "That *Asphalt Pavement* thing," he told Schary, "is full of nasty, ugly people doing nasty, ugly things. I wouldn't walk across the room to see a thing like that."

Mayer and Schary were also quarreling over *Quo Vadis*. Mayer thought in terms of a Cecil B. DeMille picture while Schary, an ardent Zionist, wanted Nero to be a symbolic Hitler killing Jewish martyrs. A compromise was worked out. Hornblow and Huston were pulled off *Quo Vadis*, which was given to the producer-director team of Sam Zimbalist (a "Mayer man" on the lot) and Mervyn LeRoy. Hornblow and Huston had already spent two millions dollars and gone through several writers and built some sets. Zimbalist and LeRoy ended up spending another twelve million dollars, but *Quo Vadis* grossed fifty million dollars. The Hornblow-Huston teaming was dissolved, Hornblow was given another assignment, and Huston was allowed to join Gottfried Reinhardt in preproduction of *The Red Badge of Courage*, which Louis B. Mayer hated even more than *The Asphalt Jungle*.

"That old classic book full of blood and killing has got no laughs, no songs, no entertainment value," complained Mayer, who had been in the business since 1907. But Schary was excited about the idea. "It can bring honor and prestige to MGM. And John promises me it won't cost too much. A million five, tops."

Reinhardt, who was seven years younger than John and whose first production job had been for Ernest Lubitsch on the film version of Noel Coward's *Design for Living*, was no longer Salka Viertel's lover but a paunchy man with a thick mane of wavy brown hair, an expression of profound cynicism, and a perpetual cigar stuck in his mouth. Married to Silvia, a slender girl with mocking air who commandeered him to take care of their dog, Gottfried had witnessed enough power struggles at

MGM to try to assert himself. Throughout the making of *Red Badge*, he tried to be all things to all men—Huston's loyal backstopper, Schary's inside overseer, and Mayer's Trojan horse, covering himself with memos to everybody and taking it on the chin from everybody.

John promised a lot of things. He would complete *Red Badge* in forty-three-days—nine days of rehearsals and thirty-four days of shooting. Above-the-line cost would be kept down by casting unknown "fresh faces" and character actors rather than stars.

When Mayer heard there would be no stars, nor any women, he threw up his hands. "I would rather shoot Huston than shoot the picture," he whined. "We could then put the money into a defense in court. No jury would convict me."

Huston *was* expensive. For *Red Badge*, he would be paid $4,000 a week and a flat $28,000 for adapting the Stephen Crane novel. And he was so deep in debt ("the ponies keep me broke!") that MGM had to advance him $150,000. Very reluctantly, the studio agreed.

Matrimony barely delayed the scripting of *The Red Badge of Courage*. John had started the screenplay on the plane to Juarez. He wanted to remain close to the book and, when he was through, prided himself for the fact that two thirds of the screen dialogue belonged to Crane.

On April 6, however, he took time out to organize a rousing birthday for his father. Walter would be sixty-six and John asked Mike Romanoff to lay on a nice affair. Friends were invited. Sam Spiegel, Jed Harris, Spencer Tracy, and Charles Grayson were to "take over" Romanoff's and give Walter an evening to remember. John's own cause to celebrate was Ricki's pregnancy. At forty-four he would finally be a father.

Celebrations started early. Walter had a birthday lunch with Paul Kohner and several other friends, but in the late afternoon he called John at MGM to say he had a curious nagging pain in the back and that he was afraid he wouldn't make the birthday party. John wasn't too worried. Walter had just arrived for a new picture—*Old 880* at Fox—and was staying at the Beverly Hills Hotel. Nan had stayed in New York to console the widow of their good friend Kurt Weill, who had died a week earlier. Before leaving New York Walter had had a complete physical and been pronounced in excellent health. Now, he told John he would be fine after a good night's sleep.

The evening wasn't the same without the guest of honor. John was there, with Ricki and Pablo, and the dozen guests. After dropping Ricki at home, John and Pablo went to the Beverly Hills Hotel. John looked in on his father and decided to rent a room across the hall and stay the night. At dawn, he was awakened and told his father's situation was serious. At 8 A.M., with his son at his side, Walter Huston died of internal bleeding and heart failure.

Nan Huston arrived by plane six hours too late. When asked for comment, all John could say was, "Dad was too tough to get sick. He just died, that's all. He went fast, the way he wanted to go."

10

SONS AND FATHERS

Ricki gave birth to a baby boy on April 16, 1950, as her husband got preproduction of *The Red Badge of Courage* into shape. The boy was named Walter Anthony Huston, after his two grandfathers.

Louis B. Mayer made one last attempt at stopping *Red Badge*. When Dore Schary was laid up at home for a few weeks with recurring back troubles, Mayer called in Huston and Reinhardt and tried to argue them out of wanting to do the film. *Red Badge* was old-fashioned, he told them. "How can you make a picture of boys in funny caps with popguns, and make people think the war they are fighting is terrible?" he asked. To make his point, he gave a vivid impression of how absurd it would be, a performance Huston later told him was one of the best he had ever seen.

Part of the film was to be shot at the Huston ranch, and—after leaving Temple Hospital with the baby, Ricki moved into a rented house at Malibu Beach, with John commuting between the beach, MGM, and the Valley ranch. Pablo was on the film too, and if Ricki didn't show up on the location every day, she was to come to Chico, in northeastern California, where the major River Crossing segment would be shot. In the meantime, she played hostess to various hangers-on John brought home. "She is a striking girl with an oval face and long dark hair drawn back right from her face, parted in the middle, and done up in a bun in back," Lillian Ross was to write in *Picture*.

Ross was a New York journalist and a friend of the Hemingways, who had met John during his trip East to confer with Nicholas Schenck and the Loew's hierarchy on *Red Badge*. "Come on out for the fireworks," John had told her when she had expressed interest in doing a series of pieces on the shooting of a major movie. The "inside story" book on the making of a movie was to become something of a paperback staple twenty-five years later, but when Ross's five *New Yorker* pieces were published in book form in 1952, this kind of acidulated reportage was without precedent.

John was in top form. First of all, he loved Stephen Crane's 1893 original and what it had to say about war. *The Red Badge of Courage* is the story of a boy soldier who swaggers to himself, is frightened, is reassured, is caught up in battle and runs, gains his "red badge" by an accident, returns, and becomes a demon of aggressive energy. And all for nothing. His regiment takes up its former position. If he has become a man, as he tries to believe, then what, asks the ironic structure of the book, is a man?

Crane doesn't give his farm boy a name until halfway through, when he becomes Henry Fleming. Huston simply called him Youth. As the others are neither types nor "rounded out" characters but individuals who only acquire meaning in their own context and in Crane's impressionistic imagination, Huston simply called them the Tattered Man, Tall Soldier, etc.

John won all the early rounds with the studio hands down. Against the better judgment of Dore Schary and Gottfried Reinhardt, he cast a non-professional, World War II hero Audie Murphy, as the Youth. "He's a gentle-eyed little killer," John said about the twenty-six-year-old Murphy. "Why, in the war he literally went out of his way to find Germans to kill. Gottfried and Dore didn't want him at first but I changed their minds. God, Audie won every medal there was—the Distinguished Service Cross, Medal of Honor, Silver Star, Purple Heart, Croix de Guerre—you name it, he won it. This gentle little guy. Greatness is often a matter of quality rather than ability. Dad had it. So has Audie. You take a great horse. Go past his stall and you can feel the vibrations in there. Audie is like that. He vibrates."

The way Schary explained it to Ross, Huston had a way of charming people. "I love John," Schary told her. "When he wants something from you, he sits down next to you and his voice gets a little husky and pretty soon you're a dead pigeon."

To back up the small, freckled-faced Murphy, Huston and Reinhardt chose Bill Mauldin as the Loud Soldier, John Dierkes as the Tall Soldier, Royal Dano as the Tattered Man and Douglas Dick as the Lieutenant—all unknowns.

With Harold Rosson again on camera, filming started August 25 at the Huston ranch, with John trying to direct from horseback—an idea he had to abandon as it was too hard on the horse. To cut costs, second-unit director Andrew Marton was hired as a "leapfrog" director: lining up scenes for Huston so that they could be shot without delay. This leapfrogging was soon abandoned, however, because Huston couldn't make up his mind on paper and once he got to a scene lined up by Marton changed things around.

The River Crossing was filmed along the Sacramento River northeast of San Francisco with 250 locally hired extras, all emerging soaked and triumphant from the white river despite MGM legal department's fears that some of them might drown. One of the commanding officers wore Huston's great-grandfather's silver-sheathed sword.

John enjoyed himself in Chico. Ricki and Pablo were with him, quartered together with the Reinhardts, and the leading members of the cast at the Oaks Hotel. He had a great time sending his assistants out into poolrooms to find tough-looking extras—"grizzled sonsofbitches"—instead of little theater amateur actors. With a three-day growth of beard he cast himself as a veteran Union soldier standing in a line of jeering, battle-weary men showing contempt for the Youth and the other raw recruits. And he bought himself a filly from Calumet Farms and named her Tryst. "God, someday I'll have a winner and then I'll be able to say, 'Well, you bastards, this is what it was all about.' Luck and the right kind of breeding. That's all I need."

Back at the studio Schary screened the rushes every night and said, "I'm really crazy about the picture."

Spiegel popped up. Since *We Were Strangers* he had produced *The Prowler* and *When I Grow Up*. Written by blacklisted Dalton Trumbo, *The Prowler* was the last picture that fellow blacklistee Joseph Losey directed in America before his lifelong exile in Britain. It starred Van Heflin and Evelyn Keyes (Evelyn would always remember it as the best thing she ever did). When Spiegel ran into Reinhardt and said he had Huston next, on *The African Queen*, Reinhardt replied that *Badge* would be a great picture.

"*The African Queen* will make a lot of money," Spiegel answered.

The African Queen was a pretty old property, a yarn Cecil Scott Forester had written in 1935 before hitting on his Captain Hornblower series. Warner Brothers had bought it, and in 1938 Henry Blanke had borrowed David Niven from Goldwyn to star opposite Bette Davis. At the last minute, however, Bette fell out with Blanke and told him she refused to be photographed out of doors. *The African Queen* had been sold to Twentieth Century Fox, and Spiegel routinely scavenged for properties that had lost their first bloom of excitement and could be had for a minimal down payment and percentages of future profits. The novel tells of adventure in colonial Africa in August 1914 and its protagonists are Charlie Alnutt, a Cockney mailboat captain, and Rosie Sayer, a missionary lady. After her father is killed, Rosie and Charlie are trapped in German East Africa, but rather than surrender they decide to make it to British East Africa and to take action against their new colonial enemy with the only means at their disposal—the mailboat named *The African Queen*—and a supply of explosives which can be used against the German gunboat guarding the mouth of Lake Victoria. The action involves a voyage down an uncharted and all but unnavigable river, over rapids and through stagnant marshes and past a German outpost in the old mailboat, which is rapidly falling apart.

Huston loved this story of initiative and endurance under constant threat of nature and hostile fellow-whites. But he wondered if the heroics of Rosie and Charlie shouldn't come to a magnificent and existential naught like the miner's trek in *Sierra Madre*, the revolutionaries' tunnel digging in *We Were Strangers* or even the Youth's regiment's return to its former position.

To turn C. S. Forester's novel into a screenplay, John chose as collaborator James Agee, *Life* magazine's movie critic and almost the only one of all the serious writers to work in Hollywood to have turned out scripts that were above average. Three years younger than John, Agee had already written one impressive script for John—Stephen Crane's psychic mystery short story "The Blue Hotel"—and the two had become friends during the deer-hunting trip with Evelyn and Gilbert Roland in Idaho. Agee was a fervent admirer of John and considered him the best thing that happened to American movies since the war. Doing features on movie directors was not the "in" thing at *Life* in 1950, but Agee had talked his editor into agreeing to a feature profile on Huston. Agee now came to the Coast and John set him up in a luxury ranch hotel in Santa Barbara and told him to get cracking.

Tryst wasn't winning any races, but John got a thirty-thousand-dollar trust fund from his father's estate. Walter's widow was the principal beneficiary of the will, receiving the eight-thousand-acre Porterville ranch and the Running Springs retreat, and there was twenty thousand dollars for Nan, Walter's sister who had never married. John had also inherited from Aunt Margaret, who had outlived her dear Bobby by only a few years. Always an eccentric, she had told her nephew she was dying of cancer, that she didn't want to know *when* and that he should "direct" her remaining years for her. "I can't trust Walter or Nan; they're all too sentimental, but you're such a cynic," she had told him. And for the last years of her life, John had indeed been in gentle control of Mrs. Carrington's life, sending her on interesting travels and cruises and keeping from her the physicians' reports on the bone cancer that slowly took her life.

John wrapped the filming of *Red Badge* only three days over schedule and the next day went duck hunting with one of the stuntmen while veteran Metro film cutter Margaret Booth began editing the footage to a seventy-eight-minute rough cut. When he returned to Culver City and saw the first cut, he told Ross he loved it. But Dore and Gottfried felt the picture needed "more story," perhaps a new scene or two in camp with the Youth. At the next screening, Booth had added ten minutes, but Reinhardt still didn't feel the Youth came across with the right amount of clarity.

John was impatient to get to *The African Queen*. MGM had agreed to suspend his contract while he made the independent picture for his own and Spiegel's Horizon Pictures. The day he left Metro, however, his weekly salary dropped from four thousand dollars to twenty-five hundred.

Jim Agee was not a strong man and he drove himself to keep up with the inexhaustible Huston when John joined him at the Santa Barbara ranch hotel. Every morning before breakfast, John played three vigorous sets of tennis. Agee, who was not in shape, made a strenuous effort to match Huston serve for serve. During one of these early morning workouts Agee collapsed on the court. A doctor warned him to "take it easy," but Agee was incapable of following such advice and he stayed on the script in an effort to have it ready for Huston's scouting trip to Africa. A few months later, Agee suffered his first heart attack—an ailment that would kill him five years later.

Writing with John could be exhilarating. Lillian Ross visited them once in Santa Barbara and jotted down Huston's ideas of how to write for the screen: "Tell me something I can understand. This isn't a novel. This is a screenplay. You've got to demonstrate everything, Jim. People on the screen are gods and goddesses. We know all about them. Their habits. Their caprices. But we can't touch them. They're not real. They stand for something, rather than *being* something. They're symbols. You can't have symbolism within symbolism, Jim."

John spent Christmas with Ricki and their nine-month-old

son and Pablo. Ricki was pregnant again. The child would be born in midsummer. In February 1951 the Hustons attended the first fully scored screening of *Badge*. Willy and Paul Kohner were there and both congratulated John, saying he had a great picture. Reinhardt was beaming. Two nights later, MGM "sneaked" the picture in a theater in Culver City with Louis B. Mayer in attendance. The preview was a disaster. The audience laughed in the wrong places and thirty-two people walked out. Preview cards said "Lousy" and "This stinks!" In the lobby afterward the mood was gloomy. "They hated it," said Booth. Mayer didn't say anything, just marched to his waiting limousine to be driven away. The following evening Huston and Reinhardt attended a sneak preview in Pasadena. The audience was young and many teen-agers booed Murphy when he ran from the advancing enemy bayonets. The death of the Tattered Man provoked howls.

"God," said John after the showing, "I'm glad I'm going to Africa tomorrow."

MGM tried to save its $1.6 million investment. With Huston somewhere along the Congo River, Schary, Reinhardt, and Booth recut the picture. They dubbed in a narration from the book, eliminated the death of the Tattered Man and edited the two main battles into one. Scenes translating the alternating hopes and fears of Crane's boy soldier disappeared altogether. By the time *Red Badge* opened to lukewarm reviews in New York it was down to seventy minutes. The first-run business was appalling and the film was soon double-billed with an Esther Williams flick. A year later Lillian Ross's book *Picture* came out, making Margaret Booth the villain of the story. *Picture* said a lot about the studio system, about the misplaced enthusiasm, the double-crossing, Schary's need to assert himself against Mayer, Reinhardt's ineffectual meddling, and, after the lukewarm previews, Schenck's less than enthusiastic release of the picture, but what would only be clear in hindsight was that *The Red Badge of Courage* was simply the wrong picture for the wrong time. In early 1951, the Communist offensive was routing GIs in Korea and American public opinion was in no mood for antiwar propaganda. "The picture was too realistic for the period," Huston told a Paris news conference in 1965. "People like you who've only seen the seventy-minute version can't imagine how much more realistic the one hour thirty-five minute version was. The producers tried to make *Badge* acceptable. I think they were wrong, nobody would have succeeded. What I should have done was show the picture to a limited public. By the way I wasn't unhappy with the producers' cut. It was clever. I wouldn't have cut it that way, but it was better than I had expected."

Picture shows how difficult it is for outsiders to understand the inner relations and workings of the film industry. Now it is Lillian Ross's indignant finger-pointing that looks naïve. In 1961, Reinhardt was involved in *Freud*, and in 1972, John had none other than Margaret Booth cut *Fat City* for him.

ZAIRE AND *THE QUEEN*

"Hey, old son, I've got a great property," John cooed into the phone. "The hero's a lowlife and since you're the biggest lowlife in town the part is ideal for you."

Bogart asked for details.

"Kid, we'll get Kate Hepburn and we'll make the whole damn thing in the Congo. Darkest Africa! It's really going to be something, you and me down there with the king pythons and the bull elephants. You're gonna love it!"

They drank lunch at Romanoff's and by midafternoon got on the phone to Katharine Hepburn in New York where she was appearing in *As You Like It*. John did the talking and managed to reveal to her the enticements of this incredible story about a skinny missionary spinster and a sweetwater rumpot who float down an African river to fire a homemade torpedo at a German gunboat. Yes, she said, he could send a copy of the script and, yes, they could come East and talk some more.

Bogart's career since *Key Largo* had been so-so. Nicholas Ray had directed the first Santana picture, *Knock on Any Door*, with Bogart as a lawyer defending a slum kid, and it had been followed by *Tokyo Joe, In a Lonely Place* and *Sirocco*. "*Knock on Any Door* was good but it could have been better and set us up on our feet because it made money," was Bogey's assessment. "*Tokyo Joe* made money too, *Sirocco* was one we had to do and it stank." He neglected to mention *In a Lonely Place* because he hated that moody melodrama about an eccentric screenwriter, which Ray had directed and his wife, Gloria Grahame, had costarred in.

Bogart listened to John's common sense about doing a color picture in deepest Africa. Santana Production and business worries were a bore. "I like to work with John," he said. "The Monster is stimulating. Offbeat kind of mind. Off center. He's brilliant and unpredictable. Never dull. When I work with John, I think about acting. I don't worry about business." Bogart had never worked with Kate Hepburn, but he had seen her on Broadway twenty years earlier and remembered her shapely legs. He had heard she was difficult, that her real interest was the stage, that she wouldn't sign autographs for film fans and had been fired from plays because she tried to direct them and now insisted on cutting her films.

She proved charming, however, on their first meeting—not dinner, as John had suggested after he and Bogart landed at La Guardia, but breakfast. She loved the script, had a thousand ideas for revisions, of course, and, she added, she was writing her autobiography and Africa would make "a wonderful chapter." But she, too, listened. Since the war she had been in six pictures and only *Adam's Rib* had been a real success. She was going to be forty-two in November and she had sharp feelings of regret over the decline of MGM. If she wasn't exactly ready to invest in an exciting picture she was ready to, well, perhaps defer her salary.

Huston was off, he told them, to look for a jet black river.

During his London stopover, he told Spiegel and Horizon's British backers that one way of making half a million dollars extra at the box office would be to shoot *The African Queen* in color. Yes, it was expensive—exposed negative would have to be flown to Technicolor's London laboratory every day—but he insisted. Africa meant color. While Spiegel and his backers mulled over the added expense, he got himself properly outfitted—boots from Maxwell's and, from T. Tauntz in New

Bond Street, a jacket with long, flaring tails nipped in at the waist, to go with drainpipe pants and a red-and-green Tattersall vest. He wasn't totally happy with the script that Agee and he had fashioned between tennis sets in Santa Barbara—the ending, especially, didn't satisfy him so he called Viertel in Switzerland and had the writer agree to come along for a polishing job.

The Congo where Huston and tag-along Viertel went location scouting in December 1950 was still ten years away from independence from Belgium and twenty-one years from renaming itself Zaire. Kinshasa was still Leopoldville, and Kisangani, where John and Peter were heading, was called Stanleyville.

Huston spent the better part of January and February 1951 flying across endless jungles looking for his black river. When Viertel wasn't rewriting, he went along on these scouting trips that totaled 25,000 air miles before Huston settled on the Ruiki, a tributary to the Lualaba, which, seventy-four years earlier, Sir Henry Morton Stanley had established as the mainstream of the Congo and not, as David Livingstone had hoped, the headwaters of the Nile. The Ruiki is ink black, the result of decaying vegetation, and it was also infested with blood flukes, a genus of parasitic microorganism which cause an intestine and liver disease characterized by dysentery and the passage of blood in the urine. There is a cure for vesical schistosomiasis—shots of potassium antimonyl—but no immunization.

To shoot a picture 1,100 miles up the Congo was not only unusual in the early 1950s; it was unheard of. Movies were made in studios with backdrops and transparencies or within civilized radius of Hollywood and Vine. Conveniently forgetting interior Mexico of *The Treasure of the Sierra Madre*, Bogart told a friend when he and Betty Bacall took off, "Before I met The Monster my range was Beverly Hills to Palm Springs. Maybe 120 miles. Now Huston wants me to fly 12,000 miles into the Congo. And the crazy thing is I've agreed to go!"

For production headquarters, John chose Kindu (then Ponthierville), a cluster of tin-roofed warehouses and huts at the end of a quaint little railway line carrying river cargo past the unnavigable Stanley Falls to and from Stanleyville, one hundred miles downriver. Next, he invited Peter Viertel to come hunting. "Ever shot an elephant, Pete?" Viertel hadn't and didn't want to and, he said, he was going to finish polishing the script in cool Entebbe in British Uganda, five hundred miles to the east across Lake Albert and the Ruwenzori Mountains.

While Betty and Bogey and Kate rendezvoused in London, Huston went on his first safari. To Ricki, who sensibly stayed in Malibu with one-year-old Tony and was expecting in July, he wrote that if he hadn't yet bagged an elephant, a lion had recently feasted on some locals although he had not personally run across any lions. "Stalking elephants is most exciting," he wrote her. "They don't see at all well and if one stays downwind of them one can get very close. Yesterday morning we were after them in some forest and we weren't more than six or eight yards away from them finally. Just a little wall of vines between us and them. I tell you it gave me a very funny feeling."

To escort his stars to the location and settle last-minute money squabbles, John flew to London. When he arrived, Spiegel told him the British backers had withdrawn. The little producer's finances had always been something of a mystery, but his persuasive powers were intact. He persuaded Bogart, Hepburn, and Huston to defer part of their salaries. Bogart agreed to $35,000 cash, $125,000 deferred plus 25 per cent of the film's future profits, if any; Hepburn took $65,000 cash, a like amount deferred and 10 per cent of the profits. John was the craftiest dealmaker of course. He owned 50 per cent of Horizon, his director's fee was $87,000 to which was added $40,000 in "overtime," and he still received another $25,000.

While Spiegel stayed in London to raise more money, cast and crew flew to Rome on the first lap of the journey to Kindu. Kate was horrified when she saw the airport swarming with paparazzi and eager fans. She locked herself in the plane's toilet for most of the stopover. When one reporter intercepted her on the way to the washroom, she hit him with her umbrella.

From the moment Bogey set foot in the Congo, he hated the place. When he heard about the blood flukes, which Huston had conveniently forgotten to mention on the way down, he swore he would only drink scotch and eat canned beans. Kate pronounced the country "utterly divine" and demanded a private dressing room, a toilet, and a full-length mirror. When she found out that John had been elephant hunting, she accused him of being a potential murderer. What's more, she objected, she had heard that he drank as much or more than her costar. "That's true, dear," John admitted. "But you must take the bad with the good. On the Ruiki we're all going to be in the same boat."

The African Queen was actually made with a number of floating contraptions. Besides the thirty-foot steam-powered *Queen*, looking exactly as Forester had described her in his novel, were several rafts. The biggest was designed to carry lighting equipment and most of the thirty-four-man crew. It was made by strips of planking laid over three pirogues. For the launching scores of Congolese hitched a ride. When in midstream it began to sink under the weight of the enthusiastic "natives," Huston yelled, "Bail out the pirogues, then get this thing back to shore and dump the hitchhikers." Kate's dressing room and toilet were built on buoyant oil drums, "a portable palm leaf affair," John called it. She loved it and filled it with flowers in water jugs and retired to it whenever she was not in a shot. The propman bought every piece of mirror in Kindu, glued the pieces together and put a frame around the whole thing. When they presented it to her, she accepted it with regal appreciation.

She thought Huston's big-game hunter persona was as much of a put-on as his tough director-with-a-streak-of-sadism act, but when he invited her to come elephant hunting with him one day, she went along. "He couldn't hit a tin can with a peashooter," she would say, "but he liked to give the impression he could kill an elephant." She carried a gun, but the only shooting she did was with her 16mm camera.

Bogey was miserable and wondered where the laughs were John had promised. "You wait for the laughs he promised, but you can't stand the dame," he told newsmen after it was all over in his mock tough-guy rasp. "She won't let anybody get a word in edgewise and she keeps repeating what a superior person she is. Later, you get a load of the babe stalking through the African jungle as though she had beaten Livingstone to it. Her shirttail is carefully torn for casual effect and is flapping out of her jeans. She pounces on the flora and the fauna with a home movie camera like a kid going to his first Christmas tree, and she blunders within ten feet of a wild boar's tusks for a closeup of the beast. About every other minute she wrings her hands in ecstasy and says, 'What divine natives! What divine morning-glories!' Brother, your brow goes up . . . is this something from *The Philadelphia Story?*"

Filming started in mid-May. A modern towing vessel pulling the *Queen*, followed by the generator, lights and reflector platform, followed by the camera raft, another raft with props and sound equipment and, finally, Kate's floating dressing room cum toilet. A camp was built for the opening sequence where Charlie (changed from Forester's Cockney to a Canadian to accommodate Bogart's speech pattern) meets Rosie and her missionary brother (Robert Morley). The camp was complete with bucket-showers and a bamboo dining room. Betty Bacall took a hand in the cooking and declared herself an expert in python soup (which Bogart didn't think was funny). "Both Hepburn and Bacall were like a couple of Florence Nightingales," camera operator Ted Scaife said, "making sure that members of the unit had their antimalaria pills, their 'stoppers' and 'starters.'"

Cardiff and Scaife got some excellent jungle footage. And the Congolese were not the only curious observers; thousands of chattering monkeys peered from trees along the river. "We had this one older group of baboons who'd come down to the shore and squat there in the afternoon, just to watch us shoot," John remembers. "They were a great audience—better than most ciritics I know—and after a scene we'd look over at them to check their reaction. Sometimes they'd clap for us. I tell you kid, we all got so we dreaded the day those baboons would shake their heads!"

Hepburn and Bogey didn't hit it off too well in the beginning. She acted haughty and kept telling Bogart everything was "divine" until he exploded one day and, calling her an ugly bag of bones, told her come down to earth. "Down where you're crawling?" she laughed back.

The first scenes brought out a curious vein of biting wit in both of them that wasn't in the script. This humor didn't grow, however, it just laid there, heavy and baiting, until Huston was inspired to remark that Kate should play her Rosie as if she were Mrs. Roosevelt. Things fell into place after that and she and Bogey played together with the right touch for their improbable love to become both inevitable and perfect.

Bogart groaned about the insects, the humidity, and the sheer misery of trying to sleep in a jungle alive with strange sounds. He managed to get plastered night after night. Later he wrote, "While I was griping, Kate was in her glory. She couldn't pass a fern or berry without wanting to know its pedigree, and insisted on getting the Latin name for everything she saw walking, swimming, flying or crawling. I wanted to cut our ten-week schedule, but the way she was wallowing in the stinking hole, we'd be there for years." One day he saw her, loaded down with camera, fly swatters, tape recorder and butterfly nets, Bogart said, "Would you mind carrying my makeup kit?"

Another time, Kate asked him, "Can you help me?"

"To do what?" he growled. "Swat flies?"

"I'm trying to find a bamboo forest, Humphrey."

"What the hell for?"

"To sit in and contemplate."

Diluvian rains affected the filming. Kate came down with dysentery, cameras were ruined and had to be replaced from London, and the *Queen* sprang a leak and settled on the river bottom. It took the crew and nearly two hundred Congolese three days to refloat her. The heavy boiler which powered the boat was raised with makeshift pulleys attached to overhanging trees, and a mechanic was summoned from Kindu to get the sensitive steam engine started again. Viertel kept rewriting the ending. In Forester's novel, Rosie and Charlie are chivalrously spared by the German commandant, who admires their courage. Successively, Huston and Viertel invented endings that saw (1) a British warship rescue them after a heroic battle with the German gunboat; (2) Rosie propose marriage before the first available British consul and (3) Charlie remembering the wife he has in England and hadn't thought about for twenty years. As Huston finally shot it, Rosie and Charlie's marriage is celebrated at the foot of the German mast they will hang from. But rains free their abandoned *Queen* from the reeds and the current carries it toward the German gunboat. Finally, absurdity triumphs, when the *Queen* sinks the German boat. In the fadeout nature itself seems crazily on the side of our odd couple.

Communications were tenuous. They had been promised daily mail service but letters arrived in two-week batches. Cables to America took two days. They had no newpapers and scant knowledge of what was happening, although they all managed to lay bets on the Sugar Ray Robinson–Randy Turpin fight in London. The Turpin victory—broadcast on short-wave radio—was a nice boost in morale for the English crew. There was sad news, as when Kate learned of the death of her good friend Fanny Brice. And there was happy news—Ricki giving birth to a daughter. Bacall remembers that John received the news in typical Huston fashion. His comment, "Hmmmmm." The daughter was named Anjelica.

Late one night the camp was awakened by torch-wielding Congolese. "We were in our huts and Bogey started to get out of bed," Bacall remembers. "He put his foot on the ground and felt something moving. He slapped at his pajamas and I could see the floor was alive with ants. Since the legs of our bed stood in cans of kerosene, we were safe for the moment, but it was ghastly."

The army ants could only be stopped by fire and yelling, and Bogey, drink in hand, joined the Africans on the torch line. Hepburn came out on the balcony of her bungalow and gave him a tongue-lashing for staging a drunken brawl in the middle of the night.

"Bogey was wonderful," John recalls. "With simple dignity he explained to her, 'Katie, old girl. Ants.'"

Although diverted by torches and screams, the ants stubbornly returned, forcing Huston to abandon the campsite. "It's their jungle," he said, ordering the Queen out of the water and onto a flatcar for transfer to Lake Albert and the Murchison Falls on the Victoria Nile. "The big tuskers are up that way."

Alarmed by the costly delays, Spiegel flew in.

"I thought we were leaving," said Bogart.

"We are," John told him. "I know how to get rid of Sam."

When Spiegel arrived, Huston greeted him with open arms—as did one hundred chanting, drum-beating Congolese, crying "Wel-kum Sam!" Endlessly. Spiegel couldn't get away from them. They followed him everywhere chanting and beating the drums and shouting "Wel-kum Sam!"

"It's no use," sighed Huston. "You're too popular here. We can't talk business now. Go back to London and I'll meet you there soon."

Spiegel took the next plane out. Huston paid off the natives and put cast and crew aboard the ancient, wood-burning train for Stanleyville. From there, a chartered plane took them to Entebbe where, waiting for the Queen, they managed to lose a cricket match, 51–160, to the Ugandans.

For the next five weeks cast and crew lived aboard an old sidewheel steamer which Lauren Bacall called "woefully inadequate but at least the ants couldn't get us." While they awaited the arrival of the Queen and the equipment, Kate's dysentery didn't improve, and assistant director Guy Hamilton came down with it. They both had to stay behind when Huston and his entourage were invited to watch the felling of a giant mahogany tree. Remembers Hepburn, "I wanted to go desperately, but I was sick with dysentery and half a dozen other things. I was wasting away and had to lie down. John and Bogey were very annoyed. Well, they went, a huge storm blew up and a lightning bolt hit the tree. The branch fell off and nearly killed them all. I was grateful for the dysentery.

"And the reason I got dysentery was my temperance. I was so busy complaining about Bogey and John drinking hard liquor I tried to shame them by drinking water in their presence at mealtimes. Well, the water was full of germs. They never got sick, and I had the Mexican trots and was in bed every day for weeks."

When they started working at the Murchison Falls, Hepburn's first scene had her clamber overboard to free the *Queen* stuck in reeds. When she objected that the river was full of crocodiles, John said she shouldn't worry. He'd have his propmen fire a few rounds into the water. "You'll find the crocodiles get scared by the noise and they'll vanish," he told her. Kate thought about this for a while then came back, "Yes, but what about the deaf ones?" She went in anyway.

Disease took its toll. Huston was obliged to shut down production for four days during one of Kate's severest attacks of dysentery. Nine members of the crew had to be sent home with dysentery, malaria, or both. Areas of jungle growth had to be chopped away by hand; many of the crew actually stood and arranged lights when they were shaking with fever. Kate often walked unsteadily from her own sickbed. Only Huston and the Bogarts remained healthy. During the four-day shutdown, the Bogarts went hippo-hunting with their cameras and John tried to bag his elephant, without success. A mountain of empty scotch bottles testified to his frustration. If Kate's health didn't improve, he said, he would move the production to studio sets in England.

Kate recovered, but sickness so decimated the crew that everybody begged to get home. Two days before the end of the shooting, however, John dropped a bombshell: "I want to shoot three extra days," he said calmly.

Bogey exploded. He was burning to put Africa behind him and accused Huston and Kate, the two Africa fans, of hatching a plot. John turned on all his charm, arguing that the picture required three extra days. He made no headway with Bogey this time and in desperation called a meeting of the crew. They, too, were homesick, but a compromise was arranged. Bogey, Kate, and the camera crew would remain an extra two days, working almost until plane time; the others would return to Entebbe. John would get the shots he wanted, yet everyone would fly back to London together. John accepted the decision, but retired to his cabin with a bottle of brandy to pout.

There were two more months work in London. Ricki came over for what promised to be an extensive stay in Europe if *Moulin Rouge* could be put together. John had first thought of doing a picture on the life of Henri de Toulouse-Lautrec in 1944 when, on a leave in newly liberated Paris, he had discussed the idea with fellow Hollywoodite GI Tony Veiller. Now, it was the idea of James Woolf, one of Spiegel's British backers who had read the newly translated novelized biography by Pierre La Mure. John had read the book one weekend and immediately called Jose Ferrer in New York, telling the actor he would be the first and only choice for the role of the impressionist painter. "Anyway, have you read La Mure's book?" John asked on the transatlantic telephone.

"Have I read it? I *own* it," Ferrer shot back. "I plan to do it for the stage, and I've got the author working on a play version right now."

"Forget the stage," Huston snapped. "This thing has got to be done for the screen—in color, in the streets of Paris, with interiors at Maxim's and the Deux Magots. I'll get Tony Veiller to do the script. We'll fill it with cancan girls in black stockings and music and brothels and champagne! With you as a bearded dwarf in a top hat. Well, kid, what do you say?"

Ferrer said yes, and a deal was falling into place with United Artists. *The African Queen* seemed to finish itself. Everybody was happy to be back in civilization at Shepperton Studios. Art director Wilfred Singleton surpassed himself in matching the Ruiki River camp sequence with the interior and Morley joined Bogey and Kate for the tragicomical opening. For the closeups of Bogart burning leeches off himself with a cigarette, Huston had a jar of real bloodsuckers brought to the set.

"You're not gonna put those damn things on me, are you, John?" Bogey asked.

"Absolutely," said John. "I want you to shudder as you burn each of them off with the tip of your cigarette. Now, kid, you just wouldn't shudder if the leeches were phony."

Bogart shuddered and Huston shot the last of the endings—

the gorgeously improbable torpedoing of the German gunboat. In September, cast and crew disbanded, with John and Ricki staying in England. Kate went home with her bags full of souvenirs and her 16mm record of the experience and told New York newsmen, "I adored it all—Stanleyville, Ponthierville, Entebbe, the Murchison Falls, Lake Albert—it was the most interesting experience. I would love to have gone back and done more work there. We were working in a wild game preserve at the Murchison. I walked a lot. Wonderful flowers there. The crew brought me such great flowers—thrilling!"

For Viertel, the picture resulted in *White Hunter Black Heart*, a novel about a writer named Peter Verrill who is summoned to London from his Swiss skiing resort to doctor the final script of a movie that a tough sly, unreasonable, selfish, and brilliant director named John Wilson will shoot along the Congo River and the Murchison Falls. Writer and director leave for Africa before the cast and crew and Wilson turns a preproduction safari into an obsession that nearly wrecks the film and the lives of Verrill and others trapped into a venture with a man who might very well be mad.

The African Queen turned out to be one of the most charming and entertaining movies ever made. It became Kate's greatest success, gave Bogart an Academy Award, made Spiegel and Huston rich and surrounded them with that sweet smell of success that seems to make everything possible. Everybody loved the story of love progressing in bursts of ill-temper, frustrations and courage amidst heat, mud, and savaging insects. Huston turned what could have been a patriotic epic into a personal adventure—Rosie and Charlie aboard the lovable *Queen*, learning about the kind of courage that isn't the epic feat but victory over oneself. "This picture is not like others," says Huston. "The ideal movie seems to me to be one where the spectator projects what he wants to see on the screen as if he had both camera and projector inside his own head."

12

PARIS '52

They had buried Paul Signac, the last of the intellectual top-hatted Impressionists, in 1933 when John had sketched tourists on Montparnasse. Just before he hit Paris, they had buried La Goulue, the toast of the gayest nineties, demi-mondaine, cancan dancer of the devilish Moulin Rouge and model for Henri de Toulouse-Lautrec in some of his most famous cabaret canvases. La Goulue ("the greedy one") died in utter misery only blocks from the townhouse she had owned during her heyday when bankers and Impressionists drank champagne from her slipper and she could do the split and starred in a cancan quadrille in the arms of Valentin-le-Désossé (Boneless Wonder), Grille d'Égout (Sewer Grate) and a lady known as Nina Patte-en-l'air (Feet-Up-Nina). It was in her Bois de Boulogne mansion that La Goulue (born Louise Weber, the daughter of a cab driver) was once invited to dance before a gentleman who afterward covered her, literally, with banknotes and turned out to be the Grand Duke Alexis of Russia. Going to jail after some lark was the beginning of the downfall. She became a lion tamer and a dancer in a wagon show. Toulouse-Lautrec painted curtains for her, but she forgot them in some barn and rats gnawed at them until some art dealer got hold of them and cut them up into salable sections. Later, the curtains were reassembled and restored and now hang in the Louvre.

Toulouse-Lautrec was twenty-six and had behind him five years as amateur painter of horse racing subjects and magazine illustrator when he began to paint his first Moulin Rouge pictures. Until his death eleven years later, the deformed son of a nobleman haunted the bars and cabarets of Montmartre and produced his brilliant posters, drawings, and paintings of singers, dancers, whores and fellow-artists—Aristide Bruant, La Goulue, Jane Avril, Yvette Gilbert, the female clown Cha-U-Koa, and many more. During his last years he produced a series of lithographs and paintings of his favorite music halls, cabarets, and circus performers, went to London and made a drawing of Oscar Wilde, became a habitué of whorehouses, and did a large number of drawings and paintings of the girls, whom he treated as his friends. He exhibited only twice in his lifetime and, despite some praise from critics, neither show was a success.

For Huston, 1952 promised to be a wonderful year.

Romulus Films, London, and UA quickly finalized a deal that made him his own producer. *Moulin Rouge* would be filmed entirely in Paris during July and August when Parisians traditionally fled their city and, despite the tourists, a maximum of landmarks could be turned into 1890s sets with a minimum of inconvenience. The picture would be in Technicolor and the first man hired was Oswald ("Ossie") Morris. The British cameraman, who had started as a clapper boy and had just finished *So Little Time* for Compton Burnett, responded enthusiastically to Huston's idea that *Moulin Rouge* should *look* like a Toulouse-Lautrec painting. Together with fashion artist Marcel Vertes and color still photographer Eliot Elisofon, Morris worked out a method of using filters on the set lights to mute the brilliant Technicolor hues toward a more impressionistic palette. Technicolor objected and sent strong letters asking that the film stock be treated to Technicolor specifications. "We were after a tonal range which would correspond to oil paint," said Huston. "It drove them crazy, but later they wrote again, mightily impressed after they'd seen the results, to ask us how we did it."

For himself, Ricki, and the children, Huston rented a

château in suburban Chantilly, and, while Tony Veiller toiled over the script, prowled Left Bank art galleries, bought a Monet for ten thousand dollars, and went to the races. No American jockey was riding at Longchamp and Huston soon wired Bill Pearson, inviting him to come and stay at the château and maybe ride an Irish thoroughbred Huston was importing at the Chantilly steeplechase. Pearson came over and Huston threw a lavish party for the leading French riders, introducing Billy as "a fierce contender."

"By 3 A.M. we were all happily drunk," recalls Huston. "So it seemed a good idea to go out and jump some fences. Luckily, no necks were broken."

Americans in Paris became John's cronies—and Pearson's supporters. They included the "gang," Joyce and Jules Buck, the Viertels, Paulette Goddard, now divorced from Burgess Meredith, and Tola Litvak, plus such newcomers as Art Buchwald of the *Herald Tribune*, Gene Kelly, and John Steinbeck. After they had all lost betting on Pearson, John suggested they enter Billy in the Grand Prix de Saint James and, fair play or foul, make him win. They plotted Pearson's triumph in detail. Pearson would use his boots and his elbows, foul every jockey he could reach and provoke confusion with Indian war cries. If, after the race, the crowd attacked Billy, John would set fire to the main grandstand in order to create enough confusion for Billy to escape.

The plan worked beautifully. Billy threw his horse against other mounts, shouted insults, blocked in the curves and crossed the wire first as an angry French crowd roared its displeasure.

"Naturally, Billy was disqualified," says Huston. "Every jock in the race protested him. He was booed off the track. It was wonderful." That night Pearson was feted by the Americans and champagne toasts were raised to his courage and endurance.

Willy Wyler had finished *his* first away from Hollywood— *Roman Holiday*, with Gregory Peck and a delightful newcomer, Audrey Hepburn—and he and Talli had rented a house for the summer in St. Jean-de-Luz on the Basque coast. John and Ricki popped down and met Paul Kohner, who brought with him Allied Artists' new vice-president Harold Mirisch and his wife, Lotti.

Back in Paris, John realized he was broke. Billy Pearson, however, told him not to worry. "Let's head for the gallery on the Left Bank," he said. "I want to talk to the guy who runs it." Huston agreed and waited outside while Billy talked with the gallery owner. When Pearson came out he had a check for 300,000 francs ($600). "I told him I was your agent and demanded ten percent as my commission on the Monet he sold to you. Told him you were stinking rich and would buy more paintings from him only if he cooperated. So I got the dough. Now let's eat."

Evelyn Keyes popped up. She was in *C'est arrivé à Paris*, directed by blacklisted exiled director John Barry, playing a rich American girl coming to Paris and taking up with a French gigolo. One evening when she joined the gang—the Viertels, the Irwin Shaws, Litvak, Robert Capa, and John (Ricki was nowhere in sight) at Alexandre's café on the corner of the Champs Élysées and Avenue George V and everybody had had enough to drink, John began talking about art and soon leaned toward her saying he had always thought it a pity their pre-Columbian collection had been separated in their divorce. She said she agreed and jokingly told him to send her *his* half. He was not amused, but said he had a splendid way of settling the whole thing. "We'll toss for them!" Everybody laughed. "Don't listen to him, Evelyn," said Viertel. But John insisted and ceased to be funny. Evelyn could feel the discomfort around the table and in exasperation finally said, "Oh, for Christ sake, John, go ahead and toss." He made a fine ceremony out of it with a twenty-franc piece. Evelyn shrugged, "Heads," when he asked her. The table watched in silence as he flipped his coin and lost.

As the *Moulin Rouge* crew was half French and half English, so the cast was passably international. Zsa Zsa Gabor was set to play Jane Avril, the cafe entertainer who inspired Lautrec's most famous poster, Katherine Kath played La Goulue, Walter Crisham was Valentin, and Suzanne Flon was Lau-

127

trec's lost love. To duplicate Toulouse-Lautrec's diminished size, Huston invented a pair of cutaway boots that Ferrer could kneel in. This "torture rig," as Ferrer called the boots, reduced him from his normal five feet ten to Toulouse-Lautrec's four feet eight. The boots were formed like short artificial legs which allowed him to walk. When he faced the camera the effect was quite startling. Every half hour, however, the torture rig had to come off and Ferrer have his legs massaged to get the blood circulating in his feet again.

Huston and Gabor didn't hit it off too well. Her accent irritated him. "Zsa Zsa, if you go dead once more at the end of a line I'll personally murder you, so help me," John snapped once, but on Bastille Day, July 14, when he invited the entire cast to dine with him at the Tour d'Argent, their fights had ended.

"John really became a darling man," she says. "When I finished my part in the film he drove me to the airport in his special hunting clothes. He knew I was wild about horses, and the sweet thing had gone to all the trouble of putting on this wonderful riding outfit from Tautz, just to see me off."

Since a number of outdoor sequences were night scenes, Huston had had to make arrangements with the city. A reporter from Le Figaro got wind of this and ran a story saying the film company would pay 20,000 francs to anybody whose sleep was disturbed. "By the next morning, we had hundreds of letters from people in various neighborhoods, begging us to shoot our night stuff along their streets," John remembers. "Naturally, we got Figaro to run a retraction." It was at one of these night locations near the Odéon that this then very adolescent biographer first met Huston.

The crew admired the director's sang froid. "Here we were in front of the Deux Magots on a busy Saturday in the middle of a blistering summer, trying to create a scene out of the 1890s," assistant director David Mage remembers. "On the right of the square was a five-way intersection, and on the left a three-way intersection. The whole area—forty-five thousand square feet— had to be cleared of all cars, bicycles, motorbikes, buses, pedestrians, and animals. For this we had a task force of thirty policemen and three assistants, plus three men in charge of the extras who double as auxiliary police. We had a hundred and fifty extras, a trio of horse-drawn carriages and a horse-drawn van running around in the square. Traffic was backed up for three miles in all directions. And there sat Mr. Huston, perfectly composed, with a kind of soft little smile on his face, for him this was Paris in the Gay Nineties."

Interviewed at one of his night scenes on Montmartre by two young film buffs from *Positif*, Huston said everything had drawn him to Toulouse-Lautrec—the man, his work, the period, the setting. "La Mure's novel gave me the excuse I was waiting for." When the two interviewers told him it had been hard to see *The Red Badge of Courage* in France and he said he had never wanted to see MGM's final release version, they asked him if he was afraid of seeing it. "I probably am," he answered with a Homeric laugh.

Visiting Huston setside was the thing to do for Americans in town. Milton Berle was among the numerous visitors who got a taste of John's sense of humor. As the comedian stood engrossed in one of Ferrer's scenes, two husky gendarmes grabbed him, turned to Huston, and asked if this was the man he had told them about.

"Glad you got him," Huston sighed in seeming relief. "He's extremely dangerous."

As Berle was being handcuffed, he pleaded, "I know it's a great gag, John, but tell 'em to take it easy on me, willya? I've got a weak back."

"You should have thought of that before turning to a life of crime," said Huston. "I'm afraid it's far too late for pity."

Berle sighed and was carried away.

For three weeks Pablo Picasso was one elusive visitor, and it wasn't until the shooting was over that Huston heard about it. "Someone tipped him off as to where we'd be shooting each afternoon and he'd rent a room in a house or hotel there and peek out and watch what was going on," says Huston. "Maybe he thought seeing what the movies were doing with Lautrec would be some kind of clue to his own future fate. It was tantalizing as hell to find out he'd been spying on us all that time." *Moulin Rouge* wasn't the only filmic story of a solitary artist Picasso was interested in that year. In October, the painter saw *Limelight* three times and got Jean-Paul Sartre to introduce him to Charlie Chaplin.

During postproduction, Huston thought of filming *Matador*, a novel by Barnaby Conrad, with Ferrer as the bullfighter. Always fascinated by bullfightings, Huston had been in a ring once—on a dare—and barely escaped the horns. Barnaby Conrad was a bullfighter aficionado who had written several volumes on tauromachy. If his 1952 novel remained a stillborn project for John the reason was the Society for the Prevention of Cruelty to Animals which opposed the showing of a *corrida* involving the actual killing of a bull on the screen.

Moulin Rouge turned out to be a sparkling if uneven film. The Technicolor photography was ravishing and ranged from misty pastels to violent tones suggesting Toulouse-Lautrec's own palette. The story, however, was heavy going. It portrayed Toulouse-Lautrec as a man overwhelmed and morbidly obsessed by his deformity and by love for the self-torturing Colette Marchand and not, as he really was, the witty devotee of night life and the sporting scene. But as John had promised Ferrer, the cancan girls in black stockings were there, as were the brothels, the champagne, Maxim's, and Montmarte.

The West Coast première on December 23, 1952, was picketed by members of the American Legion Un-American Committee, carrying placards reading COMMUNIST PRESS PRAISE JOHN HUSTON and FERRER LEADER OF U.S. COMINFORM. When star and director arrived at the Fox Wilshire Theater in Los Angeles, the press noted that Ferrer seemed miffed, while Huston took the picketing in stride.

Huston was not at the January 1953 première in New York; he had discovered Ireland.

PART II

13

IRELAND AND
THE DEVIL

Huston had discovered Ireland while fox hunting in the late fall of 1952 and now rented a huge Georgian house near Kilcock, forty miles southwest of Dublin, and brought his family over. Ricki walked with John in the February drizzle along River Barrow, and shared his enthusiasm. Kilcock was in County Kildare, nestled in the lowland to the west of the Wicklow Mountains. Big, fertile farms and manor houses surrounded by deep forests spread toward the Barrow. In Norman times more than a hundred castles had been built in the country. By the fireplace John read avidly about the earls of Desmond, Ormonde, and Kildare who had fought for control of the Dublin government and about the Fitzgeralds who, during the Wars of the Roses, had helped capture Henry VI and ended their days in the Tower of London.

"The country is simply beautiful and the people are straightforward eccentrics," he enthused. "No nonsense about it. It's the only place where you can get drunk and not wake up the next morning with a guilty conscience. In fact, drunkenness in driving is a mitigating factor. They sort of shake their heads and say, 'Well, you know the poor fellow was under the influence. You can hardly hold him to blame for a bit of an accident.' It's delightful and fantastic."

Besides the beauty of the land and the whimsy of the Irish soul there was another, more compelling, reason for the new residence—the Internal Revenue Service. John had made—and spent, an awful lot of money during the past three years. MGM had paid him nearly $100,000 for *Red Badge*. His *Queen* earnings had totaled $153,000 and on *Moulin Rouge* he had been back on his comfortable five grand a week. The *Queen* and *Moulin Rouge* had been made outside the United States and U.S. tax laws were rather generous toward expatriate Americans. A concomitant unpleasantness was that in December 1952, Evelyn Keyes had filed a Los Angeles Superior Court suit for the collection of $20,673, claiming her former husband had never paid her a nickel.

And why go home, indeed, when everybody was running in his direction? Corporate Hollywood was discovering Europe and the mid-1950s were the beginning of a prodigious expansion—its unions would call it "runaway"—which ten years later saw "swinging London" become Beverly Hills-on-the-Thames, and the Shepperton and Cinecitta studios wholly extraterritorial American enclaves.

Ireland was quaint and soothing. If Huston thought the locals were eccentric, the locals thought the same thing of this Hollywood bigtimer who oozed confidence, whimsy, and money. The local gentry adopted him with open arms. He was a superb horseman and was soon riding with them behind baying hounds. To go fox hunting in style, he laid down several hundred dollars for a traditional scarlet coat, white cravat, and black top hat and, for the grooms, terrier men, and earth stoppers, stood hefty rounds at the local pub. When he wasn't jumping hedges with the Black and Tans and the Killin' Kildares, he attended the horse shows in Carlow and the races in Leopardstown. And there were good trout streams, good whiskey, congenial company and enough space at the rented Courtown manor to stable thoroughbreds.

Friends and hangers-on poured in, guests staying overnight,

for a weekend, and by the month. Peter Viertel left wife and child in Klosters, Switzerland, and popped up with his girl friend, Bettina. The newly published *White Hunter Black Heart* hadn't disturbed John and Peter's friendship despite the scathing portrait of "John Wilson" in the novel. Shortly after Christmas 1953, Peter's mother, Salka, stopped over on her way from New York to Switzerland and found the huge, gray mansion crowded with people—hunters, writers, and John's assistants and secretaries. "The occasion for the gathering was Tim Durante's marriage to an American divorcée, which had been planned to take place during [a racing] meet, with everyone on horseback," Salka Viertel was to write in *The Kindness of Strangers*. "It had to be postponed, because a few days before a woman had been killed riding to hounds and there were six weeks of mourning. Ricki, Huston's beautiful wife, was an emphatically gracious hostess."

The life of a country gentleman was ideal, John told Paul Kohner on the transatlantic phone. The only things that could add to his bliss was perhaps to make a film in Ireland.

For such a picture, he combed the local folklore and soon had something going, a story in which Burl Ives would play a wandering minstrel of the early eighteenth century. The untitled project wouldn't be made, but over the years John got to make hunks of various movies in Ireland and eventually a whole picture—*Sinful Davey* which was, perversely, the story of a Scotsman.

Then Bogey phoned and said they now owned *Beat the Devil*.

James Helvick's novel was a book someone had tossed into Bogey's lap in the Congo, the story about an American lowlife bound for British East Africa with his Italian wife and four "business associates" to swing a big uranium deal. John had read the book and agreed they might make a picture of it. What Bogey loved was "some cute touches on how a woman's lie confuses a gang of cutthroats."

Knowing that big-spender John had no capital to invest in screen rights, Bogey had bought *Beat the Devil*. While John made *Moulin Rouge*, Bogey had starred in *Deadline USA* and

Battle Circus, both directed by the *Key Largo* coscripter Richard Brooks, and Lauren Bacall had been in *How to Marry a Millionaire* with Marilyn Monroe and Betty Grable under Jean Negulesco's direction.

When Bogey sent "development money," John had Tony Veiller start one script in Paris and Peter Viertel go back to Klosters to work on another, while he himself got Helvick to come to Ireland for a rewrite of the drafts Veiller and Viertel sent in. A first and pretty melodramatic version was sent to Bogart in Hollywood. When John called and asked Bogey if he had read it, the long distance reply was, "Couldn't finish it. It was awful."

"Neither could I," John hummed. "Stinker, isn't it?"

Preparations nevertheless went ahead, with John becoming director-producer and Bogart the star and moneybag, eventually forking over $600,000 of his own money. *Beat the Devil* would shoot in Italy, John decreed, and if they could decide on who should play Bogey's Italian wife, Selznick agreed to loan them Jennifer Jones to play his love interest. *Beat the Devil* would be one picture Lauren Bacall couldn't be in, since she was pregnant.

Director-producer and star-financier rendezvoused at George's American Bar in the back of the Rome Excelsior Hotel. The next day when they were sitting behind their respective drinks, someone threw a copy of the *Daily Variety* on their table. In stark headlines, the Hollywood trade paper announced that revolution was hitting the film industry and over five pages, proceeded to tell how flat, black-and-white pictures were passé and three-dimensional color movies the new thing. Bogey ordered double scotches. Not only did they have a lousy script; they also had a picture scheduled in flat, normal-sized black-and-white. The 3-D hysteria was not confined to the pages of *Variety*. Selznick cabled ABANDON PROJECT. TAKE ONE OF MINE. YOU WILL RUIN YOUR CAREER AND JENNIFER'S. After a couple of more drinks, lights struck John. If no one was making good flat pictures any more there would soon be a famine of flat movies for all those tens of thousand of movie houses that hadn't had time or money to convert to 3-D. Ergo: be in a

Going to work for Metro. (Academy of Motion Picture
Arts and Sciences)

St. Clerans — a home in Ireland.

The Asphalt Jungle
Jean Hagen and Sterling Hayden. (Collection Cahiers du Cinéma)

John and Ricki.
(Ralph Crane/Black Star)

The Red Badge of Courage. (Collection Cahiers du Cinéma)

Katharine Hepburn and Humphrey Bogart aboard *The African Queen*.

Moulin Rouge
John (with cigarette) at the Deux Magots. Jose Ferrer, who played
Toulouse-Lautrec, is at the far right. (Collection Cahiers du Cinéma)

Johnny O'Clock
This was Evelyn's favorite movie. She played opposite Dick Powell.
(Collection Cahiers du Cinéma)

Gregory Peck and the great white whale in *Moby Dick*.
(Collection Cahiers du Cinéma)

The Roots of Heaven
From left, Errol Flynn, Juliette Greco, Friedrich Ledebur, Olivier Hussenot, and Trevor Howard. (Collection Cahiers du Cinéma)

The Unforgiven
Burt Lancaster and Audrey Hepburn. (Collection Cahiers du Cinéma)

The Misfits
Montgomery Clift, Marilyn Monroe, and Clark Gable. (United Artists)

Arthur Miller and director Huston on the set of *The Misfits*.
(United Artists)

seller's market when goods are in short supply, and make a *good* flat picture, which this one could be, if only we had a script.

The light dazzled Bogey, too. John suggested they get Truman Capote to work up a new script. "Instead of trying to do *Casablanca* and *Maltese Falcon* over again we'll make a picture with heart and humor." Capote, who was in Rome anyway, was hired, as was the new Italian sensation, Gina Lollobrigida, for the part of Bogey's wife. Legend has it that Bogey cabled his agent to the effect that Lollobrigida at least was not flat. In reality he was not, as he said, "a tits man" and Bogart and Lollobrigida never got along too well.

While Capote began working on the script, and Robert Morley joined the cast, John went to the hills above Amalfi in the Bay of Salerno where he wanted to shoot the picture. The production was headquartered at Ravello's Palumba Hotel, which had only one telephone.

When Bogey flew down, John was there to greet him at the Naples airport. Bogart climbed into John's rented limousine and the Neapolitan driver started the climb toward Ravello. The chauffeur was a man who apparently hated to make decisions, for at a fork of the road, he chose to go neither left nor right, but straight into a three-foot wall. Bogey crawled out of the wrecked car with two loose teeth and a split tongue. John was unharmed. "Drove us right smack through the wall," he said, shaking his head. "The Italians are an amazing people, eh, kid?"

While Bogey had his teeth fixed, Capote came down. He left his pet raven in Rome and when the bird refused to talk to him on the telephone, the writer got John's permission to go back to Rome to see if the raven was ill or just sulking.

When Angela and Robert Morley arrived in their stately car, having driven all the way from London, the production manager told them Capote was in Rome, Huston in Naples, and Bogey at the dentist. A few days later, however, everyone was there, including Capote, whose raven had died, and a cable went off to Mrs. Selznick to join *Beat the Devil*. Jennifer Jones had originally agreed to do the picture without reading the story because it was to be directed by John, with Bogey as her co-star. She arrived in Ravello to find she was to play an English girl wearing a blond wig and married to an Englishman.

As Capote remembers the writing assignment, "John and I decided to kid the story, to treat it as parody. Instead of another *Maltese Falcon*, we turned it into a wild satire on this type of film."

Morley remembers Capote writing the script page by page and reading it aloud to the assembled cast, page by page every morning. "He never seemed to manage to write very much on any one day, but then as we didn't film very much either, it didn't matter," says Morley. "The dialogue was at least always mint fresh."

"We sort of lost Helvick's novel along the way," admits Huston. "But we had a helluva lot more fun making the new version."

The evenings at Ravello were given over to poker and the main victims of John's and Bogey's hands were Capote, who lost 200,000 lire to them, and John's photographer pal Robert Capa, hired to do special photo layouts. "Capa was the worst poker player in the world," says Huston. "Even worse than Capote. He didn't cost us anything. We won his salary back each night."

John was inevitably the target of a number of David Selznick memos. David now devoted himself to his wife's career and although he had no business in *Beat the Devil* began firing off wires from New York. After the third memo, John sent back his answer, numbering the sections "Page 1," "Page 2" and "Page 4." The rest of the Selznick correspondence was largely concerned with what happened to page 3.

But even from New York, David managed to interfere. One day Hubert de Givenchy arrived from Paris, saying he had been summoned by Selznick to redesign Miss Jones's wardrobe. In one evening, he and his assistants fashioned the cotton dummies, wrote down all measurements. The next morning the Givenchy task force had disappeared. As Morley remembers it somewhat laconically, "Miss Jones played her role dressed entirely in white. The story was that Givenchy produced the toiles of her dresses for the fitting and that they were mistaken by David for the finished product."

Peter Lorre joined the cast. He had not been in a film for six years, was still recovering from a lengthy illness, and had to be given special consideration on the set. The character he played was both saintly and sinister—a German from Argentina who has changed his name to O'Hara but pronounces it O'Horror.

In the script Capote improvised day by day, Bogart and his wife, Lollobrigida, are on board a ship sailing for British East Africa; their traveling companions are Morley and his gang of uranium swindlers, and a creative liar, Jennifer, turns up, married to a bogus British lord (Edward Underdown). Then there's a shipwreck . . . With her fractured English, Lollobrigida had a hard time understanding the humor of the script—and of her director—but Bogey had to admit she was a trouper. She was always punctual, went to bed early, and arrived on the set groomed and alert.

Work with The Monster was Bogey's delight again. The unit called Bogart "Mr. President" in deference to his status as bankroller. "Having money in the film makes matters a trifle confusing for the other players," he said. "They never know whether I'm speaking as actor or executive. No one takes much notice, anyway."

Morley's considered opinion on that score was that actors should only take money out of pictures, never put money in. "Actors take themselves too serious," Morley said. "When approaching a part I incline to the principle once put forward by A. E. Matthews. There were only three questions: 'How much?' 'When do we start?' and 'Where?'" Heaving his portly frame into a chair, he added that his own future would be safe in 3-D movies.

As filming progressed, John got the idea that the Ravello monastery, founded in 1300, was just the background they needed for several scenes. With the monks' permission, generators and camera were moved in for shots of rough wooden tables and long rows of simple iron beds. Some of the monks looked as if they didn't quite believe it when Jennifer and Gina walked in—through a door which no woman had passed in over six hundred years. Part of the monastery had to be "decloistered" before actors and technicians were allowed to enter, and reconsecrated when the filming was over. Bogey thought it a big laugh to be shooting a movie called *Beat the Devil* in a monastery.

To keep everybody cheerful, Huston rented a small freighter and for a day off invited everybody to sea. Somehow they teased Jennifer into climbing the mast. Almost at the top, she lost her nerve and climbed down again. John besought her to try again. After an argument, she left in a speedboat. Hours later, she returned, ready for a second try, but John declined her offer. "When the sun went down they decided to turn the boat around and sail for home," Morley wrote in his memoirs. "To the surprise of everyone except the captain, who had presumably worked out that the time taken in any direction must equal the time taken on the return journey where the same route is followed, we didn't get to bed till six in the morning. Meanwhile, there was nothing to eat or drink. All work stopped for two days, in protest."

Judo wrestling was a setside pastime, with diminutive Capote claiming he could pin down Bogart from behind with one hammer lock and Bogey confiding to Huston he would actually squash Capote "like a bug on the wall" anytime. While talking to Morley one day after a scene, Bogart suddenly felt his arm being pulled up behind his back. He winked at Morley and began to groan. The pressure increased and Bogey let out a real howl and managed to twist himself around to see his assailant. Capote was nowhere in sight. It was John trying the armlock.

The villagers of Ravello took a liking to the movie people. Here was their own "Lollo" caricaturing herself. Here, every morning soon after seven, Hollywood's Humphrey Bogart rode the main street to work on a donkey. When John injured his back, he rode in a sedan chair to the location for several days.

John and Bogey loved to discuss each other. "Work gives John a sense of power," Bogey would say, "although sometimes he just lays in bed and lets them come to him. If you want to get him roused tell him something that appeals to his sense of justice or courage. 'I'm against anybody,' he says, 'who tries to tell anybody else what to do.' John often used to speak of the influence his father had on him. One day when John was a boy, his father took him walking in the woods. It was spring and everything was in bud. Suddenly his father seized a stick and started beating the tree with it. 'I'm trying to stop spring,' he roared. John never forgot.

"Risk, action, and making the best use of what's around is what makes him tick. When he isn't actually on the set, he sees his surroundings as a forest of windmills, bottles, women, racehorses, elephants and oxen, noblemen and bums."

John underlined their differences. "I'm a notoriously bad husband—not like you, Bogey—morbidly faithful to each of your wives. I'm a much better father than I am a husband." Bogart took his acting seriously and said he worked hard. John declared, "I hate people who claim to be hard-working. Anyone with brains doesn't have to work hard all the time." He advised Bogey to amass a fortune of twenty million so he could live properly. "My life span would probably be lengthened if I had that much," Huston sighed. "It's only trying to make twenty million that cuts short a man's years. Spending it would be healthy."

Visitors arrived at Ravello and John's Italian assistant threatened tourists and locals alike to make them appear in a crowd scene. "I've never seen such an example of slave labor," John commented, shooting the scene.

After pickup interiors in London, Huston flew to Los Angeles to edit *Beat the Devil* for a United Artists release. It was funny to be staying at the Beverly Hills Hotel when Los Angeles had been his home since childhood, but the Kohners, the Wylers, and the Bogarts were there to see to it that he didn't get into too much mischief.

Beat the Devil courted—and achieved, disaster. When it was released in March 1954, Bogey called it "a mess." In self-defense, John said, "The formula of *Beat the Devil* is that everyone is slightly absurd." Posterity was to be kinder to the fluke classic. Wrote Pauline Kael a decade later, "*Beat the Devil* is a mess, but it's probably the funniest mess—the screwball classic—of all time. It kidded itself, yet it succeeded in some original (and perhaps dangerously marginal) way of finding a style of its own."

14

THE WHALE

It would have to be a big picture and cost a great deal of course, but what a story! John made a pregnant pause and glanced across at Jack Warner. Death, mystery, affliction, evil! The high seas, the great white whale and the torment of a man trying to wrest from heaven the secret of human woe! Jack didn't like the fact that there were no women in the story, but John glowed with charm. It could be a winner, he said in his most persuasive voice.

Postproduction was always a bore, but the editing of *Beat the Devil* was suddenly enlivened. The Warners lived an easy walking distance from the Beverly Hills Hotel in Coldwater Canyon and John kept after his old boss. Herman Melville's characters were tortured, episodes were lurid, tension diffused, and a lot of the climaxes were given away too soon, but *Moby Dick* was the central masterpiece of American fiction. It was the greatest romance of the sea and it was the greatest chase story. Its theme was the equal of any attempted by Sophocles or Shakespeare and it was all acted out on the storm-tossed deck of a whaleboat. Moby Dick was a symbol of evil and Captain Ahab's fight with the leviathan a Promethean struggle with evil. Or the whale was goodness and Ahab, with his insane pride and crazed passion for revenge, was evil. Either way, it was a thrilling story.

Moby Dick was actually an old standby for Warner Brothers. The Melville classic had been made twice before, both times with John Barrymore as Captain Ahab, so Jack said yes—if a star could be found to play Ahab.

While Kohner settled the finer points of a contract, Huston set out to find somebody to help turn Melville's 1851 novel into a screenplay. The search wasn't long. A thirty-three-year-old science fiction writer came to mind.

Ray Bradbury had been an admirer of Huston's movies for years and when Doubleday had published *The Martian Chronicles* in 1950, he had sent the director an inscribed copy. Since the *Chronicles*, Bradbury had published *The Illustrated Man* and many short stories that were considered essays in fantasy and the subjective rather than "straight" s.f. John had liked the *Chronicles*, expressed interest in bringing it to the screen, and exchanged letters with the California author who, in turn, had continued to forward copies of his books as they were published. "The reason Huston selected me," says Bradbury, "was that he saw in my books a kinship with Melville. Melville is a poet and a Shakespearean and I've been influenced by poetry and Shakespeare all my life. In high school I was an actor and I read all Shakespeare and was influenced by the wonderful sound and look of his plays. Huston had enough sense to see the poet in my writing."

On their first meeting at John's hotel, Bradbury was given twelve hours to decide whether he would come to Ireland and write what would be his first screenplay. Bradbury went directly from the hotel to a bookstore and bought *Moby Dick*, which he had never read. The next day he called Huston and said yes.

In September, Bradbury sailed to Europe with his wife and children, finishing reading *Moby Dick* on the aft deck of the S.S. *United States* in a hundred mile-an-hour hurricane. He met Huston in Paris and they began discussing the script at the Longchamp racetrack. To a friend, Bradbury wrote, "Huston says he is out to corrupt me; he looks forward to putting me on a horse, riding me to hounds, jetting me in a speed plane and burying me in dope, drink and dames."

The seduction of Ray had to be postponed until after the

script had been licked. The Bradburys came to Courtown, and while wives and children got to know each other, director and writer walked the Irish moors discussing *Moby Dick*. To understand the book, Ray did twenty outlines while John flew to Los Angeles to agree with Jack Warner that Gregory Peck should be Ahab. They had missed each other on *Quo Vadis*, thank God, John said, but this would be it. "Greg has colossal dignity and great masculinity," John told a news conference. He revealed that Peck would have a long jagged scar on his bearded face and stump the deck of the *Pequod* on a peg leg. The rest of the casting was easy. Leo Genn became Ahab's first mate, Starbuck; Dublin drama critic Seamus Kelly became Flask; Count Frederick Ledebur, an Austrian sportsman friend of John's, was cast as Queeqweg; and Edric Conner, a calypso singer from Trinidad, became Daggoo. For a time John Godley, Lord Kilbracken, was supposed to portray Ishmael but Huston felt he needed an experienced actor for Melville's narrator and eventually chose Richard Basehart. Miffed, Lord Kilbracken wrote a nasty portrait of Huston in his autobiography, *Living Like a Lord*. Orson Welles had the small part of the preacher in New Bedford, Massachusetts, who, from a pulpit shaped like the bow of a ship, delivers a sermon that recounts the story of Jonah and the whale.

Bradbury wrote and wrote. By the time he was through he had written twelve hundred pages of outline and screenplay in order to get the one hundred and fifty final pages. When he was banging away on his portable, John was usually out jumping hedges. "John had several bad falls," says Ray, "and would come limping in on a cane. Every time he went out again, the rest of us at the house murmured a little prayer for his safety because all of our jobs hung on that damned horse he was on."

One afternoon a crestfallen Huston came into Ray's workroom and mutely handed the writer a telegram, CANNOT PROCEED WITH FILM UNLESS SEXY FEMALE ROLE ADDED. JACK WARNER.

"Has he gone insane?" Bradbury shouted. "This is terrible. We can't stick a woman on board. My God, he can't be serious!"

"That's Hollywood, Ray," John sighed. "Warners are paying the bill and if they want love interest we'll just have to get it in somehow. Maybe Ahab could have an affair with Gina Lollobrigida as a disguised stowaway . . ."

Furiously, Bradbury crumpled up the telegram and threw it on the floor. Then he looked at Huston.

"John was doubled up on the couch, laughing like a big monkey. That's when I knew *he* had sent the thing. I was so relieved I couldn't get sore."

Bradbury managed to turn the tables during one of Huston's chi-chi dinners for the local gentry. In front of visiting Peter Viertel, John kept insisting that Bradbury must attend the dinner and the writer kept repeating he had no formal clothes to wear. Finally, when John stepped out of the room, Peter hustled Bradbury to the attic, saying, "Let's show the bastard." In various chests and lockers they found an old skirt, black leggings, a fringed purse, and a dinner jacket.

"When the ultra-distinguished guests had arrived," remembers Bradbury, "I came down the stairs while John was playing the casual host. From the doorway, Pete announced me as 'Laird McBradbury!' in a ringing voice. All the lords and ladies turned in my direction. I saw Huston's jaw drop three feet; it was a lovely moment."

Huston and art director Ralph Brinton found a hundred-year-old three-master in a Yorkshire coastal village after a search that extended to Holland and Scandinavia. Huston bought the wooden-hulled ship and Brinton had his team set out to turn it into the *Pequod*, building an actors' deck above the real deck, a new stern, and a false bow to give it the appearance of an 1840s New England whaleboat. During the filming, the actors on deck would seem to be sailing the *Pequod* while a real crew helmed the real wheel on the original deck below. The actors' tiller was as Melville described it, made from the skull of a killer whale and the jawbone of a sperm whale. For Ahab's wooden leg, Huston insisted on a whalebone peg, pointing out that the skipper had lost his leg in the South Pacific and wouldn't have what old salts called a "Chelsea peg." Said Peck, "John wanted the one I wore to look as if it had been made at sea under rough conditions. He even showed me how to walk on it."

Bradbury finished the script during three weeks in March 1954. "The last three weeks of work turned out to be the best three weeks of the whole six or seven months' experience," he remembers. "I got out of bed one morning in London, looked in the mirror, and said, 'I'm Herman Melville.' On that day I rewrote the last thirty-five or forty pages in just a few hours, seven or eight intense hours of banging away like crazy because I was inspired. I truly was. The ghost of Melville was in me. I ran off across London to Huston's hotel and I threw the script at him. I said, 'There! I think that's it!' And he read it and said, 'Jesus Christ, Ray. This is it. This is the way we'll shoot the ending!' My inspiration was to have Moby Dick take Ahab down and wind him in the coiled ropes and bringing him up among the harpoons on this great white bier, this great cortege, this funeral at sea. Then we see, 'My God, these two should be together forever through eternity, shouldn't they?—Ahab and the whale?' I like to believe, in fact I do believe, that Melville would have approved. I'm proud of that touch. Then the motion of the whale in the sea causes Ahab's hand to beckon the men. They get maddened again and they charge in and are destroyed."

For Bradbury the battle with the whale was over. For Huston it was beginning. Oswald Morris was the cinematographer again and Technicolor was a little more receptive than on *Moulin Rouge* to suggestions of desaturated color processing. "I want the final print to have the strength found in steel engravings of sailing ships," John told the Technicolor lab in London. Together, he and Ossie also decided to deliberately shoot on overcast days to get the effect of washed-out blues of wintry sea weather. Filming began in April 1954 with the opening sequence. It was shot in Youghal, an Irish seaport village stripped of power lines and all modern signs and refurbished with quayside fronts to duplicate New Bedford. The departure of the *Pequod* featured the only women in the film, a line of gaunt and silent women in black on high widow's walks, watching their menfolk set to sea. Next, Huston took cast, crew, the *Pequod* and two mechanical models of the whale to the waters between Madeira and the Azores where Portuguese whalers still hunted the Atlantic whale from open longboats. The sea was rougher than John had expected, and the first of the ninety-two-foot dummy whales, with its steel frame under latex skin, broke its towline and disappeared. The second dummy broke away with Huston on board but was caught before it carried the director to its brother's watery grave. For hard cash the Portuguese whalers let the second unit film their hunt and Huston joined in: "In a single day we killed twenty whales, killed them the old way, with harpoons. This can be incredibly exciting and unless you've harpooned a whale in rough seas you haven't really hunted."

Seamus Kelly was to remember dozing off at day's end during the filming off the Azores and being marooned on a tugboat while John and everybody else slipped away to dinners and snug rooms ashore. Kelly succeeded in giving the master prankster a bad turn by staggering into his bedroom dripping wet late that night, claiming he had been forced to swim ashore through shark-infested water. Stricken with remorse, John could only rasp, "Gee, kid, I'm sure as hell sorry!"

From the mid-Atlantic Huston sailed to calmer waters in the St. George's Channel between Wales and Ireland. Damage to the *Pequod*, weather, and cast casualties pushed the schedule beyond the contractual three months. By the time Peck was through he had put in twenty-seven exhausting weeks. "When John told me he was going to shoot the typhoon scenes right on the ship during an actual storm we told him such a thing had never been done and that it was impossible," remembers Peck. "It's a mistake to tell John that something is impossible."

In the script Ahab insists on keeping all sails flying while the storm rages and that was the way Huston filmed it. He had Morris suspend cameras from the mast on elastic ropes to show the crew battling mountainous waves on the rolling, storm-washed deck. He allowed saltwater to break over camera lenses which he then had dried with an air hose for retakes. "We began to think of John as a real-life Ahab," says Peck. "Three times we were sure we'd lose the *Pequod* and three times she was demasted." Basehart broke three bones jumping into a whaleboat, Genn slipped a disc and got pneumonia, Peck hurt a kneecap, and a dozen men of the crew were injured at sea.

Since Bradbury had gone home to California and refused to fly under any and all circumstances, Huston got Lord Kilbracken to rework parts of the script. Still disappointed at not playing Ishmael, his lordship put three scenes from Melville back in again, but working for Huston, he wrote, was trying. "On a Monday, for example, we would be precisely on the same wavelength, thinking in precisely the same way and fully understanding one another. On Tuesday, inexplicably, there would be no point of contact between us, and collaboration was impossible. On Wednesday he would suddenly speak with violent enthusiasm of what I had written—then the next day, tear the same scene to pieces. I was liable to be called any time from 7:30 in the morning to midnight. Working with Huston was exasperating, degrading and inspiring."

As fall turned to winter, Huston headed toward the equator and in February 1955 finished the exteriors off the Canary Islands. Still to be shot was the ending and closeups of Moby Dick.

In the 80,000 gallon tank at Elstree studios outside London, oceanographer and whale expert Robert Clark had supervised the construction of the head, tail, and midsection of Ahab's enemy. A mixture of aniline dye and chemicals were added just under the latex allowing the skin to "bleed" when harpooned. The three sections were mounted on articulated frames so the beast could be filmed swimming, diving, chewing men and boats, and spewing streams of water into the air. Peck was suffering from a severe head cold when he was lashed to the back of the midsection in a tangle of harpoon lines. "The wind machines were roaring and I was half drowned by torrents of water," Peck remembers. "Huston said, 'I want you with your eyes staring open as you slowly come out of the sea on that whale's back—with your dead hand beckoning the men to their doom.' What I didn't know was that the winch they were using to rotate the section I was tied to was hand-operated. Later I learned that when they'd first tried it out the damn thing had jammed! I could have really come up dead, which I think would have secretly pleased John—providing the last touch of realism he was after."

Huston was after more than realism. As Bradbury would say, "It misses because Peck couldn't bring madness to it. A dear sweet gentleman, but he's not mad. Greg Peck is never going to be a paranoid killer or a maniac devourer of whales. He can play in *To Kill a Mockingbird* and make a beautiful film. That's a different quality. In some scenes it works. The quiet scene in the cabin where Ahab is awakened from a nightmare and in very quiet terms madly describes his obsession to Starbuck. That's a good scene because he doesn't have to go too hard with it. If I'd been old enough to advise Huston, which I wasn't, I would have advised him to play the whole thing that way, a quiet madness that's very inner, very intense, so that you don't have to try for the big thing. I think Peck could have carried that off and you'd have had a different kind of Ahab. I saw in Huston the same confusion I suffered."

Moby Dick had taken two years and cost Warners $4.5 million, but it was not a success. Still Huston would often call it his best film and even defend Peck's portrayal: "Most critics that attacked *Moby Dick* attacked Greg Peck. I swear by him. I thought he was very good in a very demanding role. I was afraid of a melodramatic approach to Ahab, someone fierce and pyrotechnic. That would have been too easy."

Moby Dick, it seemed, would not be the end of Melville for Huston. Allied Artists wanted to attain major studio status and in early 1955 authorized vice-president Harold Mirisch to sign up Wyler, Billy Wilder and Huston to make major-budget films. Wyler's picture would be *The Friendly Persuasion* (John suggested that Willy hire Bradbury to write the screenplay of the Jessamyn West Civil War drama, but the exhausted writer said no), Wilder's would be a May-September romance with Audrey Hepburn and Gary Cooper, *Love in the Afternoon*, and Huston's would either be Melville's *Typee* or Stephen Crane's short story "The Blue Hotel," which James Agee had scripted for him in 1950. *Typee*, written five years before *Moby*

Dick, is an episode in young Melville's real life, a lightly colored retelling of the months he spent with reputed cannibals on one of the islands of the Marquesas after he and another New Bedford youth had jumped ship. *Typee* is a hymn to the noble savage uncorrupted by the vices of civilization in general and Christianity in particular (early editions deleted Melville's more mordant reflections on missionaries in the South Pacific). "The Blue Hotel" is a gambler's story. Set in Nebraska in midwinter, it is the tale of fear and death in which the murder of a professional gambler is an act of necessity and the force that makes it inevitable is beyond any single person in the hotel.

John was in New York and Los Angeles in November 1955 to settle the finer points of the Allied Artists contract and to deliver the *Moby Dick* negative to Warners. In Hollywood, he was camping at the Beverly Hills Hotel and seeing friends, including the Bogarts. Bogey was finishing *The Harder They Fall* under Mark Robson's direction for Columbia and next Betty and he were to do *Melville Goodwin, U.S.A.* together. Director H. C. Potter had bought the J. P. Marquand novel seven months earlier and thought the Bogarts would be perfect as the hard-bitten general (the U.S.A. stood for United States Army) and the society lady who had a fighting love affair. The producer was Milton Sperling, a Warner son-in-law, and the scripting was long and tortuous, but, as Betty said, it would be their first together since *Key Largo.* Bogey looked tired and had a small, dry cough that made him touch his breastbone when he coughed, as if to locate the source of the twinge. The doctor's theory was that it was an acid condition and he told Bogart to cut out the breakfast orange juice.

Was there anything John and Bogey could do together? Well, there was *The Man Who Would Be King.* For his Allied Artists debut, Huston chose *Typee* because Peck was available to star, but the most important aspect of the AA contract was that John had convinced Mirisch to buy the rights to the Kipling short story from the Kipling estate. "The Man Who Would Be King" was a wild story of two ex-soldiers of the British Army in India who through ingenuity, guts, dumb luck, and vestigial honor among thieves carve out their own kingdom in a remote Afghan mountain range where the white man has not been a burden since Alexander the Great. John had originally wanted his father and some other top actor to play the ex-soldiers. Now, as he got Peter Viertel going on a first draft, he agreed it would be ideal for Bogey and Clark Gable.

Typee and *The Man Who Would Be King* were not the only projects piling up. Another was to direct two ninety-minute television spectaculars; another was a remake of *The Devil and Daniel Webster,* which Walter had starred in under William Dieterle's direction in 1942. Yet another project was Aristophanes' satire on sex and war, *Lysistrata.* On his own John was seeking to buy Terence Rattigan's play, *The Sleeping Prince,* in which he hoped to star Laurence Olivier and Marilyn Monroe. Also there was a possibility of filming the untitled life story of his photographer buddy Robert Capa, who had just been killed doing combat photography in the French Indochina war.

Toward the end of his Los Angeles stay, John ran into Evelyn at a party. She was in the third year of a rollercoaster affair with the mercurial Mike Todd, who was even borrowing from her to pay the weekly bills on *Around the World in 80 Days.* John talked her into visiting him at the Beverly Hills Hotel, to talk about serious things as he said. She was on her guard—the last time she had nearly lost her half of the pre-Columbian collection. He plied her with a stiff martini before coming to the point—a painting she had, Juan Gris's *Harlequin.* "It's yours, John," she smiled. "I've always meant to give it back." He had expected resistance and was silent for a long moment. "I'm glad," he said simply "Leslie gave me that picture." They drank more martinis, talked about Ireland, an Italian painter he admired, and Pablo, who had married and moved back to Mexico. When Evelyn got back to Todd, late for their dinner with UA president Arthur Krim, she was subjected to an uncalled-for outburst of jealousy that ended with Todd's storming out of the house, her calling John and spending a chaste and drunken night with him before flying with him to New York for another patchup with Mike.

John was on his way to Ireland, but in New York he heard

that Marilyn Monroe had been hospitalized and decided to pay a visit to the actress who remembered him and *The Asphalt Jungle* with worshiping fondness. At Manhattan's Doctors Hospital he met Marilyn's new husband, Arthur Miller, who, in the waiting room, got to talk about something that in John's mind sounded very much like a movie possibility.

To get a fast divorce from Mary Slattery, his wife of sixteen years and mother of his two children, Miller had decided on a Nevada procedure. He had spent his compulsory six weeks as a Nevada resident at Pyramid Lake near Reno and had fallen in with a trio of cowboys who divided their time between roping wild horses and proving their virility with Reno's overflow of would-be divorcées, usually impatient to prove to themselves that they were ready to regain their freedom. The three wranglers had taken Miller in tow to the dry lake where they hunted mustangs and told him how, in the 1930s, there had been a substantial market for the wild little horses as children's ponies. "Now, we sell 'em for dog food," one of them had said. The way they hunted mustangs was mechanized. From a plane, one of them flushed the herd out of the mountains and onto a dry lake where the two others roped in as many as they could with a pickup truck. Their catch was worth six cents a pound. Miller had done an *Esquire* piece on this trio of misfits who lived a degenerate version of their former cowboy trade.

Until Miller met Huston at the Doctors Hospital, the *Esquire* article had been the end of the Nevada wranglers. Now, John prodded him to tell more and, intrigued, came back the next day to talk some more. "Every day while Marilyn was there, Arthur and I would meet in the hospital waiting room and he'd develop a little more of the idea," John remembers. The obvious thing to do, John suggested, was to involve the wranglers with one of those Reno divorcées, a lady who in her own way might be just as much of a misfit. Miller nodded. He would like to write something for his wife, but he had never done a screenplay. John told there was nothing to it and had him promise to forward whatever he got down on paper.

With that Huston flew to Ireland, bought himself a Georgian manor and went tiger hunting in India. The house was St.

Clerans, near Craigwell in County Galway, an estate with a hundred acres of rolling grassland on the edge of Galway Bay, an hour and a half's drive from Shannon Airport. The house had been built on the site of an eleventh-century monastery 150 years before and had suffered neglect in recent decades, but it stood out beautifully in the green, wet, and windy countryside. The manor itself was imposing, and had a colonnaded courtyard with fountains in the middle and stone lions flanking the main entrance. The hall had black marble floors and there was a giant fireplace in every room. A staff of eight was necessary to serve John, Ricki, and the children and to maintain the grounds.

"When I was a kid I never had a home," John told Louella Parsons in announcing the purchase. "I was always on the prod, living out of dressing rooms and hotels. So, all my life, I've been looking for the right place to settle."

While Ricki and a Dublin architect supervised preliminary remodeling which included stripping a layer of Victorian icing from the façade, the construction of a sunken Japanese bath and the refurnishing of the whole house, Huston flew to India to scout locations for *The Man Who Would Be King*. In Calcutta, he met an Englishman and an American on their way to hunt Bengal tigers in the Himalayan foothills in Assam state. John joined them and their host, the Maharajah of Kumar. The quartet hunted in style. Their jungle camp came equipped with dining room on stilts and a well-stocked bar. Each morning the hunters mounted ladders to the shooting platforms of their respective howdah elephants and rode off into the jungle where hundreds of beaters worked the bush. On the fourth day their elephants sensed the presence of a tiger and became unruly. Both the Englishman and Huston fired at a tiger from the backs of their swaying elephants and missed. On the eighth morning, Huston bagged a Bengal with a 125-yard rifle shot. When the tiger was laid out it measured nearly nine feet.

Back in Craigwell the new master of St. Clerans organized his first fox hunt. Ricki, who had taken lessons with a local riding master to improve her skill, was among the dozen people who were thrown jumping hedges. John saw her fly out of her saddle. "I thought, God, there goes the mother of my children! But she was lucky and only broke most of her lower teeth. I shipped her back to our dentist in the States."

Ricki was back—and ready to ride again, for John's big birthday celebration.

15

OUR HERO AT FIFTY

John celebrated his fiftieth birthday as if he were a rich man. "I will live to be a hundred," he grinned on August 6, 1956. When a reporter asked him how he could be sure, he said all anyone had to do was to promise himself, at bedtime, a shot of Bourbon the next morning. "That way you've got something to wake up to."

The restoration of St. Clerans and the attendant lifestyle proved to be costly. What was worse was that projects began to collapse left and right. Wyler's *Friendly Persuasion* had been budgeted of $1.5 million and had come in at over $3 million and Wilder's *Love in the Afternoon*, now filming in Paris, was marred by bad weather that drove up the cost. *Typee*, Harold Mirisch decreed, simply would have to wait. The Capa life story was far from ready and, Paul Kohner reported from Hollywood, *The Man Who Would Be King* script needed extensive revisions and, more important, Bogart was stricken with cancer. In February, the small, dry cough that had made Bogey touch his breastbone was diagnosed as the symptom of a malignant growth on the esophagus and in March he had undergone a brutal, nine-hour operation. He was home now, feeling he would be all right if only he could put on a little weight. If he could get back to work, he'd feel even better. In the meantime, however, H. C. Potter was filming *Melville Goodwin, U.S.A.* with Kirk Douglas and Susan Hayward (Warner retitled it *Top Secret Affair*).

Huston needed money badly. *The Sleeping Prince* was shooting—with Laurence Olivier directing Marilyn Monroe and himself—and the Cannes Film Festival revealed that Christian-Jaque [no first name] made *Lysistrata* one of the sketches of his *Destinée*, with Martine Carol playing Aristophanes' heroine. On the long distance phone, John told Paul he couldn't afford to turn down any decent offer. Kohner did his best—the box office failure of *Moby Dick* didn't exactly strengthen his hand—and when the dust settled, Huston was in the thrall of Twentieth Century Fox for three movies.

Fox was in the reign of Spyros Skouras, the onetime shepherd from Greece, with the day-to-day operation in the hands of Buddy Adler, like Darryl Zanuck a Warner Brothers alumnus. After producing *From Here to Eternity* at Columbia, Adler had house-produced a succession of major Fox pictures, including *Love Is a Many-Splendored Thing* and *Bus Stop* and was now slowly dying of cancer.

John came to Los Angeles to sign in and Adler assigned one of his yes-men, Eugene Frenke, as the on-line producer of the first Huston picture—a turkey not even Wyler had been able to put into filmable shape. In 1952, Fox had bought *Heaven Knows, Mr. Allison*, a World War II novel by Charles Shaw with a nun-and-marine-trapped-together-on-South Pacific-island theme. Catholic authorities had expressed reservations and Willy had had Adler submit a treatment to the League of Decency in which the girl is revealed not to be a real nun after all, but someone who, to escape the Japanese, disguises herself in nun's clothing. This version had won church approval, but Wyler had given up and moved to Paramount and, with Bogart, made *The Desperate Hours*.

The present *Heaven Knows, Mr. Allison* script was the kind John would have lit his cigar with ten years earlier, but the bills were piling up. Valiantly, he set to work and, with John Lee Mahin, wrote a screenplay in which Sister Angela had not yet taken her final vows and nothing censorable takes place be-

157

tween her and Allison. Not on the surface at least. Huston couldn't help making the picture Hustonian, a meditation on what happens when circumstances force people to question fixed certainties. In *Red Badge*, the Youth becomes a hero through cowardice. In the beginning of *Heaven Knows*, Allison believes in his machine gun and Sister Angela believes in her crucifix. In the fadeout neither can reintegrate former roles and beliefs without shedding individual freedoms.

Huston wrote and filmed powerful scenes. In one, a drunken Allison shouts to Angela, "We're like Adam and Eve in Paradise." Frightened, she runs away. When two days later, he tells her he is sorry he provoked her, she answers that she didn't run away from him, but from the truth. Other images show her receiving in the folds of her robe the fruits he throws to her from atop a tree, their lingering gazes and, at a moment when she is frightened, his hands on her praying, folded hands. When the Japanese land on the island, their military ceremonial is satirized with shots of weapons exercises, orders barked, and the raising of the colors. At the end of the picture, Huston comes back to the flag raising, this time with an American flag going up the same pole.

Before taking off for Trinidad and Tobago to start production, with Deborah Kerr and Robert Mitchum as Sister Angela and Allison, John spent a couple of quiet cocktail hours with Bogey. The actor knew he had cancer, and he felt this was nothing to be ashamed of, or to be whispered about. He could no longer walk, but at five o'clock every evening he would have his nurse shave and groom him and dress him in gray flannels and scarlet dinner jacket. Then his emaciated body was lifted into a wheelchair and pushed to a dumbwaiter. His nurse helped him in and, sitting on a little stool, he was lowered to the kitchen where another transfer was made, and again by wheelchair he was taken through the house into the library and to his chair. And there he was, sherry glass in hand and cigarette between the lips when, at five-thirty, a few friends arrived. He kept smoking because, as he pointed out sourly, your esophagus has nothing to do with your lungs, and he kept drinking because he liked it, and he was not about to change the habits of a lifetime just because he was a little underweight. The selected friends who dropped by included Spencer Tracy and Katharine Hepburn, Nunnally Johnson, Sam Spiegel, the Sinatras, the Nivens, and literary agent Irving Lazar. Bogey never whimpered or complained; everybody knew that he knew he was dying, but he wisecracked, and Betty played along. John was impressed by Bogey's courage: "After the first visit—it took that to get over the initial shock of his wasted appearance—one quickened at the grandeur of it and felt strangely elated, proud to be there, proud to be his friend."

The major difficulties in Trinidad and Tobago were to find extras who could play Japanese soldiers and a giant sea turtle to tow Mitchum for an underwater sequence. Says Huston, "There was not a single bona fide Japanese in the whole Caribbean—and we finally ranged as far south as Brazil. We needed eight men who could speak Japanese fluently. They didn't have much to do—just talk casually to one another for scenes in the officers' mess. It should have been easy to find them but it wasn't. We finally found them in Sao Paulo. The other 'Japanese' in the picture were really Chinese. We imported them from Trinidad, along with a hundred U.S. marines for the beach fighting stuff."

The turtle the crew finally captured was a three-hundred-pound monster. Mitchum was supposed to catch it for food, but it almost became the other way around. The turtle towed the actor for what seemed miles and almost dragged him into a coral reef. Mitchum saw the razor reef just in time. On other occasions he sustained a deep cut on one foot in a battle sequence and took several layers of skin off his chest sliding down a coconut trunk.

Ricki came over with the children. Anjelica was three, and Tobago was to remain one of her earliest memories: "We had a house right on the beach. The fact that my father was making a movie was not so extraordinary for me, it was my life. Some people had fathers who were bankers and farmers; my father made films, that's how I saw it. As for the movie stars they just were around, some of them were friends, others weren't, it was all just part of my everyday life."

Midway through the filming, Huston received word from Fox that No. 2 of the contract would be *A Farewell to Arms* for David Selznick. The salary would be $250,000, double the current pay. A week later, John also received the visit of a studio representative who said he was sent out by Adler to check out any elements in the *Heaven Knows* script that might offend Catholics. John handled the representative in his own manner, telling him they had added a new sequence to be shot the next day. "Thought you might enjoy watching us shoot it," John cooed.

Sitting in a canvas chair next to Huston, the censor watched Kerr and Mitchum. As the scene progressed he turned pale. "Mr. Mitchum is *seducing* her," he gasped. "This is absolutely horrible! You cannot allow this!"

Huston told him to be quiet, that it was too late now to make further script changes. What the studio representative was only told later was that there was no film in Ossie Morris' camera.

The rest of the four-month location shooting went by serenely, and John invested in a local heavyweight named Erwin Allen. "I always like to keep some money tied up in a good fighter," he said, sending Allen to England to train.

John returned to Hollywood for the editing on New Year's Day 1957 and to see Bogey one last time. Bogart died January 14, three weeks after his fifty-sixth birthday. Betty asked John to say a few words at the funeral service at the Beverly Hills' All Saints Episcopal Church. "He loved life," John said in his eulogy before several hundred film notables. "Life meant his family, his friends, his work, his boat. He could not imagine leaving any of them, and so until the very last he planned what he would do when he got well. His boat was being repainted. Stephen, his son, was getting of an age when he could be taught to sail, and to learn his father's love of the sea. A few weeks' sailing and Bogey would be all ready to go to work again. He was going to make fine pictures—only fine pictures from now on." Huston also talked about Bogart's hospitality, saying he "fed a guest's spirits as well as his body. He would ply you with goodwill until you became drunk in the heart as well as the legs." In private, John said that although he had kicked around with Bogey for some thirty years it was only in the last few years that he had come to understand him.

In February 1957, Huston flew home for a short vacation before the Hemingway classic, which was to shoot in northern Italy. St. Clerans was coming along fine. His Monet and Utrillo paintings were hung next to the Toulouse-Lautrec posters, and other rooms were decorated with Louis XV mirrors, Indian jade deities, African sculptures and what was left of the Aztec and Maya collection. *Heaven Knows, Mr. Allison* was released in March, another Hollywood flick effectively destroyed by Cinemascope and censorship. Members of the writing branch of the Academy, however, saw enough distinction to nominate Huston and Mahin for Best Screenplay Oscars.

Selznick was something of an anachronism in 1957, a hangover from the Golden Era of the producer as autocrat, ultimate Hollywoodizer, and believer in his own publicity puff. He had not produced a picture in nearly ten years and he plunged into *A Farewell to Arms* with a vengeance. Frank Borzage had directed Paramount's memorable 1933 version with Helen Hayes and Gary Cooper as Hemingway's nurse and soldier and Michael Curtiz had made Warner Brothers' less creditable 1951 edition, called *Force of Arms* and starring William Holden and Nancy Olson. Selznick was convinced that neither picture had captured the full scope of the war theme nor the intrinsic beauty of the love story, and he was hurt when the New York *Times* dared refer to his production as a "remake." He was pleased that Jennifer Jones was in demand and since *Beat the Devil* had appeared in three pictures, but he believed that none of these had realized her true potential as a romantic star. *A Farewell to Arms* would be the vehicle that would allow him to show his wife's true talents as an actress.

With Fox financing and distributing, Rock Hudson was borrowed from Universal to costar with Jennifer in what David thought was the century's greatest love story. The shrewd Ben Hecht, who in one frantic week in 1939 had whipped the *Gone With the Wind* script into shape for David, was hired to do the screenplay and Selznick agreed that Huston would be the right director. When the producer's one-time production manager, Ray Klune, heard this, he called up his former boss and told him Huston was a mistake.

"Why?" David asked.

"Because you'll kill each other. It's the old law of physics about an immovable object and an irresistible force."

The initial meetings, however, went smoothly enough. Together with Hecht, they held script conferences in New York and Beverly Hills. John thought Λ *Farewell to Arms* was more than a love story in a war setting. To him, it conveyed a sense of the impermanence of the best of human feelings—love, and implied comments on the futility of war in its description of grace under pressure, Hemingway's favorite theme. After only a few meetings, John and David clashed over Hecht's rewrites. Huston attempted to remove parts that had not been in the novel and to put more of Hemingway in. In some instances Selznick agreed, but he argued it would be impossible to please the author, since Hemingway disliked any changes in dramatizations of his books.

In March, the company moved to Italy, David setting up headquarters in Rome and John proceeding to the first location at Cortina d'Ampezzo, a ski resort six thousand feet up the Dolomite Alps. In his hotel room, John found a new script—by Cesare Zavattini and two other Italian writers. The attached sixteen-page Selznick memo said this script was "more commercial" than any of Hecht's rewrites. Memos were flying thick and fast to everybody on the location. To production manager Arthur Fellows, who had been John's assistant on *Red Badge*, David wrote that precautions must be taken to prevent loss of life. To Rock Hudson—practice rowing so you will look professional in the lake sequence. To Ossie Morris, imposed by Huston, went twenty pages of instructions on how to photograph Jennifer. To the publicity chief in New York went a memo criticizing the preparations for the publicity campaign. Rolled out, the cable extended down the hallway and ended with, ON SECOND THOUGHT, I TAKE BACK EVERYTHING I SAID. PROCEED AS YOU SUGGESTED. The memos to Huston were increasingly snappish. John wanted Hudson's hair cut to the severe style of

World War I; David accused him of trying to ruin Rocky's sex appeal.

On the eve of shooting start, Selznick dictated a memo to Huston saying he was desperately unhappy with how things were going; that their differences would not help the picture, that he was not asking John to resign but telling him the conditions under which they could proceed, that they were both individualists but on *A Farewell to Arms* only one individualist could prevail, and that was David O. Selznick. Arthur Fellows was instructed to deliver the memo and the production manager phoned John in his room and said, "I've got something to give you, and I don't think you'll like it. I think he's nuts, and you'll hit the ceiling when you read it."

Huston read half the memo and phoned Fellows' room.

"I not only hit the ceiling; I'm stuck up there," said John. Half an hour later he had packed his belongings and left Cortina d'Ampezzo.

Selznick issued a widely quoted remark, "In Mr. Huston I asked for a first violinist and instead got a soloist," and flew to Hollywood to consult with Skouras and Adler, telling reporters en route there was no truth to reports that Huston had quit because of differences over Jennifer's portrayal; that he was himself usually an easy man to get along with and had only changed directors on *Viva Villa, Gone With the Wind*, and *Duel in the Sun*. While Fellows took over the direction of location scenes on a temporary basis, Selznick chose Charles Vidor to replace Huston. Evelyn Keyes's second husband lasted through a long, hot summer of filming, a production halt declared by David so more love scenes could be written, and Fellows' actually smashing his fist against the producer's bespectacled face. Everything went wrong. The reviews called the picture old-fashioned, overproduced, poorly acted, and ineffective, and David's publicity gesture of promising to pay Hemingway $50,000 of the picture's future profits turned into a public humiliation. In his reply to Selznick's cable, Hemingway deprecated the chances of a profit for the remake in which the forty-one-year-old Mrs. Selznick portrayed the twenty-four-year-old nurse of his novel, but that if such a miracle should occur, Selznick should change the fifty thousand into nickels and shove them.

John and David met a year later in the lobby of the St. Regis in New York and exchanged a few words. Later, Jennifer invited Huston to a party at the Selznicks', but he declined, saying, "I'm still sore." *A Farewell to Arms* was Selznick's last production. He died seven years later.

Huston spent part of the summer in France, jokingly promising to be a character witness for Peter Viertel in a British court, getting Jean-Paul Sartre to agree to write a Sigmund Freud screen biography and going to the Cannes Film Festival with Willy and Talli Wyler and Paul and Lupita Kohner. Peter and Deborah Kerr had fallen in love and were both fighting messy divorce proceedings, Viertel to shed Virginia, to whom he had been married since 1944; Deborah to dissolve her twelve-year marriage to Anthony Bartley. Christopher Isherwood *was* Peter's witness in Santa Monica, but the London proceedings were more dramatic. Bartley named Viertel as corespondent and, as was possible under British law in 1958, sued him for damages.

The Sartre connection was Suzanne Flon, who hadn't done much acting since *Moulin Rouge* but was involved with the excited young movie buffs surrounding André Bazin and his *Cahiers du Cinéma*. She got busy translating once she brought Sartre and Huston together and philosopher-playwright and director plunged into Freud. John's interest, he explained, went back to the documentary on psychological combat shock he had made for the U. S. Army. His scriptwriter back in 1945 had been Charles Kaufman and the two of them had promised each other they'd one day make a picture about Freud. In 1947, Kaufman had approached Fox and almost pulled it off, but Anna Freud had warned she would not tolerate any film biography of her late father and Fox had shied away from the subject. Anna, and Freud's son, Ernst, still opposed the idea, but, John explained—and Suzanne translated—they had all decided to ignore the Freud children. "Freud belongs to the ages," he said, "and we have found that his life can be dramatized without permission of the heirs as long as we portray no living characters and don't malign the subject."

Sartre answered it was ironic that Huston should come to him, who had always denied the existence of the unconscious, but he was—well, broke. John grinned and said the writing fee might be twenty-five million francs, or $50,000. What *also* made Sartre sit up was John's idea of showing Freud before he was famous, in fact, showing him when, at the age of thirty, he was completely wrong and his ideas had led him into hopeless error.

The following Sunday, Simone de Beauvoir joined the trio for dinner. Sartre's longtime mistress thought Huston had that "American attractiveness, despite a big stye on his eye" and the four of them talked a lot about Freud, who had been a virgin until his marriage at twenty-seven, and a totally faithful husband. Sartre felt the most enthralling time in the life of any great discoverer is when he seems muddled and lost but has the genius to correct himself. Of course it was difficult to explain this development to an audience who didn't know Freud. In order to arrive at the right ideas, it would be necessary to explain the wrong ones. Sartre, it was agreed, would write a script that began when Freud actually believed the cause of feminine hysteria was fathers' raping their daughters and follow his career to his discovery of the Oedipus complex.

Gottfried Reinhardt's brother, Wolfgang, who had co-scripted *Juarez* with John, would produce *Freud* and, before leaving Paris for Cannes Huston had him work out a hefty advance for Sartre, who promised he would deliver the script by Christmas.

Willy's *The Friendly Persuasion* was in competition in Cannes, running against Ingmar Bergman's *The Seventh Seal*, Andrzej Wajda's *Kanal* and Jules Dassin's exile picture, *Celui qui doit mourir*. On the terrace of the Carlton, Wyler, Huston, and Kohner sipped Veuve Cliquot and ruminated over the changing cinema. Willy and John could smile at the intense fervor of the new movie crowd thronging the Croisette, but both were keenly aware of Hollywood's growing insularity. Television had proved a major threat after all and neither 3-D nor widescreen revolutions had brought back the twice-a-week moviegoing habit. Hollywood could still sock it to 'em, but another kind of cinema was becoming relevant and Cannes was full of pale young Frenchmen who spent their waking hours in cinemas and talked about *mise en scène*—that virtually untranslatable Gallicism meaning as much elucidation and creation of mood and ambiance as, literally, visualizing a text in three dimensions and directing actors from camera-left to camera-right. Wyler was a fallen star in the canary-colored *Cahiers du Cinéma*, where Huston was also regularly zapped. But Huston had a respectful following in the rival Parisian highbrow magazine, *Positif*, which had already dedicated two issues to analyses of the Hustonian *oeuvre*. What was irritating about these intense young buffs was that they were as ignorant about the movies as an industry as they were knowledgeable about its product, but the business was changing. Willy told how he was forced to tackle Technirama in *Big Country*, his next with Greg Peck and Charlton Heston, and John mentioned how Selznick had been offended when Rod Steiger and others in the new generation of actors had refused to sign term contacts. The irony was of course that the studios were quietly dismantling their stables of players, writers, and technical staffs. Everybody, it seemed, was becoming a free-lance, and Kohner and his fellow agents were moving into the vacuum.

Maybe it was time to move toward a totally international cinema. Lots of European pictures were now coproductions and the Italians and the French were especially good at it, although everybody along the Croisette groaned and said the arrangement was rarely ideal. With the exception of American and British bigtimers, virtually no major director seemed to escape this *cinéma apatride*, as the French called this flag-of-convenience moviemaking. The Hollywood majors were themselves in the game, especially United Artists, which wasn't just an Italian production firm but even an Italian distribution company. Paul had more and more European clients—he was about to sign up Ingmar Bergman, who, like Wyler and Huston would remain a steadfast client—and why not? Why not, indeed. Huston was the first to agree. His last picture in the

States had been *The Red Badge of Courage*. With British technicians, he had shot *The African Queen* in Africa. He had made *Moulin Rouge* in France with a mixed French-British crew, *Beat the Devil* in Italy with a half-Italian crew, and, again with British staff, *Moby Dick* on the high seas, and *Heaven Knows, Mr. Allison* in Tobago and Trinidad.

John ordered a round for everyone when *The Friendly Persuasion* won the Palme d'or grand prize. When he got back to St. Clerans, a big brown envelope from Fox contained a proposal to make a picture in Japan.

"If I have one heritage from my father, it's respect for the source," John told a Hollywood news conference announcing the production start of *The Townsend Harris Story*. "Dad told me to go to life itself for my material. Well, after I saw *Rashomon* and *Gate of Hell* I wanted to make a Japanese picture using Japanese crews, shot over there from first frame to last. And now that I have the right property I'm going to make it. I'm going to the source."

The studio release said Townsend Harris was the first western diplomat to enter Japan and somebody asked the director who would play Harris.

Huston grinned and sucked truculently on his cigar. "Only one man is right for him and that's John Wayne. I want to send Duke's gigantic form into the exotic world that was the Japanese empire in the eighteen hundreds. Imagine! The massive figure, with his bluff innocence and naïveté, with his edges rough, moving among these minute people. Who better to symbolize the big, awkward United States of one hundred years ago? Duke's our man."

The historical Townsend Harris landed at Shimoda on the tip of Izu peninsula in 1856—invited after Commodore Matthew Perry had showed America's naval strength—and set to work with patience and tact. He had no ships at his disposal, but he made effective use of news of Chinese setbacks at the hands of British and French expeditionary forces. He insisted on presenting his credentials personally to the shogun, or military commander, in Tokyo, and over the two following years worked out the first modern treaty. Its provisions governed duties, currency exchange, and freedom of religion for Americans with rights to reside in six ports. The court in Kyoto didn't like the treaty, but officials of the shogun ratified it on their own authority.

When Harris set up his first residence, he hired a young washing woman to maintain his quarters. On her second visit, he noticed that the girl had a skin infection and promptly fired her. From this brief encounter, however, a Japanese legend flowered about the love between a beautiful geisha and her "barbarian" from the West. In reality, Harris was a devout Christian who never touched liquor and refused to work on Sundays. He did not like Japanese women—perhaps he didn't like women at all, since he died a bachelor at the age of seventy-three—and he would never have condoned such immoral conduct. Legend was more powerful than facts and the severe diplomat became a romantic folk hero at the dawn of Japan's fateful opening to the West.

The authentic Harris and the first resident barbarian of Japanese folklore were much too tame for John's taste—and Wayne's persona. The way Huston saw it—and his friend Charles Grayson began writing it in the screenplay—Harris would indeed become involved with a beautiful geisha but he would also be spied upon and attacked by a combative samurai, become the enemy of the governor of Shimoda and, to combat a cholera epidemic, burn down a village.

Between them, director and star cost Fox a cool million. Wayne was paid $700,000 for fourteen weeks, the highest salary any actor had been paid up to 1957. Huston's stipendium was $300,000. Eugene Frenke was the producer again and in July, Huston, Frenke, Grayson and cameraman Charles Clarke were off. The beauty of traditional Japan, especially Kyoto with its eight hundred shrines and temples, overwhelmed John and he decided to shoot the main action in the ancient capital. Interiors would be filmed at Kyoto's Eiga studios while a relatively unspoiled fishing port on Izu peninsula was picked for Harris' landfall and sanitary burning of a village. Huston wanted to make a *Japanese* movie and he quickly surrounded himself with Japanese technicians. As script superviser he man-

aged to hire a fellow-director of statue—Teinosuke Kinugasa of
Gate of Hell fame. John was eager to duplicate Kinugasa's
breathtaking exteriors and tried to hire his cameraman as well,
but Kohei Sugiyama was busy elsewhere. Minoru Hirotsu became technical superviser and Kisaku Itoh art director.

While Grayson and two other writers, Alfred Hayes and
Nigel Balchin, plugged away on the script, John and his Japanese assistants began looking for someone to play the legendary
geisha. They saw clips of 150 actresses and actually tested
twenty-nine before Huston discovered a lovely seventeen-year-
old in a geisha house. The house mother agreed to let him give
her a screen test if he paid the girl twelve hundred dollars "pil-
low money" in advance. Huston agreed, but the test was never
made. "The poor dear got appendicitis," says Huston. "So we
had to keep on looking."

The final choice was Eido Ando, a singing stripper Huston
found in a Tokyo music hall. "I knew she was our gal. For one
thing, she was tall for a Japanese—five foot seven—which
would help in scenes with Wayne, who is six foot four. Addi-
tionally, she possessed a lovely, low-pitched voice and moved
with a dancer's natural grace. Of course she couldn't speak a
word of English."

To play the governor, Huston chose So Yamamura, the
"Laurence Olivier of Japan," according to Fox publicity.

A minor crisis occurred early in the shooting. Huston was
setting up a shot next to a Buddhist temple when Grayson
handed him a Hollywood trade paper saying the new title was
The Barbarian and the Geisha. John exploded and wired Adler,
declaring he would withdraw his name from the finished film if
it bore that "ridiculous title." Frenke managed to soothe Huston. "I like it," said the producer. "After all, John, we do have
a barbarian and we do have a geisha. It makes sense." John
got his revenge by conning Frenke into playing a splendidly
dressed samurai and seeing to it he got dumped head first into
a lake.

The row over the title was only a warmup to the fights with
Wayne. When the actor saw the rushes of the early scenes, he
objected that nothing suited his screen image. "Huston has me

walking through a series of Japanese pastels. Hell, my fans expect me to be tall in the saddle.

"Usually, I gain a director's confidence, but when I go up to Huston's room and ask what's coming up for the day, he sighs and points out the window. 'Duke, just look at that view. Isn't it magnificent?'"

Huston ignored Wayne's recommendation that he photograph his right, not his left, profile and when it came to Harris' fight scene, he pitted his star against a tiny judo master who tossed the 220-pound Duke as if he were a child. Wayne wondered darkly what his fans would think of this fight, but Huston was delighted with the footage.

Huston had never been so free and ready to use the fortuitous. At the fishing village, three hundred fishermen hired for background action and dressed in period costumes became highly agitated one morning, quit the movie and hopped into their sampans to head for the open sea. A school of dolphins had been sighted and it took the fishermen three days to herd the dolphins to shore and slaughter them. Instead of tearing his hair out, Huston filmed the whole thing and even paid another three hundred men to keep their modern boats out of sight. When a small boy laughed at Harris walking past him in a scene, John didn't yell "Cut!" but kept the take. "If that kid thinks he looks funny today, then a kid of a hundred years ago would have thought so too." When an intricate shadow pattern cast by several actors caught John's attention, he shot the shadows instead of the actors. When a gnarled caretaker of a Kyoto temple refused to allow the felling of an old cherry tree, even if the movie company planted a new tree in its place, John made the tree the center of his scene.

The Barbarian and the Geisha was fast becoming the most expensive movie ever shot in Japan. The interior set for the shogun's palace where Harris presents his treaty was too big for the sound stages of Eiga studios and the company had to build it in Kyoto's Exhibition Hall, requiring special soundproofing and electrical equipment. To simulate spring, 32,000 artificial cherry blossoms were manufactured and hung on bare December branches, but setting fire to the village proved the most trying and expensive. When everything was ready for Harris and his interpreter (Sam Jaffe) to put torches to the first houses, John told Grayson the scene didn't make any sense. "Why would they let Harris live if he tried a stunt like this?" John asked the writer. "Why wouldn't they just chop the bastard?"

Grayson reasoned they wouldn't do it because the picture is just starting. Unimpressed, John stared at the fishing boats and hundreds of waiting technicians, actors and extras and Grayson got the idea that the governor might allow Harris to set the fire in order to arrest him and ship him back to America as a criminal.

"Go do it," John said.

To write anything with several hundred people looking on was beyond Grayson and he dashed off to the production shed. When he returned with the new scene, John said, "Uh-huh," edited a few lines and handed the new scene to Angela Allen, the script girl who pecked out copies on her portable and Japanese assistants frantically coached Yamamura. When the Duke got his copy and told Huston one important line had been lost in the revision, John told him just to go ahead and speak the line.

The first take went on cue. Wayne and Jaffe put torches to the first straw roofs, extras scampered about in mock terror. The governor and his retainers appeared, shouting their new lines. The barbarian was accused of criminal action and hauled off by the samurai after an angry exchange of dialogue. Said Grayson, "the entire set was an inferno. The only spot still clear of the holocaust was the area where the governor arrested Wayne. And even it was being seriously threatened by the spreading fire. John ordered another take of the dialogue scene. 'Again, from the governor's entrance!' The scene was repeated as things grew hotter. 'Again!' yelled John, and the sweating actors obeyed. 'Once more!' John commanded. This third take was it; Houston had what he wanted. By now Jaffe's pants were smoking and Wayne had scorched one arm and burned his leg."

When Huston called Ricki on New Year's Eve to wish her

and the children Happy 1958, she told him there was no script from Sartre. Not that John had time for *Freud*. There was still one more month of location work on *The Barbarian and the Geisha*.

They struggled through January and by the time the location shooting ended in February, director and star were no longer on speaking terms. When Huston arrived in Hollywood for postproduction work and reporters asked him about his rumored differences with Wayne, he smiled crookedly. "Suppose you just say that there is no great meeting of souls."

Huston also quarreled with Adler and left the picture to the studio to complete. Wayne was called back for a couple of retakes. Years later, the Duke would squirm at the mentioning of *The Barbarian and the Geisha* and call Huston one of the slowest directors he had ever worked with, a man fascinated by petty detail. As an example Wayne would mention an opening sequence in Townsend Harris' cabin aboard the navy ship taking him to Japan.

Huston remembers it differently: "You won't believe me but the way I did it, *The Barbarian and the Geisha* was a beautiful picture. I managed to do excellent things on the formal level and to develop a pretty subtle way of telling the story, a narration that wasn't as dramatic as it was linear; in short a narrative I was entirely happy with. A man I have no great esteem for, John Wayne, took over, shot scenes I hadn't planned and threw out others I liked, in short changed completely the picture which I now disown." By the time *The Barbarian and the Geisha* was released to devastating reviews in October 1958, John had another picture in the can, an African caper produced by Darryl Zanuck, who was just about to stage the palace revolution that would lead to the firing of Skouras and Adler. And twenty years later, John was back with producer Frenke on *Saud*.

16

WOBBLING

The French consul in Los Angeles followed an honorable tradition. Like Chateaubriand, Stendhal, Claudel, Morand, and other distinguished members of France's diplomatic corps, he was a writer. Not a moony bookworm but a raffish *lettré* as famous for the beauty of his ladyfriends as for the elegant cynicism of his novels. Invitations to the parties he gave at the consular residence on Hollywood's Outpost Drive were eagerly sought after.

If there was a theme to Romain Gary's books it was an aversion to modern barbarism. To this forty-four-year-old Parisian of complicated Russian-Jewish origins who had spent the war years in the entourage of General de Gaulle in London, authorship was justified by ethics. Since his ironic and cynical wartime novel, *Education européenne,* he expressed the confused generosity of a moralist troubled by the growing inhumanity of the modern world, an inhumanity falsely justified by the imperatives of war and technology. His latest book was *Les Racines du ciel,* winner of the prestigious Goncourt Prize in 1956 and now out in English. *The Roots of Heaven* was an ironic plea for something that didn't have a name yet—ecology. It is the story of Morel, a Frenchman in Africa, who one day decides to oppose the hunting and killing of elephants.

Love for the big beasts, idealism, and a need to challenge society are the motives behind the action of this former conscientious objector. For Morel, the elephant is the symbol of gigantic freedom, a freedom that he finds all the more precious since it doesn't have to impose itself by force. Acting with superb logic, Morel defies the law in the name of nature because he feels that humanity has taken a wrong turn and is heading down a road at the end of which looms the atomic holocaust. "Come on now, you're not going to destroy a race just to make billiard balls and paper-knives," says Morel. The sentence brings with it the specter of ends and means and eventually turns Morel into an anarchist.

Darryl F. Zanuck—DFZ, as he liked to style himself—was a frequent visitor to Outpost Drive, but it was in Paris that his girl friend, Juliette Greco, had drawn his attention to *Les Racines du ciel*. Like Huston, Zanuck had sensed a shift toward Europe and moved to Paris with the intention of producing two or three films a year for Fox, each personally chosen and supervised. The first had been an adaptation of Hemingway's *The Sun Also Rises*, directed by Henry King.

John was a logical choice for *The Roots of Heaven*, since the picture would have to shoot where the elephants were—in Chad, and feature a large international cast headed by William Holden as Morel. John was leery of embarking on a picture with a headstrong producer, but he loved the book and the chance to make another picture in Africa. After several meetings in St. Clerans and Paris, they agreed to give it a try. Each had his prerequisites. Zanuck kept veto power over casting and wanted Gary to write the screenplay; Huston insisted on Ossie Morris on camera and for a rewrite imposed Patrick Leigh Fermor, an Irish novelist he admired. Fermor's draft would introduce a couple of incongruous characters of the kind John affected.

When Holden proved unavailable, Trevor Howard took his place. Errol Flynn, who had been surprisingly good as a mock-Flynn in *The Sun Also Rises*, was cast as a drunken English ex-officer, Orson Welles as a bulbous TV commentator, and Eddie Albert as a pain-in-the-neck journalist. Juliette got the only feminine part, the role of a sad lark of a concentration camp survivor who finds a new commitment to life in Morel's mission to save animals from extinction. It had been during Mexican locations of *The Sun Also Rises* that Mel Ferrer's wife, Audrey Hepburn, had suggested torch singer Greco for a still uncast minor part. A May-September affair had blossomed between the raven-haired torch singer and DFZ and, as Zanuck would remember it, "I foolishly started looking for stories for her."

Welles was not required to come to Chad but would do his bit at the Boulogne studios in Paris after location filming. The technical staff was the most multinational team Huston had worked with and included American, British, Chadian, French, and Italian crew members. The budget was a comfortable three million.

When compared to this picture, *The African Queen* was, in retrospect, a lazy bob on a sunny black river. Daytime temperatures in southern Chad range up to 140° F. and dip to 90 and 100 at night. Here in the savanna and the huge marshy basin of the Bahr Aouk, the fauna is extraordinarily rich and only a few robust tribes sustain a marginal existence, the sun is a blast furnace and drinking water a taboo treasure. Fair-skinned people have a tendency to sweat out liquids before they reach the interior of the body, provoking a dehydration that often leads to delirium. The marshes where the elephants themselves cool off are the breeding grounds for a billion insects and malaria and amoebic dysentery are a bigger danger than the huge crocodiles. During the second week on the location, an Italian crew member who neglected to take his antimalaria pills contracted the most virulent form of the disease and died. Bobby Jacks, Zanuck's son-in-law, also came down with this form of malaria, but survived. Another member of the company was so badly bitten by sleeping without mosquito netting next to an insect-attracting kerosene lamp that he was hospitalized for two weeks. In all, the company doctor logged 960 sick calls and many members of the troupe had to be sent home. Eddie Albert collapsed from sunstroke, became delirious, and, in John's words, "was out of his head for a couple of days." Despite his claim of immunity to tropical illness, Flynn suffered a touch of malaria, Greco came down with a rare blood disease that caused her blood pressure to fall dramatically, and DFZ suffered an attack of shingles.

John of course was in perfect health. As Errol Flynn wrote in *My Wicked, Wicked Ways*, "Huston was obviously very good in the bush. I thought I was pretty good, but ole Johnny leaped along through the jungle like a big spider. He was hard to keep up with."

Filming started in March to beat the summer rains which make the huge plains inaccessible from July to November, but the heat soon cut back the daily schedule. Shooting started at dawn, but at noon John had to call it a day. Still, people collapsed from the heat. Trevor Howard had to wear a tan makeup because his brick-red complexion didn't photograph right. The makeup caused his face to boil if it was left on more than an hour. The other actors sweated so much they doused their heads every ten minutes and had makeup reapplied. The camp was decimated by sunstrokes, malaria, dysentery and several diseases of unknown origin. A French driver went crazy and said he was going to make a picture in Africa.

Tempers flared. Greco fought with Zanuck and found Huston's direction frustrating. "He never says I am good or I am bad. First I think he must hate me. Then he looks at me like a snake with little, slitted eyes, and he says through his teeth, 'Fine, honey, fine.'"

To make her happy, DFZ flew in a number of her Left Bank friends, including Anne-Marie Cazalis, who had discovered Juliette. Cazalis was put on publicity, but instead of calming Greco down, seemed to excite her. Zanuck finally shipped Cazalis back to Paris. In retaliation, she collaborated with Juliette on the torch singer's memoirs, which were to describe in embarrassing, unflattering detail the Greco-Zanuck courtship, romance, and breakup, all of which seemed to happen at the same time.

By Zanuck's estimate more liquor was consumed than on any other film in history. The producer stayed with beer, downing twelve bottles a day, but the others were on hard stuff. Huston and Howard were famous boozers, but Patrick Leigh Fermor outdid them. The most pathetic drinker was Flynn. He brought twelve cases of vodka with him, drank it all, and sent for more. "He would sit all night with a bottle of vodka, an open book, and a Coleman lantern, and never look at the book," says John. "He was never drunk when working but whenever we shifted to another location he would drink too much and to recover he needed drugs. Errol was on his way out of course, he was dying." During one of the moves, John invited Errol along on a private safari. Flynn loved it and wrote in *My Wicked, Wicked Ways,* "I shall never forget it. I didn't shoot anything . . . Huston got one of the largest pair of horns for a trophy and he was like a kid with his first lollipop."

Like Morel, John was often more interested in the elephants than in human company. His most fortunate moment came one dawn when the company accidentally came upon an immense herd at a river bank. "We got some fabulous color footage," he says. "Ossie and I both knew we'd really lucked into something. You don't bump into six hundred elephants every day in the week—not even in Africa."

He fell in love with the tamed elephants the company used for staged scenes, especially one huge female. He stood and talked to his lady elephant before shooting a scene with her. "I marveled at her patience," he said. "Animals are among the best actors I've ever worked with. They know exactly what they want to do, without remorse and without misgivings."

Huston was his old self when he directed Errol performing one of his own stunts—crossing a river clinging to the tail of his horse. In midstream, Flynn heard pistol shots and realized crew members were trying to discourage several gregarious crocodiles from closing in on him and his horse.

"John, you sonofabitch," he shouted. "Get me out of this stinking river before one of these bastards has me for lunch!"

John smiled sympathetically and called for another take. When Flynn and horse were safely out of the water, Errol was told that a week earlier a French army officer had been seized by a big crocodile a couple of hundred yards upstream.

Widespread sickness caused Huston to postpone several key scenes and fly out his company. "We barely made it," said Trevor Howard. "Huston got us out of there just half a day ahead of the rains. Twelve more hours and we might all be there yet."

While the director shot Welles's scenes at Boulogne, assistants found a sandy plateau ringed by trees and boulders in the Forest of Fontainebleau south of Paris. Animals were hired from a circus and several dozen African students rounded up in St. Germain des Prés, given grass skirts and spears and rehearsed to dance fiercely around a car. When John arrived to film the scene, the students danced on cue around the car containing Flynn and Juliette Greco. They howled and brandished their spears, but Huston groaned. "They're not looking hostile enough," he told the assistant who had rehearsed the scene. "Tell them I want lots of scowling and spearshaking. God, you'd think they were a welcoming committee."

While the students were taken through new frenzies, John played *boules* with background extras. He was winning heavily at this Marseillais sport when animals howls, followed by pistol shots, were heard from the direction of the circus enclosure. When he and others reached the spot, two hyenas were locked in battle. One had bitten off the other's tail and the trainers were howling helplessly and firing their pistols into the air.

Said John, "Now *that's* what these natives should look like."

The Roots of Heaven was released in November 1958 to less than enthusiastic reviews. In hindsight, it was one picture Huston would take all the blame for. "There are some so bad that it would pain me a little bit to think about them," he would say in 1972. "I wasn't responsible for a couple of them being as bad as they are. For one I was entirely responsible and I regret that failure as much as any sin I've committed in my time. That was *Roots of Heaven,* which could have been a very good film. And largely owing to me it was not." Romain Gary had another fall guy. Zanuck had loved the author-diplomat's original script and assured him he would rather cut his own throat than change anything. "I have fifty cables assuring me that there would be no changes. Then," adds Gary, "he fucked it up."

Huston had corresponded with Arthur Miller about the wranglers' story and during postproduction of *Roots*, Miller's screenplay arrived—even if Sartre's didn't. John thought *The Misfits* was one helluva script and he wired back his enthusiasm. Immediately, things were set in motion. Marilyn Monroe would of course play Arthur's divorcée, and the playwright wanted Clark Gable for the role of Langland, the head wrangler. *The Roots of Heaven* finished the contract with Fox. Sartre was still working on *Freud*, but even if it had been ready, Reinhardt wasn't. Wolfgang was now producing a major musical in Austria for Universal, *The Sound of Music*.

John was restless—and in demand. He hated to rest on a failure. Besides, the remodeling of St. Clerans and his jet-set lifestyle made another three hundred grand highly desirable. "St. Clerans will never be complete in my lifetime," he told members of the Dublin press corps when workmen uncovered several dozen human bones while restoring the stern façade with hand-hewn blocks of gray granite. The local policeman had declared the remains to be evidence of a recent mass murder, but when Huston checked with an archaeologist and a historian, the bones were found to belong to members of the monastery who had lived in the tenth century. "The constable was let down," John told the press. "He had counted on becoming world famous with his multiple-slaying theory. Too bad. We Irish love a good murder."

To be able to pay for the continued restorations, John squeezed in *The Unforgiven*, a picture that he reckoned was his first Western, although Warner Brothers had called *The Treasure of the Sierra Madre* just that. *The Unforgiven*, adapted from a novel by Alan LeMay, was for Hecht-Hill-Lancaster Productions, Burt Lancaster's independent outfit. Harold Hecht was not related to Ben Hecht but was the brother-in-law of John Garfield, and James Hill was a screenwriter who had long worked for Lancaster as his story consultant. Hecht-Hill-Lancaster had hit paydirt—and respectability—producing

Marty and, as a corporate entity, its three associates saw themselves as fearless anti-establishment freebooters. Besides, wasn't it time to be bold? *The Man with the Golden Arm*, Otto Preminger's adaptation of Nelson Algren's netherworld of drugs, had been a smash hit despite censorship trouble, and so had *The Defiant Ones*, Stanley Kramer's plea for interracial brotherhood. *The Unforgiven* was about racial prejudice on the Texas frontier, a story that pitted upbringing against blood, society against race.

For John, it was a throwback to *The Laughing Boy*, which Willy and he had seen go down the tube because the sexual mixing of the races had been too hot to handle in 1931. This time, the miscegenation was in the fadeout, coupled with an odd whiff of incest. The plot hinged on whether or not the adopted daughter of a Texas family is really an Indian.

Audrey Hepburn, fresh from *The Nun's Story*, was quickly chosen to play Rachel, the girl who is not the daughter of the Zachary family but a Kiowa Indian. Lancaster is Ben, the head of the Zachary clan, and the man Rachel has always considered her brother but whom she ends up promising to marry. When the Kiowas finally storm the house, she must fire upon her people to save the man she loves. Audie Murphy was chosen to play Ben's quick-tempered brother and Lillian Gish their widowed mother who, when the Indians are heard over the hill making war medicine with drums and flute accompaniment, has the family piano carried outside so she can answer the war cries with Mozart. Charles Bickford plays the Zacharys' nearest white neighbor and John Saxon a Portuguese who tracks down a vengeful old man who starts the rumors of Rachel's true ancestry.

The Unforgiven was no spaghetti Western. Lancaster, Hepburn, and Huston each got $300,000 and the final budget for the United Artists release came to $3.7 million. Over $300,000 was spent on a complicated set built on a windswept prairie in the Durango badlands in central Mexico. The centerpiece was a replica of the 1860s "sod house." Built with a steel frame, the structure was invisibly hinged to provide breakaway walls to admit the camera crew and allow filming from all angles. A man-made hill, landscaped with grass and cactus, covered part of the "soddy."

"In a way it was almost as ingenious as the whales built for *Moby Dick*," said John. "It served as a studio as well as our main set because we did our film cutting right there, in the back of the house under the artificial hill." On his orders, a London lab was chosen instead of the usual Hollywood processing, adding daily Durango–Mexico City–London air freight to the production cost.

John hired Emilio (El Indio) Fernandez as supervisor of outdoor action and as an actor playing a bloodthirsty Kiowa. Fernandez was a tawny *mestizo* with an improbable life story that included riding with Pancho Villa as a thirteen-year-old, teaching Al Capone's sister to tango in Depression Chicago and, in 1944, putting Mexico on the cinematic map by directing *Maria Candelaria*, a gratingly poetic look at the misery and oppression of Indian peasants. El Indio's career had peaked in the late nineteen forties and he now clowned in American pictures shooting in Mexico, sometimes off camera but mostly on screen, where his extraordinary bandit's face had a way of enhancing the most pedestrian pulp.

Audrey was delicate. After five years of marriage to Ferrer, the thirty-year-old Audrey was finally expecting a child. The pregnancy was not discovered until after she had signed her contract. She had never been an expert horsewoman and halfway through the filming she fell from her mount and broke her back. The accident caused an expensive production shutdown while she was hospitalized in Los Angeles.

John decided to visit his stepson while they were waiting for Audrey. Pablo was now twenty-five and living in Cuernavaca, south of Mexico City. He was a photographer, married, and the father of a son he had christened John Walter Huston Albarran. John was touched.

Audrey returned to Durango and finished the film but miscarried in July 1959.

The Unforgiven had instances of Hustonian poetry, humor, and inventiveness—cows grazing on top of the sod house, a twilight chase among the cactuses, a lovestruck man with his bunch of flowers under the moon and an extraordinary sequence of an Indian subduing a balking horse with sweet gentleness. Seeing a flock of wild geese flying north, Rachel says, "They're human, too, maw; they jest fly a mite higher than us, that's all." When this shot of the migrating birds is repeated at the end, it takes on allegoric overtones. Below, the protagonists have lost everything and stand, wounded, among the dead in the burned-out ruins—gaunt, intractable losers in a landscape of geological indifference.

But the story never came off and *The Unforgiven* remained another big Hollywood picture gone wrong. When Rachel is revealed to be a Kiowa who has been torn from her crib in infancy, and the Kiowas want her back, the Zacharys won't give her up. Instead of sitting down to discuss things, they all reach for their guns. The result is not a film speaking out against racism but a hodgepodge of sententious ambiguity. The Indian attack is pure formula Western, in which every white bullet finds an Indian heart.

And *The Unforgiven* was another picture Huston walked away from during postproduction. In the editing something happened to several characters, suggesting Hecht, Hill, and Lancaster were a little less fearless than their liberal swagger suggested. John Saxon's Portuguese, whom everyone thinks of as an Indian or a halfbreed, is heavily established early on and is given a suspense-filled chase sequence only to disappear in midfilm. And as Stanley Kauffman would say in his review, "That Huston could not get a good performance out of Lancaster cannot be held against him, but he has achieved what no other director has done: he has got a bad performance out of lovely Audrey Hepburn."

The Unforgiven was the fourth turkey in a row.

17

THE MISFITS

The Misfits is a movie with a long shadow. By the time of its release, Clark Gable was dead and Marilyn Monroe and Arthur Miller had broken up. A year and a half later, Monroe committed suicide and five years later Montgomery Clift was dead. Ten years later, *The Misfits* was a late-night TV perennial with its own mythology.

As a film project, *The Misfits* was the stuff showbiz fiction is made of. It was the kind of vertiginous emotional trip that John thrived on while everybody else went to pieces. Monroe was on medication and for a time too ill to work at all. The Monroe-Miller marriage was crumbling as fast as her psyche. In addition to his continued battle with a homosexuality he couldn't accept, Clift was convalescing from a car accident that had left him with many bones broken and his face disfigured. Plastic surgery had done miracles, but the shock and the necessary painkillers made him subject to the blackest of moods. Like Marilyn, he often found it unbearable to show up on the set. Out of sheer boredom with sitting around day after day waiting for his emotionally crippled costars, Clark Gable insisted on doing a lot of stunts which contributed to the heart attack that killed the fifty-nine-year-old actor. As usual, there were script troubles and Miller rewrote well past the last day of shooting. The Monroe-Gable pairing never achieved the desired chemistry because neither would allow himself to play the character Miller had in mind. The original story celebrates a kind of archaic but good-natured machismo with the three cowpokes competing for the Reno divorcée. Marilyn hated her sex goddess image and didn't want to "sleep around" on the screen; she wanted respect, and Gable's persona no longer allowed him to play someone whose younger buddies can lust after his girl, let alone steal her away from him. So Arthur wrote and wrote, making his wife's character ever tenderer, Gable's manliness ever more assertive, and their affair ever more idyllic. The two hundred people on the payroll eventually included three pilots, six policemen, a doctor, a masseur and a double for Gable's double. The campfollowers included a reporter writing a book about the whole thing and a freelance photographer who was to become Mrs. Arthur Miller No 3.

The Misfits was Huston's first in the United States in ten years, a Seven Arts production for which he was paid his usual $300,000. It was his first experience with that new phenomenon called "packaging." Hollywood was increasingly run and rigged by agents and *The Misfits* was a George Chasin Agency package. Written by Chasin client Miller, it had been proposed to Chasin client Marilyn's contractual employer, Twentieth Century Fox. Spyros Skouras had found it too highbrow, but to keep it in *his* family, he had told Chasin to go to Max Youngstein, Skouras' first cousin by marriage, who headed Seven Arts. When a deal was worked out there, a copy of the script had gone to Chasin client Gable who had responded that he liked it but didn't understand the Gay Langland part he was asked to play. No sweat, a rewrite was coming up. By production time, Chasin had 10 per cent of the salaries of Miller, Monroe, Gable and Frank Taylor, Miller's friend and editorial director of Dell Books, whom the playwright had persuaded to become the producer.

There was no doubt in anyone's mind that *The Misfits* should shoot in its natural habitat. More important than getting Reno on the screen was the fact that the wild mustangs—actually descendants of domestic horses—were in northern Nevada. This was Comstock Lode country. It was the fabulous

Tony and Dad preparing for their scene in *The List of Adrian Messenger*. (Universal-MCA)

Freud
Huston directing Susan Kohner and Montgomery Clift. (Universal-MCA)

The Night of the Iguana
Ava Gardner and Richard Burton. (Seven Arts-MGM)

Making *Reflections in a Golden Eye*, from left Brian Keith, Marlon Brando, Elizabeth Taylor, and John Huston. (Warner Brothers– Seven Arts)

Huston as Noah listening to the voice of the Lord in *The Bible*.
(Twentieth Century Fox)

The tower of Babel in the spectacular, *The Bible*. (Collection Cahiers du Cinéma)

Cece.

A Walk With Love and Death
Assaf Dayan and John's daughter, Angelica Huston. (Twentieth Century Fox)

Fat City
Stacy Keach and Jeff Bridges. (Collection Cahiers du Cinéma)

Making *Fat City*, from left Conrad Hall, Stacy Keach, John Huston, and Nicolas Colasanto. (Collection Cahiers du Cinéma)

Paul Newman in *The Life and Times of Judge Roy Bean*. (National General Pictures)

Huston playing Buck Loner with Raquel Welch and Mae West in *Myra Breckinridge* for Michael Sarne. (Twentieth Century Fox)

As Noah Cross with Jack Nicholson in *Chinatown*. (Paramount)

The Man Who Would Be King
Michael Caine and Sean Connery. (Allied Artists)

1859 gold and silver strike that had turned the round-backed, red-clay sagebrush mountains along Carson River into teeming mining camps. It was in Virginia City, twenty miles southeast of Reno, that "bonanza barons" had built Victorian mansions, six churches, one hundred saloons and one opera house. Huston and Taylor scouted locations during December 1959. They would use the Styx Bar in Reno, where Miller had actually met his cowpokes. Dayton, a ghost town south of Virginia City, would be used for the rodeo sequence and the actual mustang roping would be filmed over fifteen miles of dry lake nearby. John had two demands that were immediately met—he wanted to film *The Misfits* in sequence and in black-and-white. Shooting the first sequence first and the last scene last, he felt, would increase the film's tension and allow a well-knit and hard direction and black-and-white would enhance the picture by not intruding on its harsher qualities.

With the locations set and Russell Metty—the cameraman on *We Were Strangers*—signed on, Huston flew to St. Clerans for Christmas and New Year's, bringing Miller with him for a couple of weeks' script work. During the spring of 1960, *Let's Make Love*, in which Monroe starred opposite Yves Montand under George Cukor's direction, fell behind schedule, causing *The Misfits* to be postponed until midsummer. It was July 15, 1960, when cast and crew assembled in Reno and took over half the Mapes Hotel. Gable drove up from Los Angeles with his new bride, Kay, in his Mercedes 300XL and arrived looking tanned and fit. He had gone on a crash diet and shed thirty-five pounds for what he called his "offbeat role in an offbeat picture." The Millers flew in with Marilyn's personal drama coach, Paula Strasberg, who, despite the heat never dressed in anything but black and made John think of a fury from Greek mythology. Marilyn herself was all blond and moon whiteness, ruminating over Goethe and Stanislavsky. She was a mass of inhibitions, terrors, and indecisions and immediately imposed her no-work-before-noon rule. Eli Wallach, who played the ex-army pilot wrangler, and Thelma Ritter, cast as a cynical divorcée, bitched about Marilyn's unprofessionalism, but they—and Huston—all had to take it or see Seven Arts and

United Artists scrap the picture. *The Misfits* was made for only one reason—Marilyn Monroe.

Two weeks into shooting, the company feted its director's fifty-fourth birthday with appropriate bombast. Guests arrived from Los Angeles, Paris, London, and San Francisco. Burl Ives was due, with guitar, from Kansas City; Mort Sahl promised to entertain, and a tribe of Paiute Indians from Utah came over and made John an honorary member of their nation, naming him Long Shadow. Said he, "I'm proud to be in the tribe and I intend to be one of the best damn Paiutes there is!" Marilyn became sentimental and told James Goode, who was writing *The Story of "The Misfits"* as a diary, that if it hadn't been for John back there when she tested for *The Asphalt Jungle* on the floor, no one would have heard of her. "Working with him again, after all these years, is so good," she said. "He's an artist with a camera—and he sees like a painter. John watches for the reality of a scene, then leaves it alone. He waits till he needs something before he comes in—and I think that's just a lovely quality." Someone in the press corps said that as a social event, Huston's birthday was not something you attended but something you survived.

Neither booze, heat, neurotic actors nor very difficult wild horses got to John. The crap tables did. After a day's filming, he spent his evenings at the dice tables with a large stack of twenty-five-dollar chips. When he lost, he smiled; when he won, he left "a few hundred for the boys." More often than not he lost, standing all night at the tables. On August 16, Goode recorded, he lost $15,000 at the Mapes. One night, when a fire in the area caused a power failure, he had a couple of gaffers haul in the company's diesel generator to illuminate the Mapes Casino so the gambling could continue.

On Huston's instructions, the company's sixteen wranglers roped in a half-dozen genuine wild horses and rented a dozen mean steers for the rodeo sequence. The animal Clift was to mount in a cattle chute was almost too wild, but, said John, this was a closeup. With the camera on him, Monty settled onto the back, only to have the bronc rear back violently against the side of the wooden chute. Clift's shirt was half

186

ripped from his back. Huston thought this made a fine take. Later, in another closeup where doubles could not be used, Monty had his hands lacerated while trying to hold down a fighting mare.

One day a huge packet arrived—*Freud*. Sartre's screenplay was eight hundred pages long. Flipping through it, Huston estimated the running time would be eight hours. Before he had time to shake his head, he found Sartre's enclosed note. The author was quite aware that the script was too long and suggested they prune it together.

On August 29, Monroe was flown to a Los Angeles hospital in a state of acute nervous exhaustion. When newsmen asked Huston if he wasn't worried about the production, he said, "To hell with the picture. The girl's health is at stake. If Marilyn gets proper rest at this point she'll be okay. The picture will just have to wait. Me, I'm going camel riding."

The camel race was part of Virginia City's Labor Day festivities, an event sponsored by the Phoenix *Gazette* and the San Francisco *Chronicle*. To have a worthy competitor, John prevailed on Bill Pearson to come up and ride against him. A brave local citizen entered as the third contestant.

For the race John appeared in appropriate attire. His costume, Goode wrote, "began with a pair of English riding breeches, to which was added a mauve shirt with a Faubus-for-President button pinned to one pocket, a straw hat with a Madras band, a silk scarf and red tennis shoes." John's mount was a five-year-old camel named Old Heenan. Pearson's was a fifty-year-old one-humper named Izzy. The third camel was a fifteen-year-old female named Sheba. At the shot from the starter's pistol, Old Heenan bolted forward. The local rider was instantly thrown from Sheba, but Izzy took off in hot pursuit. Unhappily for Pearson, Izzy galloped sideways into the crowd, jumped a tiny sports car, then ran directly for Piper's Opera House, one full block off the official course. Pearson ducked behind Izzy's neck as they clattered through the doors of the opera house. Inside the lobby Pearson got off his camel, shouting, "I concede."

John crossed the finish line without his straw hat but with

his teeth bared in a triumphant grin. When reporters interviewed him, he said he owed his splendid victory to the deep understanding of the camel. "You're really living when you're up there between those humps." Asked what he thought of his chief rival, he said Billy Pearson was obviously a disgrace to the camel-riding profession. "He rode over parked cars, widows, orphans—in fact there are camel-stunned babies scattered all over these historic hills. It is a scene of carnage, owing to Pearson's mismanagement of his mount."

Production resumed September 6, when Marilyn returned from the hospital. In her wake came rumors of romantic involvement with Yves Montand and an impending separation from Arthur. The playwright, who was on the set every day, refused all comment. Huston later said Marilyn was always "sensitive, nervous and goaded." She coped with her hysterical scenes where John got her to shout—a startling contrast to her hushed, monotonous voice through the picture. She had to be coached and primed, but her attention span was extremely short and few takes lasted longer than thirty seconds. In certain shots she looked anguished and sick, knocked out and impulsive. Each day's filming was a crisis situation.

Inevitably, the media coverage increased, and although newsmen and photographers were banned from all scenes with Monroe, the press corps kept growing. One hot-shot freelancer flying in was Magnum's Inge Morath. This former assistant to Henri Cartier-Bresson drew assignments all over the world and in the high-strung confusion of the Reno location barely got to meet Arthur Miller. Six months later, however, she was his new wife.

By the end of August, *The Misfits* was $416,000 over budget, and on September 20, Marilyn had a relapse that caused a second production halt. This time, Huston went sailing on Lake Tahoe. When she returned, she was spaced out in a haze of amphetamines.

The only sane couple on the location was Clark and Kay. With her periwinkle eyes and spunky independence, the thrice-divorced Kay Williams had made Gable happy. She had become a good shot, golf player, and angler, and had even made him loosen his purse strings—the 300XL was her idea—and he, who had never had children, had adjusted to her little boy of four and daughter of three. Engrossed in his marriage, Clark was nevertheless the complete pro. He was always on time, always letter-perfect and ready to do his utmost to give his director what he wanted.

There was jubilation the day Gable announced that Kay was pregnant. "I guess there's some life in the old boy," he grinned, adding he would be a father the following February. John, whose dice losses were approaching fifty thousand dollars, ordered drinks for everybody.

In response to John's goading and in frustration over his neurotic costars, Gable did stunts that would normally be done by his first or second double. Anything was better than sitting around day after day while Marilyn and Monty doped themselves up enough to face the camera, but roping a wild mustang in searing heat and being dragged along the dried-up lake were not sensible pastimes for a man of his age. He tired easily, but blamed his exhaustion on the crash diet.

The least stir of the lake bed made the air thick with alkali dust. Afternoon temperatures hovered around 120° F. For closeups of Clark being dragged across the lake bed by a wild horse, John had the camera truck pull the actor at the speed of a galloping horse. Protected by heavy leather chaps, Gable was dragged four hundred feet through the choking alkali before John had the footage he wanted. At night, Kay doctored Clark's cuts and rope burns. She was appalled and asked Huston to try and talk her husband out of the stunting. Clark wouldn't listen. At least, *he* was a pro. One sequence called for him to be knocked down and dragged by a stallion; in another he had to run behind Wallach's departing truck.

Weeks over schedule, the location filming finished on October 18, and everybody repaired to Hollywood and a couple of weeks of interiors at Paramount. On November 2, John called Clark in to complete his final scene, where he cuts the stallion free and goes off with Marilyn to begin a new life with their child-to-be. "I think this is the best thing I've ever done,"

Gable told Huston on November 4. "Now all I want out of life is what Langland wants—to see that kid of mine born."

The following day, Gable suffered a massive heart attack. Kay moved into the hospital with him and saw him steadily improve over the next nine days. On the tenth day, he died—two months before Kay gave birth to a son.

When John was asked for a statement, he said Gable was one of the last truly great. "All he wanted every day was to do the best he could at work, and then go home to his wife. He liked being with Kay best of all. The joy over the expected baby, which was to be his first child, was shared by every one of us. That he couldn't have lived to see the child is the greatest tragedy of all."

At the cost of four million dollars, *The Misfits* was in the can December 3, and the next day John was off to St. Clerans, with Sartre's eight hundred pages in his luggage. *The Misfits* premièred February 1961 in the midst of the headline-grabbing Miller–Monroe divorce—and the quiet split-up of John and Ricki. The picture had the dubious distinction of being the most expensive black-and-white picture since the 1925 *Ben-Hur*. Its failure so shocked Spyros Skouras that he refused to loan Marilyn for *Freud*. "Never has so much talent been wasted," he huffed. It was only after the *Cleopatra* debacle removed Skouras from the Fox presidency that Huston and De Laurentiis could convince Zanuck to make *The Bible* a Fox release.

18

FREUD AND THE
INNER SELF

When John greeted Sartre on the threshold in a red tuxedo
and told him Montgomery Clift would be Freud, he was surrounded by an odd assortment of cronies and guests, who,
Sartre would remember, included an Anglican bishop, a maharajah, and an eminent authority on fox hunting. But the lady
of the house was not there.

Ricki had had enough.

John had never slunk in and out of St. Clerans. He had always been the boisterous master of the house when he was
there, his voice crackling like parchment outdoors as he loped
around in his crouching, thrusting stride, mellow and consid-
erate in the evening with after-dinner cognac by the main fireplace. He could be positively lyrical in praise of marriage and
he liked to deceive himself into thinking his family came before his career, that if he made so many pictures it was also for
them. His idea was to live, emotionally, from hand to mouth,
as Aldous Huxley had said, in good company of one's own daily
choosing, not the choosing of others or of some dead self. He
didn't "sleep around," but definitely here and there. He always
had. Ricki herself had moved in on him when he was married

to Evelyn. Once at a party when John had had some blonde on his lap, Evelyn had pulled the girl off by her hair and, pointing toward Ricki, shouted, "I'm his wife, and that's his mistress over there, and you are one too many." Everybody had thought the incident was hilarious, except Ricki.

Quiet and calm Ricki had allowed her husband to fade out of their marriage without much of a quarrel and his regular postproduction re-entries into hers and the children's lives were long accepted with little comment. Tony was a tall eleven-year-old who looked like a local lad—and talked like one. Anjelica was a slender girl of nine who attended the Sisters of Mary convent school. Both looked like their mother, both were dark and delicate.

They didn't see much of their father. As Anjelica would say later, "I was sorry that he was too busy caring for a whole lot of things that he couldn't get to us except for one week in a year. He was caring about a whole kingdom; he's a Leo you know, so he has a kingdom, and he was trying to keep his kingdom there."

Ricki had moved to London toward the end of *The Misfits* and found a quiet apartment near Regent's Park. She had taken Anjelica with her. For the time being Tony stayed at St. Clerans. For Ricki the separation was just that, a need to see clearly where she was in her life. John could see her—and did. He saw enough of her to make her pregnant in 1964 and see her give him a daughter while *The Bible* was in postproduction.

A permanent fixture in Huston's life was Gladys Hill, a woman of definite and plain-spoken strength who was all things—save mistress. Miss Hill, as John sometimes called her, had worked for Sam Spiegel when he and Huston had formed Horizon Pictures and had married an art dealer in San Francisco. "When John heard I'd gotten *un*married, he sent me the sweetest telegram: I UNDERSTAND YOU ARE WORKING TEMPORARILY AND SINCE YOU LIKE TO TRAVEL, WHY DON'T YOU COME TO IRELAND AND WORK FOR ME FOREVER AND EVER? she would tell a New York *Times* interviewer in 1977 when she had spent more than fifteen years as Huston's angel-secretary-assistant-screenwriting-companion-chauffeur. Access to Huston henceforth passed through Paul Kohner *and* Gladys Hill.

Sartre had come to St. Clerans to prune *Freud*, but John was hard to get to, even in his own home. The manor was crammed with what Sartre thought was a costly and bizarre assortment of art and with a no less incongruous human collection. People drifted in and out. Huston had a habit of suddenly leaving these guests in the middle of a conversation, which Sartre, in his tortured English, would politely try to keep going.

Wolfgang Reinhardt was there, and during the day when John was out riding, the producer and Sartre began the pruning. After a few days they had the script down to six and a half hours' playing time. But there were problems and, across the language barrier, arguments and misunderstandings. Sartre had the feeling Huston didn't understand the father of psychoanalysis and John thought the existentialist philospher was belittling Freud.

"Except in construction, the final script has little resemblance with what I wrote," says Sartre. "The fault is partly mine, and partly Freud's. My scenario would have been impossible to shoot; it would have lasted seven or eight hours. The other problem was that Freud, like the majority of scientists, was a good husband and father who seems never to have been unfaithful to his wife. We tried to blend the internal and the external elements of Freud's drama; to show how he learned from his patients the truth about himself."

Huston felt Sartre's 2,000-page effort derived too much from Freud's work and that most of the action "happens behind the eyeballs." "Freud as adventurer, exploring his own unconsciousness was basically my idea," he says. "Freud managing to clarify his own case. Sartre had the idea of fusing several of Freud's patients into the one character, Anna O. You know Freud never met Anna O., only knew of her case history through his friend Dr. Josef Breuer."

Sartre's departure was amiable. Alone, John and Wolfgang tried to cut some more, gave up and went back to Kaufman's 1947 version, eventually combining this traditional Hollywood bio with whatever they found salvageable in Sartre's dramatization. Filming started in Vienna and Munich in October 1961. An appropriately bewhiskered Clift had as his vinelike wife Susan Kohner—Paul's actress daughter and John's goddaughter. The nineteen-year-old Susannah York played the Sartrean Anna O., Larry Parks was Dr. Breuer, Eric Portman was Freud's biting superior, and British character actor David Kossoff was Freud's own father.

Mayor Frank Jonas of Vienna and Dr. Hans Hoff, the head of the Vienna University's psychiatric department, were all for the film, but there were rumblings from London that Anna Freud would sue. She and her brother said they "disassociated" themselves from the film and told the BBC they had written to Huston to express their objection.

Vienna was used for exteriors. Together with art director Stephen Grimes (who, with the exception of *The Misfits*, had been with John since *Roots of Heaven*) and cameraman Douglas Slocombe, Huston recreated Vienna of 1885, adding an unobtrusive hackney coach here and a gas light there. The weather was chilly and autumnal and the Viennese landmarks, especially chosen for their shadowy baroque, had as much of a dampening effect on cast and crew as the drama they were filming in black-and-white. John directed with his usual modulated bedside manners, and after a couple of emotional flare-ups, Clift settled into his part, telling the New York *Times* correspondent that playing Freud could become wearying on the audience if he lost hold of his character. "I have to give it electricity all the time," he explained. "Any letting up on my part would lead to an all-round reduction of the voltage. For this reason I am cutting social activities to a minimum and when I'm not on call I spend as much time as I can in my hotel room, thinking, concentrating, recharging the batteries."

When Huston was asked how Freud affected him, he answered, "Not too much, I hope. I don't think Freud 'takes' too strongly with the over-forties. My interest in him, though, has perhaps made me just a little less sure of whether, after all, I'm as much in control as I like to think. And I find myself questioning my motives a bit more. But there has been no drastic conversion, or revelation, and I don't think I'm in danger of becoming a candidate for the analyst's couch."

Interiors, including a number of electrifying and chilling dream sequences, were shot at the Bavaria Studios outside Munich. Monty developed cataracts on both eyes, and required hospitalization. Adding to his discomfort was the constant rewriting Reinhardt and Huston engaged in. "I'd go to bed knowing one set of lines and wake up to another whole new scene."

As finally filmed, the story is simple. When Freud begins to study hysterical women, they are scorned by neurologists as silly females acting up to get attention. Freud doubts the diagnosis and suggests that hysteria proves the existence of unconscious thought. Most of his colleagues laugh, but Dr. Breuer describes how one hysteric found relief in simply talking about the causes of her uncontrollable outbursts of emotions and fear. Freud takes over the case and the rest of the film is the drama of detection, in which the audience sees both a lurid mystery unfold and a momentous theory develop. Following his patient's lead, Freud successively discovers the healing effects of catharsis, free association, and finally formulates his doctrine that everything has meaning and that most neuroses result from sexual conflict. As social commentary, *Freud* deals with the conflict between freedom and hypocrisy.

In Rome, Dino de Laurentiis announced that Huston would be one of four directors directing his upcoming production of *The Bible*. The producer said the film would run eleven hours, then extended his plans and talked of two films, each running six hours, on a $90-million budget. "This will cancel out all other films ever done on the Bible," the ebullient Roman enthused. "Orson Welles will direct the Abraham and Isaac sequence, Robert Bresson will direct the Creation, Federico Fellini will direct the Flood, Luchino Visconti will direct the scene of Joseph and his Brethren and John Huston will have the responsibility of giving the entire project cohesion and continuity. Maria Callas will be Sarah, Mother of the Jews, and Sir Laurence Olivier will be God. Igor Stravinsky will write the music. It will be fantastic!"

Anna Freud never sued Huston, Reinhardt, and/or Universal, which, after a year's delay, released *Freud* in early 1963. Studio chief Lew Wasserman found the picture dry, impersonal, academic, and limited in appeal, and the launch was low-key. The critics didn't like Clift (*Time:* "Behind that bushy beard, who knows, he may even be acting"), but found newcomer Susannah York electrifying and talked about an informative, thought-provoking period piece. Universal retitled the picture *The Secret Passion* and redesigned the advertising campaign, but *Freud* never found its audience.

As usual John wasn't around to commiserate. Instead, he was reactivating *The Man Who Would Be King* with Seven Arts and signed to direct *The List of Adrian Messenger* for Kirk Douglas' independent company and Universal. This time *The Man Who Would Be King* would be coscripted by good old Tony Veiller, possibly for Richard Burton and Marlon Brando.

Before Veiller could get to Kipling, however, he had to do a quick rewrite of *The List of Adrian Messenger*, a murder mystery by British author Philip MacDonald. *The List* was a gimmick picture and the star was really Universal's makeup genius Bud Westmore and his artificial faces, which allowed the entire cast to become maddeningly suspicious characters in a charade of phonetic clues, fancy sleuthing, one fox hunt, and a lot of loose ends. The actors under Westmore's makeup, hairpieces, contact lenses, false teeth, and plastic chins included George C. Scott, Kirk Douglas, Clive Brooke, Gladys Cooper, Herbert Marshall, a couple of Hustons, plus guest bits by Burt Lancaster, Tony Curtis, and Frank Sinatra. At the fadeout, each star strips off his "other face" for the benefit of a patient if slightly incredulous audience.

Kirk Douglas had bought the MacDonald novel in 1961 and several writers had toiled on it before Huston imposed Veiller. *The List of Adrian Messenger* is in the vein of *Kind Hearts and Coronets*, the story of a retired British intelligence officer's efforts to nab a killer who has ingeniously murdered eleven men who are obstacles to his acquiring a huge fortune. The killer will become the heir to his uncle's wealth as soon as he has eliminated the twelve-year-old grandson of the Marquis of Greneyre.

With exteriors already set for London, Huston had Veiller whip up a climactic fox hunt—to be shot in comfortable proximity of St. Clerans; but what was really fun was to cast Tony as the twelfth and last heir the killer has to eliminate.

For the fox hunt, the squire of St. Clerans cast several of his titled Irish friends, including Lord and Lady Hempill from Tulira Castle, Viscount Powerscourt, Sir George and Lady Melissa Brook, the Countess of Mount Charles, and the Marquess of Waterford. The screen debut of a third-generation Huston was duly noted by the attending press. Tony was a dark-haired version of his father. When he wasn't before the camera, he dressed in cap, corduroy pants, and enormous sweaters. Huston *père* cast himself in the fox hunt, telling everybody he felt right at home in this role.

Westmore was called upon to turn a Welsh corgi hound into a fox for the closeups. He attached special plastic ears and a long tail, then sprayed the animal reddish-brown. The confused dog rolled wildly in the grass, shed tail and ears and took off for the nearest hedge. The Dublin newspapers, radio, and television gleefully reported all this, as well as the film company's desperate need for foxes. This led a lady to sell two pet foxes for twenty dollars, a row with the Dublin Society for the Prevention of Cruelty to Animals, and a compromise—the actual footage of the pursued fox was filmed with nary a hound around.

The List of Adrian Messenger was released in May 1963 to pleasant reviews that hailed Huston for directing with flair and style, George C. Scott for being a convincing Scotland Yard sleuth, but complaints about the contrived plot. The *auteur* fad was crossing the Atlantic, and New York auteurist Andrew Sarris and anti-auteurist San Francisco radio critic and art house owner Pauline Kael suddenly flung barbs at each other across *Moby Dick, Moulin Rouge, The African Queen,* and *The Misfits.* Sarris considered Huston a filmmaker whose work had gone sour, "a forgotten man with a few actors' classics behind him" and in *The Village Voice* dismissed *The List* as one "more complex example of stylistic corruption resulting from lack of conviction." The occasion was too good for Kael. If the auteur theory meant anything, Huston should now be *progressing* toward a ripening maturity, she wrote in *Film Quarterly*. "Disregarding the theory, we see some fine film achievements and we perceive a remarkably distinctive directorial talent; we also see intervals of weak, half-hearted assignments like *Across the Pacific* and *In This Our Life*. Then after *Moulin Rouge*, except for the blessing of *Beat the Devil*, we see a career that splutters out in ambitious failures like *Moby Dick* and confused projects like *The Roots of Heaven* and *The Misfits*, and strictly commercial projects like *Heaven Knows, Mr. Allison*. And this kind of career seems more characteristic of film history, especially in the United States, than the ripening development and final mastery envisaged by the auteur theory—a theory that makes it almost de rigueur to regard Hitchcock's American films as superior to his earlier English films."

In Rome, De Laurentiis was still packaging *The Bible*, but the project was coming down in scale and some of the announced superstar directors were proving somewhat eccentric. Orson Welles was rewriting the Good Book, Visconti was telling the Italian press he was only in it for the money, Bresson tested a black couple for Adam and Eve, and Fellini felt he was "wrong" for the job. More important, none of the majors was willing to bankroll De Laurentiis to the tune of ninety, fifty, or even thirty million dollars.

After the wrap of *The List*, Huston was resting up at St. Clerans, when one night the phone rang. It was Otto Preminger calling from New York. Otto was brief and to the point. Would John like to play a part in *The Cardinal*, his new picture for Columbia?

"Certainly not," Huston answered. "Me, acting in a film, what a silly idea."

"Okay, forget it," came Preminger's long-distance voice. "A pity though, I had a great part for you."

"What part?"

"A cardinal."

"I accept."

"But I thought you said . . ."

"I accept . . . if you meet my price."

Like a pair of Armenian rug sellers, the two directors eventually settled on John's fee—a Nicholas de Staël painting for his St. Clerans collection. What made John accept, he said, when he reported to work in March 1963, was the chance to wear ecclesiastic robes. Burgess Meredith, who as an ailing priest dies on screen with Huston administering the last rites, paid the neophyte actor a handsome compliment. "My death was at least three minutes quicker than scheduled because Huston was staring down into my face. He was so depressingly good it hastened my end." Preminger was of the same opinion. "Huston was a joy to direct. He behaved as we both want actors to behave; he came on the set knowing his lines. He rehearsed and did the role without the slightest critical comment about the direction or even a hint of professional advice." When *The Cardinal* was released, John was singled out by the critics (*Time:* "Huston is superb—playing with a rip-snorting vitality that all but steals the show"), but when he was nominated for Best Supporting Actor, he thought things were getting too silly. In public, he said there was only one actor in the family—Walter; but in private he was tickled pink with the nomination.

19

NIGHT OF THE IGUANA

"People have exhausted themselves surveying my movies to decide in which film the characters fail and in which they succeed. To me, the goal doesn't mean anything; it's the companionship of doing which is the adventure. To me, *The Night of the Iguana* was a picnic, a gathering of friends, a real vacation."

The events that occurred during the filming of Tennessee Williams' play on a near-inaccessible bluff at Puerto Vallarta on the Pacific coast of Mexico made it the most talked-about movie location of 1963. Richard Burton arrived with Elizabeth Taylor, who was still married to Eddie Fisher and constantly consulting Burton's agent, Michael Wilding, who in his acting days had been her second husband. Sue Lyon was living with Hampton Fancher III, whose wife shared location quarters with Sue's mother. Ava Gardner romped about in her Ferrari with a local beach boy. Peter Viertel, who had been Ava's companion on *The Sun Also Rises* was there as Deborah Kerr's husband, but he was currently Huston's out-of-favor ex-scripter (*Time* speculated the reason was that John hadn't forgiven Viertel's malicious portrait of him in *White Hunter Black Heart*). Skip Ward's wife was miffed when her husband's mistress, Julie Payne, came down. Halfway through filming, Tennessee arrived with his lover, Freddy, and Gigi, a tiny dog prone to sunstrokes. John, who directed in striped muu muus, was with a tawny Anglo-Iranian girl named Zoe Sallis and was making the discovery of *raicilla*, a 180-proof distillate of the maguey cactus.

When it was all over and Los Angeles newsmen questioned the director about Burton's thigh injury, the chiggers in Taylor's feet, Sue Lyon's scorpion bites, the food poisoning, and the sunstrokes Mr. Williams' mutt suffered, John sighed, "The misfortunes you enumerate are entirely accurate, but I try to overlook such things. One hopes for a good picture as ultimate compensation. In this instance I think we have just that. After all these years I can smell a failure and this picture smells fine to me!" *The Night of the Iguana* had indeed the sweet scent of success. It was a worldwide smash hit with both critics and the public and within a year earned Metro-Goldwyn-Mayer ten million dollars.

Ray Stark, who produced the *Iguana*, thought John was just marvelous. "He just loved the idea of making a picture with all these neurotic people," Stark said in the middle of the whole thing. "Right now he's out buying guns for me and the cast!"

Indeed, Huston presented gold-plated derringers to Stark, Burton, Sue, Liz, Ava, and Deborah. Each gun came in a velvet-lined box containing five golden bullets—engraved with the names of the other five. Wisely, John had seen to it that none of the bullets had his own name on it. By the time Huston finished the shooting—ahead of schedule—130 members of the world press had visited and reported on everything from Ava's tantrums to Zoe's smoldering eyes. Stark and MGM realized the *Iguana* was becoming a media event and that the press was giving them millions of dollars' worth of publicity. "We've got more reporters here than iguanas," Ray loved to say.

Everybody *was* a problem. When John phoned Ava in Madrid in August 1963 and offered her a part in the *Iguana*, she said she'd love it. When he told her the role was Maxine— a part Bette Davis had played on Broadway and wanted badly to repeat in the screen version—Ava had him promise to rewrite to tone down the hard-knock bitchiness. At the first script conference, John turned to Williams and said, "Tennessee, I think you have something in your craw about older women. You're trying to do something perverse with the part." The playwright answered, "Well, that's possible, John," but objected when Huston and Veiller decided to save Burton's drunken, end-of-the-rope defrocked clergyman for Maxine instead of destroying him as he was on stage.

Ava got as far as Mexico City, with her two maids, secretary-accountant, and personal hair stylist, before self-doubts assailed her and she commanded Huston to come up from Puerto Vallarta. "We had a difficult session," he recalls. "Her doubts were coming to the surface and overwhelming her. I had to be firm. I said, 'Come on, Ava, that's quite enough of this now. You're going to do it, you've got to do it, and I don't want to hear one more word about backing out of it!'" When she saw her costumes, she broke into tears. Maxine's clothes were definitely unflattering, she complained to him. "Now, now, Ava," he soothed. "You're supposed to look a little beat-up in this one—so that's how we dressed you. But you'll be the hit of the picture, I promise you."

Huston also had to use his charms on Deborah Kerr, who couldn't stand too many changes in set decorations. When drenching rains made shooting impossible, the gathering flock of journalists insisted that Ava talk about her "broken relationship" with Viertel and her jealousy of Deborah. Helen Lawrenson, writing for *Show* magazine, was especially goading, but it was the photographers who got to Ava. She kicked *Life*'s Gjon Mili in the stomach and literally drove him off the set (which made Lawrenson observe that Ava "was her customary self, as amiable as an adder").

Liz was not in the movie, but was kept busy nursing the boozing Burton. She rented a four-story villa and imported her own secretary, cook, and chauffeur, and three of her children. Locally, she added two maids and a former slot machine repairman whose job it was to massage Burton's flabby stomach. Richard's alcoholic intake was awesome and resulted in bawdy hilarity or sullen gloom. Once, after several potent mixtures, he fell out of a chair on the set and slashed his thigh. Liz was not satisfied with the manner in which the company hairdresser arranged his locks and kept fiddling with his hair, until he one day poured a can of warm Mexican beer over his head. "Now, by God, how do I look?"

Besides world-renowned cameraman Gabriel Figueroa, who became an opera singer of considerable lung power when drunk, Emilio Fernandez was the most arresting Mexican on the picture. Huston and El Indio hadn't seen each other since *The Unforgiven* and John immediately hired Fernandez as his assistant director. Later, he put Fernandez in the picture as Maxine's bartender. Fernandez, who in his heyday hadn't been above pistol-whipping slow-witted actors and interfering producers, was armed on the *Iguana* and did his part to keep the press corps happy. He provoked one flurry when he announced he was going to marry Ava and another when he supposedly killed two American sightseers in a Puerto Vallarta bar. "Emilio's only weakness is his tendency to shoot people he doesn't like," John sighed on another occasion when Fernandez wanted to defend Liz Taylor and Burton got upset.

Puerto Vallarta, and its Mismaloya peninsula with its rocky coastline, were John's idea—a memory of sailing down the coast in 1929. He felt the Mismaloya promontory better reflected the characters' torment and the smothering atmosphere than Williams' stage Acapulco. Under Stephen Grimes's supervision, nearly three hundred Mexican laborers had built a replica of the weathered hotel on the tip of Mismaloya, three hundred feet above the sea. In addition to the hotel, Huston had ordered forty cottages built as living quarters for cast and crew on the high Mismaloya peninsula. The site on a cove in the Bay of Banderas, was only accessible by water and the stars rented villas in Puerto Vallarta. Getting to work immediately became a game of "one-upwomanship" Ava chose to cross the eight miles of the bay on water skis behind her own speedboat. Liz insisted on her own launch and ended up with a sizable yacht which lacked speed but was comfortable. Sue Lyon also got a private boat, as did Deborah Kerr, but both their crafts were inferior to the Gardner-Taylor boats. Sometimes Ava gave Deborah a lift in her speedboat, scotching rumors that the two of them were fighting over Viertel.

The most upsetting aspect of Mismaloya was its stifling heat and its scorpions, midges, chiggers, civet cats, mosquitoes, flies, snakes, gnats, and giant land crabs. "Turn on a light," said one of the cottage dwellers, "and your wall is covered with insects. Walk outside and a spider lands in your hair." Taylor made the mistake of wearing open-toed sandals and got chiggers in her feet. These six-legged mites had to be dug out with a knife. Sue Lyon's scorpion bite was treated as feature news by the New York *Times*, as was Taylor's variety of bikini appearances and at least one of Burton's remarks about a peek-a-boo bolero top: "Lordy! Now she *looks* like a French tart."

Liz exhibited remarkable tolerance, munching on imported hamburgers, sunbathing, and looking after her children and Burton. Following one of his five-hour drinking bouts she confided to a reporter, "Richard lives each of his roles. In this film he's an alcoholic and an unshaven bum, so that explains his appearance and liquid intake."

The press reported Burton saying that when downed straight, the potent raicilla cactus brandy could be felt go into each individual intestine. John was quoted as adding, "I think that's because they left in the needles."

Shooting the climactic scene in which Burton cuts a captured iguana free proved electrifying for the actor. Normally a rather sluggish animal which doesn't mind being tied up, this particular iguana ignored broom handles and an application on his tail of turpentine. "I think he's a fan of mine," said Burton. John ordered one of the electricians to rig up a 110-volt charge wire. "Prod him with that when I give the word," said the director. "He'll jump."

Both the iguana and Burton jumped. The way it was explained, Burton had been touching the iguana at that moment and the current passed directly into his hand.

Ava was terrified of an on-screen swim with her two beachboy lovers. John handled that one by having her join him in several stiff drinks. Then he walked into the surf, almost naked, and with the beachboys, showed her what he wanted. Commented one observer, "If I didn't know better I'd have said he looked like a fairy."

Hampton Fancher III was a pain in the neck to several people. When Grayson Hall was doing her scene, she complained about Fancher and Sue necking on a sofa out of camera range. "Here I am, trying to concentrate on my lines, with the two of them going at it, hot and heavy on the sofa. It's just damn distracting." When Burton added to her complaint, John had Fancher barred from the set, provoking Sue to go into a crying fit. "If you want to neck, that's okay," said John. "But just don't neck on the set, honey. It bothers the people who are not necking."

Skip Ward, who played Sue's love interest and the bus driver taking the defrocked minister's elderly ladies on cross-country tours, nearly caused a major disaster. Huston wanted to film the busload of tourists as they are driven around hairpin turns on the narrow mountain road above town. When it came to shoot the interior of the bus, with Burton and his elderly ladies in their seats, Ward was at the wheel and, going around one curve, got too close to the edge. The soft dirt shoulder began to give away and everybody scrambled out as the bus teetered over the edge. Several of John's lady assistants played tourists in the bus, including Thelda Victor and Gladys Hill.

The press corps continued to grow and eventually included a representative of *The Ladies' Home Journal* and Barnaby Conrad, usually writing on bullfighting but here clicking photos for Spanish magazines. John hadn't seen Conrad since *Matador* had almost become a Huston picture. *Time* called the off-screen scene "something straight out of Tennessee Williams" and said the playwright had hustled down to talk Huston out of using a Happy Ending, but that the director was so obstinate that Williams grew a beard and tried to keep cool by going swimming with Taylor and Burton, wearing a bathing cap. Nothing escaped the notice of the press and the world was fed such trivia as Elizabeth going fishing with Viertel in exchange for his giving her his spaghetti sauce recipe. Skip Ward was reported to sit down like an avid movie fan to listen in on everyone else's interview. Many of the assembled reporters were disappointed that no one was publicly seduced or divorced, but the Mexican press pretended to be scandalized. *Siempre* went so far as to call for the expulsion of the whole *Iguana* circus, claiming Mexican children were being introduced to "sex, drinks, drugs, vice and carnal bestiality by the garbage of the United States." When asked to comment, John sighed, "I have long since ceased to be disturbed by attacks from the press. And I am far too busy to spread any carnal bestiality."

To keep their sanity in the fishbowl atmosphere, Deborah began a diary and Ava changed houses five times. Of Huston's giving the producer and each star the gold-plated derringers with the inscribed bullets, Deborah wrote, "I sensed a certain nervousness in the laughter and thanks of everyone concerned. It was almost like the start of an Agatha Christie murder novel."

Sometimes laughter broke up the setside strain, sometimes the tension oozed over into off-hour get-togethers. In a scene in which Ava was shaving Burton as he lay in a hammock, she was supposed to answer Burton's threat of tearing the phone from the wall by saying, "In a pig's eye you will!" Instead, she fluffed the line and said, "In a pig's ass you will!"

"Cut," said John. "It's the eye of the pig we wish to concentrate on. Can you remember that, dear?"

One night when diluvian rains had Kerr write in her diary while the others played gin rummy, she looked up and wondered what would happen if the rest of humanity was wiped out by an atomic war and they were the only survivors. "I suppose we'd have to repopulate the globe," she said. "The result would be interesting, wouldn't it."

Absorbed in his cards, John murmured a slow yes-dear-it-would reply when Sue yawned and said she was getting tired of being a glamour object.

"Don't give me any of that crap, sweetie," said Ava. "Not after the way you were hogging the camera in my scene today."

"Now now, dears . . ." soothed John.

Deborah continued her diary.

At the height of the rumored marriage between Ava and Emilio, one reporter persisted in trying to have her confirm the romance. "You *did* kiss Mr. Fernandez, didn't you, Miss Gardner?"

"Hell yes," she exploded. "Everybody kisses everybody else in this crummy business all the time. It's the kissiest business in the world. If people making a movie didn't keep kissing, they'd be at each other's throats."

By November, the press corps had put Puerto Vallarta on the list of new "in" places. Huston was smart enough to invest an undisclosed sum in the budding tourist resort and invite Buckminster Fuller down to perhaps join in a geodesic-dome-building boom. John thought Fuller's igloo-shaped domes were the cleverest thing in construction and when he introduced the architect-engineer to cast and crew, he told them he was thinking of having Fuller put up one giant dome over all of Mismaloya. "Lush tropical vines would cover the roof, creating a beautiful soft green light for the interior," he said. "We could all live under this immense dome, sleeping as the Japanese sleep, on slabs of polished wood." No geodesic domes were built.

On November 17, two assistant directors, Tom Shaw and Terry Morse, were injured when a balcony they were sitting on collapsed, sending them hurtling to the ground. They were both in agony, taken to the hospital in Puerto Vallarta. Shaw was flown to Los Angeles. Wrote Deborah in her diary, "We didn't get to bed until 6 A.M. and I couldn't get to sleep at all. I kept seeing them both fall like ragdolls again and again all night long, and hearing Tom's terrible groans." Huston was so upset by the crummy construction of the cottages that he walked into Thelda Victor's cottage and with one well-aimed kick, knocked down her balcony.

Five days later, grief from the outside world imposed itself when news of the assassination of President Kennedy was broadcast. Ava was sitting in the Mismaloya bar at four-thirty when a silently weeping Deborah joined her. John solemnly announced that work would continue. When assistant director Jamie Contreras called for a minute's silence during the evening's filming, Ava and Deborah clung together and cried unashamedly.

The stream of wholly imaginary rivalries invented by the press got to Ava during the last weeks, but she attended John's end-of-shooting party for cast, crew, press, and assorted "cats, dogs, and iguanas." The catered affair featured food flown in from California. A fifteen-piece mariachi band entertained, the tequila flowed, and Ava looked suitably sexy in a harem outfit which Stark had given her. Burton showed up in an old green sweater, saying he loved it because it made his eyes look light green. According to Thelda Victor, the unrehearsed part of the entertainment included "a twenty-year-old German girl, whose function on the picture was never fully explained, executing a very sensual solo dance that had her end up writhing like a snake on the floor. The party lasted twelve hours and even John's pet iguana looked stoned."

Before *The Night of the Iguana* was released there was some question of its nationality. To Seven Arts and MGM it was as American as apple pie, or at least as Tennessee Williams, but not to Hollywood's trade union battling "runaway productions." By forfeiting certain pension clauses, the picture had lost its Americanness. When asked what he thought the nationality was, John said he believed the *Iguana* wasn't Mexican although it had been filmed there with Mexican key technicians. "Hmmmm," he shrugged, puzzled. "Maybe it's Liberian, or Panamanian."

On January 3, 1964, he changed nationality himself. "I've lived in Ireland for quite some while and my children have grown up here," he said when he signed the official documents in the Dublin office of Justice Charles Haughey. "The step I'm taking represents a sincere desire to get to the roots of my ancestors. I've had this in mind for a couple of years."

Huston was a man who operated largely by instinct and was rarely overburdened by self-doubts or needs to cling to home or roots. He could make gross errors of judgment, of taste, and of understanding, but he was not a person to be insincere. He meant what he said that January afternoon in the justice's chamber in Dublin, even if it was convenient that with one stroke of his own pen he put himself out of the reach of U.S. tax authorities. It could be said in his defense that half of Hollywood was taking up residence in Europe and that, with the exception of *The Misfits*, he hadn't made a picture in the

United States in fifteen years. He had enjoyed the benefits normally accorded Americans residing abroad but managing money had never been his forte and he had never been able to catch up with the IRS assessments and arrears.

Renouncing a citizenship rarely sits well with the citizens of the country being renounced and over the years Huston learned to play down his Irish naturalization and to remain essentially American—especially to his former countrymen without whose continued patronage the expectations of the squire of St. Clerans might have to be severely reduced.

20

NOAH'S ARK AND CARSON McCULLERS

The Huston circus was rolling again in May 1964, this time in Rome, with side trips to Egypt and Tunisia. Was he worried about the size of the project? Huston was asked at the first Roman news conference. "It should be fun," he answered. "I've always wanted to create the heaven and the earth."

The Bible had come down in size since Dino de Laurentiis' last flurry of press releases. The film would run three to four hours. It would be limited to the first twenty pages of the Old Testament and it would only have one director—John Huston. Laurence Olivier and Maria Callas were no longer God and Sarah, but, at John's suggestion, had been replaced by Peter O'Toole and Ava Gardner. Stravinsky would still write the score and there would be seventy-seven sets, most of them at the new Dino de Laurentiis studios, south of Rome. An unknown couple would play Adam and Eve. George C. Scott would be Abraham; Stephen Boyd would be Nimrod; Richard Harris, Cain; and John's girl friend Zoe Sallis would play a handmaiden to Sarah.

While the producer interviewed three hundred prospective Eves, Huston flew to Hollywood for the Academy Awards. His

Cardinal nomination was popular and many friends in the industry rooted for him. He arrived at the Santa Monica Civic Auditorium escorting Stella Stevens, who told TV reporters she *knew* John would win. He didn't. The Best Supporting Actor Oscar went to Melvyn Douglas for his performance as Paul Newman's father in *Hud*. In the press "bullpen" backstage, John was asked for the obligatory loser's statement. "Ain't it a hard road we travel," he mocked. "And Purgatory at the end!"

In May, Ulla Bergryd, the nineteen-year-old daughter of a Swedish language teacher, was chosen to play the mother of us all and twenty-six-year-old Hollywood actor Michael Parks was selected for Adam, largely on the strength of footage Huston screened from *Fargo*, an as yet unreleased picture.

The Garden of Eden was a palatial seaside estate twenty-five miles from Rome. John had plastic flowers strewn about and trees spray-painted gold, but a thirteen-foot python stonily ignored him, refused to slither and to hiss on cue. Huston wasn't sure Eve should munch on an apple. "No church authority— and we consulted with all of 'em—really claims that Eve bit into an apple," he told newsmen. "They all agree that it's a piece of forbidden fruit, but that's as far they'll go. We just don't specify what kind of fruit."

The press was banned from the Garden of Eden but Huston gave daily briefings: "First we were going to use single fig leaves on Adam and Eve, but we found we needed more than one each. So we had wardrobe whip up some fig leaf girdles, but they looked like G-strings, so we just shot Mike and Ulla from unshocking angles. We naturally couldn't have outright nudity and we also wanted to avoid any coy behind the bushes stuff." What he didn't say was that Parks's vocal acting was so appalling that the voice of David Warner replaced his mumblings on the final soundtrack.

Dino milked the nude filming for all its worth, perhaps even egging on the ever-enterprising paparazzi by telling the press he had hired two dozen *carabinieri* to keep out unwanted visitors. Photographers bribed set workers, crawled over palace walls, crowded behind bushes and hung in tree tops to get pictures. For Huston, the trained lions, zebras, giraffes, cheetahs and assorted beasts were more of a problem. A baby leopard scratched Ulla's thigh when she tried to pet it, forcing him to shoot her from an angle where her Band-Aid wouldn't show. "Also," he told the next briefing, "Ulla's blond wig, where it was pasted to her bosom, kept coming unstuck in the wind. But all in all, we did okay."

Huston irreverence inevitably led to questions about his own faith. On several occasions he was disarmingly forthright. "Every day I'm being asked if I am a believer and I answer I have nothing in common with Cecil B. DeMille. Actually, I find it foolishly impudent to speculate on the existence of any kind of God. We know the world was created and that it continually creates itself. I don't think about those things, I'm only interested in what's under my nose. Also, I believe that whatever man erects, builds and creates has a religious meaning. A painter, when he paints, is religious. The only religion I can believe in is creativity. I'm interested in the Bible as a universal myth, as a prop for numerous legends. It's a collective creation of humanity, destined to solve, provisionally and in the form of fables, a number of mysteries too disquieting to contemplate for a nonscientific era."

Christopher Fry had written *The Bible* three years before Huston came on board. Fry was a British poet with a knack for giving colloquial English a sense of classic wonder. He had written the last draft of the much-rewritten *Ben-Hur* and William Wyler spoke highly of him to John. In Fry's typewriter, Willy said, a line like, "Did you enjoy your dinner?" became "Was the food to your liking?"

John liked Fry's *Bible* script so much the first time he read it that he phoned De Laurentiis and asked, "Are you serious about this?" There were no liberties as such, yet Fry had written a love scene for Abraham and Sarah that he had taken from classical Greek love poems. The language of the dialogue was King Jamesian and, to Huston's ear, contained its own beauty.

John wanted the film to show the power and terror of the Bible as "universal myth," the wrath of Jehovah, the fascination with sin. The story of Noah and the Ark—the only sweet and hopeful story—should be left sweet and hopeful, and the biblical characters should not be modernized into comfortable and safe people. John wanted his audience to be on man's, not God's side, through these tribal tales and fantasies of the origins of life. The audience should come into the Ark with Noah and the animals and not perish outside in the Flood. Eve's crime should seem disproportionately little compared to the punishment the angry godhead imposes on her and her children forever after. But *The Bible* was also size, scope, and a cast of thousands. As Abraham and Sarah, Scott and Ava toiled on Mount Etna, Cain slew his brother in a striking one-take crane shot in a field in Sicily followed by an upward pan as he strode away. The top of the Tower of Babel was shot in Egypt and the bottom in Rome, where three thousand Romans were spray-painted from head to toe to change them into nut-brown Babylonians. Katherine Dunham's dance troupe was summoned "to provide the sin," as John put it, in a plastic Sodom. Special effects turned Lot's wife into a pillar of salt.

When a television reporter asked O'Toole how he had prepared himself to play God, he said he took cold baths, gave up drinks, and submitted to daily birchings. "And the bloody nit believed me!" he shouted, when the television crew had left. In Egypt, one of the forty-five camels which Abraham leads against a tribe of robbers didn't run fast enough. Perhaps remembering his camel race triumph on *The Misfits*, John managed to sweet-talk the animal into a faster pace. When only fifteen hundred extras showed up for the Egyptian part of the Tower of Babel sequence, John sent all available assistants into Cairo in cabs to hire people off the street.

Noah's Ark was the most difficult. Five models of the ark had been built. The largest of them, a 200 by 60-foot hand-cut log model, cost $300,000. The animals had been brought from a circus in Germany and housed in a special zoo until director, crew, and animal handlers were ready to shoot the Entering the Ark.

Since no one had been cast to play Noah and John was growing a beard, the press put two and two together. In reality,

Huston was his own last choice, after Robert Morley and Alec Guinness were unavailable because of conflicting schedules.

"I scraped the bottom of the barrel," he shrugged with a mock-deprecatory gesture, "and came up with myself. Yes, I shall be essaying the part of Noah."

"Then you're the character with seven hundred wives," a lady correspondent shouted from the other end of the news conference room.

"You must be thinking of Solomon, dear," he smiled. "I've only had four."

In flowing beard and tunic, Huston tried to herd the animals, two by two, up the gangplank to the indoor Ark replica. The two honey bears would get into a quarrel that would upset the elephants and stampede the zebras. This caused the Siberian tigers to growl, the yaks to grunt, the sheep to bleat and the lions to roar, but as he told the next news briefing, "I'm at home with animals, much more than with machines. I got an electric toothbrush today and it has already betrayed me."

Among the human interpreters, George C. Scott caused the most trouble. Perhaps confusing his and Ava's biblical roles and the divine injunction to end her barrenness, Scott fell crazily in love with her and, when spurned, created scenes that the sniffing press corps soon caught wind of. One incident took place in a bar where she was having a drink with O'Toole. Another had Scott disappear for two days in Rome. According to several newspaper reports, he followed her to London once the picture was finished, stormed into her suite at the Savoy, threw her agent out, and seized her violently.

Says Huston: "He was out of his mind over her—literally, and you can quote me. I have the greatest admiration for him as an actor and the greatest contempt for him as a man. Not only did he attack her at the Savoy—my understanding is he broke down the door—but he struck her and damn near broke her jaw. She was black and blue. She was so terrorized she was hysterical. He began chasing her clear across the map—he even made a terrible scene after he had followed her to Hollywood and tracked her down to the Beverly Hills Hotel."

While *The Bible* was in postproduction in Rome, Ricki gave birth to a daughter in London. Only Tony and Ricki's parents were there. John stayed in Rome and Anjelica was in her convent school in Ireland. The infant girl was christened Allegra. Her mother was thirty-five; her father fifty-nine.

The Bible cost eighteen million dollars. Toshiro Mayazumi finally wrote the score, full of atonalism, chanting voices for Adam and Eve and pastiche Stravinsky for the climaxes. Fox agreed to distribute worldwide (except Italy, which De Laurentiis kept for himself). Released in 1966, the film was universally panned but eventually made its money back. Adam and Eve were found to be ludicrous, dashing about among filtered forests and marshlands looking cold and lonely, Richard Harris' Cain was likened to a Method actor battling against an early version of St. Vitus dance. The Tower of Babel was that—a confusing anthill of extras, Sodom and Gomorrah left most debauchery to the audience's imagination and the worship of the Golden Calf looked like a nightclub act. Fry's incantatory dialogue was found needlessly hard on the actors, although Scott was singled out for negotiating awkward passages more successfully than the rest and his Abraham was called a subdued, poetic performance. Only one sequence seemed to stand head and shoulder above the rest—the Ark and John's wise-fool Noah.

Huston turned sixty a month before *The Bible*'s New York opening. If he succeeded in ignoring his birthday, the gala première was to stand out. He escorted Ava to the Times Square ballyhoo where she lost her mantilla and, during the intermission, her seat. During the screening, she kept punching John on the arm and saying, 'Christ, how could you let me do it?' At the supper party De Laurentiis offered, they ran into old mates and Rex Reed, the new gossip columnist. Reed quoted her as saying, "We had to stand around and smile at Artie Shaw, who I was married to, baby for Chrissake, and his wife, Evelyn Keyes, who Johnny Huston was once married to."

A lot of projects were humming along, adaptations of work by Tennessee Williams and Brian Moore and—again, *The Man Who Would Be King*. To await Burton's availability, the Kipling yarn was postponed until 1967.

If the mid-1960s were turbulent, busy years for John, they were very private and quietly resigned for Ricki. With the children, she lived in a big Edwardian house in quaint "Little Venice" in the St. John's Wood area of London. She had become a Quaker, moved on the serious fringe of "swinging London" and gave intimate little dinner parties. Most important, she surrounded herself with young people. Damien Thomas was a handsome twenty-four-year-old actor who became her friend and frequent companion and whose sister was Tony's first teen-age crush. Thomas was to remember Ricki as "an utterly lovely person."

"We were very close, but not physically—there was someone and the family knew that," Thomas said ten years later. "She was an extraordinary and charming woman, but there was a kind of sadness to her, a melancholy and resignation. She made me understand what it was to have been a very young woman —starry-eyed, and married to an old man. He had made her unhappy and she seemed to have very little use for older people. Allegra was utterly divine, a blond little thing of two or three."

The conversation piece of Ricki's living room was a mural of misty, gray-blue colors she had had painted. She had been forced to bully housepainters into rubbing out the first five layers of paint and only pronounced herself satisfied with the sixth layer. She called the mural a painting of "distressed Irish skies." Holidays and vacations were spent at St. Clerans, with John joining the family, but Ricki had come to loathe Ireland.

The times were changing for Huston. The Age of Aquarius was not so much creeping up on the movies as triumphantly taking over. The message was becoming the thing and if new directors in their twenties weren't exactly challenging the big-timers, youth displayed its strength, beauty, and self-assurance. The mood was brassy, swinging, and intense. Smart money was beginning to ride on frugal "little pictures" that reflected the shift in perception and awareness. Smart money was going international in the big way. Hollywood was not only filming overseas on a very large scale, it was involved in an intense and

216

continued quest for projects, stories, personalities, and creators of worldwide appeal.

In the summer of 1966, Huston inherited a project that would allow him to move toward a delicate and impressionistic interiority, a film that was all-American but a picture that, to accommodate everybody's tax accountants, would mainly shoot on De Laurentiis' stages in Rome. The project was the minor work of a dying southern writer for whom John would go out of his way to give one last joy.

Ray Stark had taken an option on Carson McCullers' novel *Reflections in a Golden Eye*, but already in 1956 Harold Hecht and Burt Lancaster had tried to have Tennessee Williams write a script and Carol Reed to direct. With *The Night of the Iguana* so successfully behind them, Stark asked Huston if he thought *Reflections* could be made into a meaningful film. The producer had Elizabeth Taylor in mind and Liz had Montgomery Clift in mind. Clift was a mess, strung out on alcohol and drugs, his life dominated by a series of homosexual encounters. Playing McCullers' repressed homosexual might in a sense be too close for comfort, but Monty's friends Liz, Marlon Brando, and Frank Sinatra thought precisely the opposite. Playing Captain Weldon Penderton under the firm guidance of his *Freud* director might be exactly what a psychiatrist might order.

McCullers, who had once called *Reflections* a pretentious piece of gothic, was flattered by the renewed interest in her 1941 novel. *The Heart Is a Lonely Hunter* was being scripted by her friend Tom Ryan and was scheduled for production in 1967. Now Huston and Stark wanted to bring *Reflections* to the screen. It was just about the best news the forty-nine-year-old novelist-playwright could get. Physically, she was a wreck. A bone cancer victim in and out of hospitals since 1962, she lived, crippled and bedridden, with Ida Reeder, her black housekeeper, in Nyack, twenty-five miles north of New York City. For a year doctors had talked about amputating her left leg, which she needed to have elevated and held out straight if she were in a sitting position. She was most comfortable lying in bed, although circulatory problems ensued, accompanied by excruciating pain in her leg.

Huston read the various attempts at scripting *Reflections*—Tony Richardson was supposed to have directed a screenplay written by Francis Ford Coppola, and Peter Glenville to direct his own script with Burton as Captain Penderton—and decided to start from scratch. As he had done with *The Maltese Falcon*, he made up his mind to *follow* the original as faithfully as possible, indeed, to put the more grotesque happenings on the screen as though they were the most natural thing in the world. McCullers had written her story in a matter-of-fact manner: "There is a fort in the South where a few years ago a murder was committed. The participants of this tragedy were two officers, a soldier, two women, a Filipino, and a horse."

A certain briskness had always worked for Huston when it came to handling intractable material. He always preferred to state rather than to imply, to set forth rather than suggest or insinuate. McCullers' fiction was filled with deformed conflicts, frustrations, pain, and grief, and *Reflections* was more extravagantly scored by violence and perversion in a variety of forms than her other work. John knew exactly the writer he needed to help him adapt McCullers—Chapman Mortimer, a little-known English novelist whose strange, haunting novels he had read for years. But Mortimer was nowhere to be found, and at St. Clerans John and Gladys Hill began adapting *Reflections*.

When he wasn't writing with Gladys or riding to hounds, Huston was trying to put his adopted country on the map of the new European cinema. For some time he had been saying that Ireland should have a film industry of its own. London seemed increasingly destined to become the world center, with Michelangelo Antonioni, François Truffaut, and Roman Polanski sharing crammed studio space with the onrushing Americans, but John looked more toward Scandinavia and Poland as examples. He was impressed by *Hunger*, a Danish-Swedish-Norwegian coproduction based on the Knut Hamsun novel, by Mai Zetterling's *Night Games*, and Polanski's subtle *Knife in the Water*, but more than any specific film it was the climate of Scandinavian and Polish filmmaking that he found propitious. Small countries produced decent films and new, significant film artists.

Elections, which saw Eamon de Valera re-elected with an unexpectedly narrow margin, resulted in a cabinet shuffle that made Jack Lynch Prime Minister. The trade gap was widening despite the inauguration of a British-Irish free trade pact. Taxes were up and labor launching major strikes. Only tourism, which brought in over two hundred million dollars a year, was a bright spot in the Irish economy. John was ready to journey to Dublin and to dangle before the Lynch government the value of films in promoting trade and tourism, but first he needed a suitable project, ideally an American-financed picture of his own to the filming of which he could invite the entire Lynch cabinet.

Before *Reflections in a Golden Eye* got under way, Huston was one of five directors in pursuit of the big spy joke, *Casino Royale*. Shooting had started in late 1965 and went on for most of 1966, with each expensive day seemingly bringing a new "name" to the cast of Peter Sellers, Woody Allen, and Ursula Andress. John directed David Niven in a pivotal segment and, for good measure, played M, 007's boss, himself.

"It's just as well that my father can't see me now," John said in mock horror while shooting at Pinewood. The explanation he offered for casting himself in this picture as in *The Bible* was that he couldn't find other actors to do these roles.

Casino Royale was a mess. The screenplay had started twelve years and countless versions earlier, but when producer Charles Feldman had been unable to land Sean Connery for the lead, it had been decided to make Ian Fleming's first Bond book into the Bond movie to end all Bond movies. The late Ben Hecht, with whom John had worked on *A Farewell to Arms*, had had three bashes at the script. It had been rejiggered by Billy Wilder, who in turn had been rewritten by Joseph Heller. The script *du jour* was by Terry Southern, Wolf Mankowitz, and John Law, except that Sellers had winged most of his scenes and Huston was redoing his. After shooting karate-chopping scenes with Niven at Pinewood, John and David and a full crew went leisurely on location in Ken, Scotland and, at

Huston's insistence, Ireland. The other directors of this cannibalizing of earlier Bond films were Ken Hughes, Val Guest, Robert Parrish, and Joe McGrath. The final price tag to Columbia, Feldman's bankroller, was ten million dollars, or the cost of the first four James Bond pictures together.

While bivouacking at Claridge's—a fifteen-minute cab drive from Ricki and the children—John managed to locate Chapman Mortimer and to seduce the author into working on *Reflections*. "I'd never been able to find anybody who knew him or knew of him, but I finally located him in Sweden and got on the phone," John recalls. "I asked him if he wanted to do film work and he said no. Then I told him what the project was and he said, 'Ah!'" By midsummer, Huston was in Nyack, reading most of the *Reflections* script aloud to McCullers. A few days later, she wrote a letter to the three adapters, saying she had just reread the screenplay and found it full of eerie power and splendor.

Reflections in a Golden Eye started shooting for Warner Brothers in October 1966. The film was the break Monty never got, since he died of a heart attack, at forty-five, two months before production start. Instead, Marlon Brando played Weldon Penderton, boldly and brilliantly interpreting the Huston-Hill-Mortimer script and turning the repressed army officer into a grotesque and painful impotent man with an overpowering nostalgia for the simple masculine comradeship of his young soldiering and an obsessive yen for one of the young privates on his Georgia army post. Elizabeth Taylor played Leonora Penderton, the silly, sensual "southern lady" who is virtually the only sane person around, a woman who hates her husband and divides her time between a neighboring colonel and her beautiful stallion. Robert Forster was Private Williams, who is the object of the major's attention and who divides *his* time between riding around the countryside—"barebacked and bareassed," as Mrs. Penderton puts it—and stealing into her room at night to stare in mute wonder at her sleeping form. Brian Keith and Julie Harris are the other army couple—he the harebrained lover of Mrs. Penderton; she the sparrowish, half-crazy wife-victim whose epicene houseboy

(Zorro David) is hardly less mad, but essential to the murder plot.

Filming began with a brief week of exteriors on Long Island, with several hundred men of the Rainbow Infantry Division of the Brooklyn National Guard exercising for the camera, followed by two months of interiors in Rome. At the end of the Long Island shooting, John visited McCullers at Nyack and invited her to come to St. Clerans.

"Are you serious?" she asked from her bed.

"Very serious. As soon as I finish—after we come back from Rome—you and Ida must come to Ireland."

When the New York *Times* interviewed Brando during the Long Island location and asked why he wanted to play a neurotic impotent, he grinned and said, "Seven hundred and fifty thousand dollars, plus seven-and-a-half percent of the gross receipts if we break even."

The filming was placid. To watch Brando become Penderton was to witness a privileged moment of acting, John felt. No other actor would dare to play so unflatteringly and so painfully to the camera and Huston stood back and watched, barely addressing himself to his leading man. In line with his experiments on *Moulin Rouge* and *Moby Dick*, Huston persuaded Technicolor to desaturate the color film until the final climax so as to give *Reflections* a ghostly sheen.

His invitation to McCullers gave the author something to live for. As he had done with Aunt Margaret, he now directed McCullers to go into serious training so she would be strong enough for the trip. By return mail she assured him she was not only eating enormously, sitting up more and working hard with her therapist, but had successfully given a large cocktail party for some forty-five guests at New York's Plaza Hotel.

Talks and preparation for the long overseas flight extended for almost five months. On January 5, 1967, Huston wired her to come. Tentatively, he arranged with the Irish Army to helicopter Carson and Ida from Shannon to his front lawn, but it was finally in a Volkswagen bus that, on April 2, McCullers and her housekeeper were transported from the airport to St. Clerans. To bid her welcome, John had champagne popping and McCullers said she wanted to see all of the house and the grounds. "Carson took everything in with those great eyes," says Gladys Hill. "In our innocence, we quite believed she might be capable of one brief look." After a sip of champagne, McCullers was carried upstairs, but in the afternoon she was brought down again, dressed in one of her Chinese robes and placed in a wheelchair. "When she kept slipping down in the chair," says Hill, "we began to realize that her expectations— and ours, exceeded her strength. She was taken back upstairs and never left again until her return to Shannon."

McCullers was flown home sixteen days after her arrival. Three months later, John received a wire from Robert Lantz, her literary agent, informing him she had suffered a massive stroke. For six weeks she survived, without mental and physical faculties. On September 27, Lantz attended a Warner Brothers screening of *Reflections in a Golden Eye*. Two days later she died.

21

FAMILY PICTURE

"*The Man Who Would Be King* has been reactivated as a film project, this time as a big budget roadshow production from Warner Brothers–Seven Arts," the August 7, 1967, announcement said. Executive production vice-president Kenneth Hyman termed the acquisition "the most important one" since the merger of Warners with Seven Arts (and Jack Warner's shrewd selling his own interests). *The Man Who Would Be King* would be made in Hollywood and on locations, in Panavision and Technicolor.

It was eight years since Universal president Milton Rackmill had announced the imminent start of the Kipling story, with Huston as producer-director of a screenplay written by him and his *Juarez* writing mate, Aeneas MacKenzie. It was four years since John and Tony Veiller had scripted the Seven Arts version (Veiller had died in 1966 while polishing Tennessee Williams' *This Property is Condemned* for Huston) and it was just a year ago that Paramount had quietly dropped the project when Richard Burton had proved unavailable.

Kipling's two soldiers of misfortune would reach the screen finally.

While Warners finalized the details, John was trying to get an Irish cinema off the ground. He had managed to shoot bits of four pictures in Ireland. Youghal in County Cork was Melville's New Bedford in *Moby Dick*, the English fox hunt of *The List of Adrian Messenger* took place in County Meath, the cliffs of Moher appeared in *The Bible* and Sallygap became a Scottish moor in *Casino Royale*, but now he was shooting the whole of *Sinful Davey* in the Wicklow Mountains in County Kildare and at Dublin's Ardmore studios with American money and, largely, local talent.

Sinful Davey was not Irish, but Scottish, the story of Davey Haggart, a young highwayman who wrote his memoirs while under sentence of death in 1821. "The only reason we have for filming in Ireland is that I like to be here and my associates, who know this, are humoring me," Huston told setside visitors. He explained that *Sinful Davey* was a romp. "It's amusing to do a chase. That's what this picture amounts to, a chase. It's a prank."

John Hurt, the English actor whose first screen appearance was as Master Rich in *A Man for All Seasons*, plays Davey who sets out to avenge his father by committing all the crimes his poor dad failed in. He is surrounded by a host of Irish Equity members, plus a violinist named Pecker Dunn and a midget known as the Mixer.

Huston invited members of the Irish Government to the location, and with appropriate gravity plugged his Scandinavian- or Polish-style-industry idea. What he had in mind was a picture that would be financed partly by the government, partly by moviehouse owners and partly by private capital. Such a picture could have a budget that would only be a quarter of the *Sinful Davey* cost and it could be made with a handful of craftsmen. "How to go about it?" he wondered aloud to the assembled Lynch Cabinet as he squatted in a canvas chair in a Sherlock Holmes cloak. "The way to start a film industry is to make a film. And the way to ensure it will develop is to plan a program of films. Now, a small country like Ireland could never hope to make millions, or to make superproductions. It must choose themes suitable to itself and go where its talent shines —writers and actors—and train technicians abroad."

The incentive he dangled before Lynch and Cabinet was trade and tourist dollars, "It's likely that John Ford's *Quiet*

Man has attracted as many tourists as Bord Failte with all its inducements," he said. A board should be set up to decide the program of, say, six modest-budget pictures. The aim should be higher than "purely commercial targets"—creative and artistic values and the education of young Irishmen in the film business, he said, inviting the Ministry of Education to send students to follow the making of *Sinful Davey*. The government left, with Lynch assuring everybody he and his Cabinet would seriously consider Huston's ideas.

The Man Who Would Be King fell through on the casting, but John was all set to team up with Katharine Hepburn on *The Madwoman of Chaillot*. The filmization of the Jean Giraudoux comedy was only a viable project because Kate felt she owed producer Ely Landau one for having gambled his resources on bringing O'Neill's *Long Day's Journey into Night* to the screen. She liked Edward Anhalt's *Madwoman* script and loved the idea of working with her *African Queen* director again. Landau lined up Danny Kaye, Charles Boyer, Edith Evans, Yul Brynner, and John Gavin for the picture, which would shoot in Paris. When Landau came to St. Clerans, however, Huston and he couldn't reconcile their interpretations of Giraudoux and the producer signed Bryan Forbes instead. Kate was upset but did the picture anyway. Because of Forbes's inept directing and because of Hepburn's softening of the madwoman, the picture was a total fiasco.

Sinful Davey wasn't much better. The Walter Mirisch production was indeed a prank and a self-indulgent "lark," as Huston began calling his lesser efforts when they bombed. *Sinful Davey* was a costume comedy with a lot of horses, an obligatory hunt sequence, and an undemanding storyline that is part *The Beggar's Opera* and part *Tom Jones*, and its only redeeming factor was Robert Morley in the final third. As the Duke of Argyll, a massive figure in kilt and sporan, Morley proved again, as one reviewer said, that he can dominate any scene in any movie by standing in front of the camera and raising one eyebrow. At the 1972 Cannes festival where *Fat City* was a surprise hit, Huston tried a limp excuse. "I should have removed my name," he said in self-defense. "*Sinful Davey* was in the hands of the Mirisch brothers. One of them [Harold] was dying and the other [Walter] hesitated. So when I saw the finished picture, I said, 'Forget it!' Now that it's dead and buried I couldn't care less."

A *Walk with Love and Death* was John's birthday present to Anjelica. Producer Carter De Haven was a friend. When he asked Huston to read a first draft screenplay of Hans Koningsberger's 1961 novel, John immediately thought the starkly simple love story was a picture for his daughter. When he was accused of favoritism in his choice of leading lady, he disarmingly answered, "Absolutely!" Anjelica was equally to the point: "It wouldn't have happened if I'd been a plumber's daughter."

John spent every Christmas with Ricki and the children at St. Clerans but rarely showed up at the house in London. Tony was going to London University and planned to major in English literature. His goal was to become a writer. Anjelica was attending London's French lycée and was totally unhappy. Besides normal adolescent problems, she hated the school and invented all sorts of excuses for not attending. She felt out of tune with her competitive French classmates and played hooky whenever she saw a chance to. Neither of her parents had actually asked her outright whether she wanted to act, but it was sort of understood that she would be an actress.

Koningsberger's story is set nineteen years into the Hundred Years' War and concerns a young student and a girl wandering through war-ravaged France. The year is 1358, but the *Romeo and Juliet* theme carries all sorts of modern overtones. It touches on protest against war and defiance of authority. The hero looks like a campus radical in revolt against an endless war and against the posture of the Church. Koningsberger, a Dutchman who had lived for twenty years in New York, meant his story to be modern, "the story of two young people, with a curtain of violence behind them."

When De Haven and Huston cast Assaf Dayan as the medieval student hero they claimed they had no idea he was the son of Israeli Defense Minister Moshe Dayan. The twenty-year-old Dayan was something of a student dropout himself who, after his tour of duty as a private in the Israeli army, had some minor league acting experience behind him in Tel Aviv and Rome. "Assaf had a kind of nobility and intelligence, a good face and lovely manners," John hummed at the press conference announcing Dayan's engagement. What Huston, De Haven and Fox kept a closely guarded secret was that no insurance company would extend coverage to Dayan because his notoriety made him such an obvious Palestinian target and that *A Walk with Love and Death* was that one-in-a-thousand exception, a major picture shooting without life insurance on its leading man, and therefore a picture without a completion bond. If Dayan's screen career never went further it was because he was literally uninsurable.

Huston got Leonor Fini to do the costumes. This Buenos Aires-born painter-illustrator-poetess would give the film some of the strange seductiveness and suffocating sumptuosity of her surreal paintings, drawings, and theater sets. Fini, who lived in Paris and had just won the Prix des Critiques for her stage designs, immediately began working and came up with a wardrobe of arching expressions in green—winged robes and flowing caftans.

Dale Wasserman had written the screenplay, but three weeks before production start Koningsberger arrived, uninvited, at Huston's Paris headquarters saying he couldn't bear to see his story altered for the screen without having a hand in its transformation. John liked the Dutchman, and Koningsberger stayed with the company, writing, rewriting, and working on the script with Huston over and over again, sometimes well into the night. The experience was something of a shock for him: "What is difficult for me is that when you write a book you look at it from inside out, it feels natural to you, you don't try to analyze the motivations of your characters. Huston looks at things completely analytically, from the outside. He says, 'Why did they do that?' It's like a painter who is asked what a painting means . . . He accepted the whole but weighed each part and if I couldn't convince him, not only of its naturalness but indeed of its unavoidable necessity, he wanted it rewritten, or at times rewrote it himself." Koningsberger was full of praise for the director's respect for books, his patience and aversion for triteness: "Real books are seldom seen circulating in the movie world; its dealings are with story outlines, as if what mattered in literature was really and only what the personages ended up doing to each other and the rest just decoration—a parallel to saying, Never mind whether this painting is a Vermeer or a Picasso or a Smith, just tell me the subject. Huston wanted to film a novel; not the movements of the people in a story but the *idea* of the book."

A few days into production, French student agitation erupted into what was to become the May Events of '68 that eventually led to President Charles de Gaulle's downfall. As the days went by, the student unrest escalated from "occupations" of campuses to full-scale Latin Quarter riots, a one-day general strike, and militant disruptions of thousands of businesses. "Wildcat democracy" was everywhere as the country seemed to slide toward anarchy. Wage-boost offers were jeered, government offers of a referendum booed and the leftist cadres, including the Communist Party, was revealed to be totally out of touch with youth and even organized labor rank and file.

A *Walk with Love and Death* moved to Austria and resumed filming at Mauerbach, a former monastery near Vienna, and in medieval towns across the border in Czechoslovakia. Visiting media people were only interested in the father-daughter relationship.

"What really counts in film acting is that rare moment—just a flickering," said John, "when through the eyes you get a glimpse of the real meaning of the character. It is not technique or professionalism, just truth. Garbo had it. Monroe had it. I can see it in Anjelica."

From the ease with which she carried herself and the intelligence of her face the news people gathered Anjelica possessed the inherent talent of a born actress. When they interviewed her it became evident that her father and De Haven had told the media before they had told her about her starring role. "I never wanted to make films earlier; it's a bit nasty if you start off as a child star, and it's very difficult to get out of the child star image. The first day I was out of my mind. My heart was going boom, boom, boom."

228

The press admired her riding big Noriker war horses with elegant expertise and quoted John as saying he was probably the only director who had directed both his father and his daughter. He loved the Norikers and told how they were useless in the modern world, even as draft animals, and only bred for their own sake in southern Germany. He used a white Noriker for a signal effect: It is when one of these great, clumping horses is slaughtered that the war becomes obscene.

In August, Russian armor moved into Czechoslovakia to squash Premier Alexander Dubček's "socialism with a smile" and *A Walk with Love and Death* moved to northern Italy where the filming was completed in October.

In hindsight, Anjelica was to consider her father's birthday present a gift of dubious value: "It's really hard to make a movie on another person's territory, especially when that person is your father, therefore too close to the situation. It was a situation where I couldn't speak up properly or understand properly, and maybe I didn't want to. It's hard being directed by one's father; he was impatient and at the time I had no point of view, I never let on what I wanted for myself."

Some stage acting followed for Anjelica before she became a model. In London, she understudied Marianne Faithful in Tony Richardson's *Hamlet* and got to play Ophelia five times. Huston also did a quick acting stint during the winter, playing the Abbé de Sade who first sowed the seeds of depravity in the young Keir Dullea entrusted to his care in *De Sade*. Director Cy Enfield called the picture "a story of protest," Huston called it a "welcome relaxation." As for playing a dirty old man, he said in the proper reverent tone that the Abbé de Sade "is rather a fascinating character. I might add that being him for a while is a thorough pleasure." The July 1969 *Playboy* featured a spread of *De Sade* which included two shots of the clerical Huston fondling a semi-nude Senta Berger.

The family was together at St. Clerans for Christmas. John was planning a picture on the 1916 Easter Uprising, De Haven and he were getting ready to follow up with John Cheever's new novel, *Bullet Park*, to be filmed in New York, and Dino de

Laurentiis wanted him for his big Soviet-Italian coproduction, *Waterloo*.

John was in Rome in January 1969 talking *Waterloo* and possible substitute projects when Ricki, and Brian Anderson, a twenty-nine-year-old English musician, decided to share a ride through France and Italy to Rome. In the late afternoon of January 29 they were approaching the town of Gray, two hundred miles southeast of Paris, on the two-lane Route nationale 67, when Anderson lost control of their sports car, swerved to the left, and collided head-on with a van driven by Gilles Marcoux, a local motorcycle dealer. It took police and firemen one hour to free the victims from the wreckage. Anderson's face suffered multiple lacerations and Marcoux's left leg was severed. Ricki was pronounced dead on arrival at the hospital in Gray.

22

FAT CITY AND CECE

Huston flew to London and took charge. In silence, he attended the Quaker funeral for Ricki, benumbed and bewildered by the absurdity of death by accident. And who was Brian Anderson, Ricki's lover? Another sensitive young person she had picked up? No one knew. John was not given to personal ruminations in public and throughout the busy year of 1969 gave few hints of his inner feelings. Sometimes such feelings bubbled over, but he immediately suppressed them. As when he was interviewed by Associated Press reporter Hal Boyle a few months after Ricki's death. "Now I just make pictures, ride horses, collect paintings and regrets," he said. "Most of my regrets, however, are of such a private nature that they would hardly bear either repetition or printing."

The Edwardian house in "Little Venice," with Ricki's painted wall of "distressed Irish skies," was vacated. Tony had dropped out of London University, feeling that one way not to become a writer was to study English literature. Anjelica was living in New York and discovering her Americanness with a vengeance. Four-year-old Allegra was with her devoted Spanish nanny.

A Walk with Love and Death was a disappointment. This fable about youth and dropping out was a strong antiwar movie but it was a slow, gloomy voyage toward tragedy and as such stood in dire contrast to the amplified "now" of *Easy Rider* and *Alice's Restaurant* and the tense, subversive hedonism of *Woodstock*. Filmic relevance was a matter of texture and pitch. A *Walk with Love and Death* was about the right things —young, romantic people in a long war that wouldn't go away —but it lacked urgency. The strong, seductive hits of 1969 were full of light reflected on shiny surfaces, devastating cityscapes, foul-mouthed closeups and hand-held riots. It was all a matter of complicity, indiscretion, and playfulness.

Did Huston understand the young and what they wanted? When he was asked in May by the Los Angeles *Times*' Marika Aba, he grinned and said, "I haven't the vaguest idea what *they* want. But I sure as hell know what I want. I think that is always a good start."

In the fall of 1969, he was involved in a piece of absurd studio counterculture—*Myra Breckinridge*, directed by twenty-nine-year-old Michael Sarne. The salary was irresistible and John thought it could be fun to play Buck Loner, Gore Vidal's hysterical takeoff on the Hollywood cowboy and acting school owner. John had a couple of ideas on how to incarnate Buck Loner, but on the second day of shooting, the Los Angeles *Free Press* quoted Sarne as saying Huston was such an "old hack" that he, Sarne, had almost walked off the picture when Twentieth Century Fox had cast Huston. After that John never refused to take directions, but, according to his fellow-actor Rex Reed, he never responded to anything Sarne did as a director. He would say, "Yes, yes" and do a scene exactly the way he had planned to do it. In the mounting bedlam of the filming, John kept a steely eye on his contractual cutoff date. The morning of that day all his bags were packed and outside his dressing room, with a car and chauffeur waiting for him at the sound stage. Yet to unit publicist Don Prince, he was the only friendly face on the picture, an exemplary pro and gentleman who kept his thoughts to himself about Mae West's senility, Sarne's tantrums, Raquel Welch's insecurity, and the studio forces tussling and losing the battle of salacious scenes, disconnected jokes, and mod sickness. When one night Prince asked Huston why he cavorted in front of the camera in this abandoned battlefield of a movie, John said because of "the beautiful money." When Prince objected that John must have enough money, he was told, "No one has enough money."

Tony and Anjelica had told their father to see 2001, A Space Odyssey. When he did, he felt the Stanley Kubrick film was too much technology and too little character. Tony was traveling around the United States with Buckminster Fuller. Tony's job was to record and transcribe the architect's campus lectures. Anjelica was making her debut as a model in New York and loving every minute of what she called "the inspiring competitiveness." "New York is more honest," she said. "New York is mythically ugly. It's going through a mythical disaster. However, it's the only exciting city there is. I love London; it's a village in comparison to New York."

With *The Kremlin Letter*, John got to make a Twentieth Century Fox picture that, like his own assessment of 2001, was more technology than character, a preposterous movie about a group of secret agents from some supersmart U.S. agency prowling around Moscow in search of a compromising letter. Shot at De Laurentiis' studio in Rome, with exteriors in Finland, *The Kremlin Letter* featured a starry cast in improbable roles. Max von Sydow is a political strongman within the Soviet hierarchy. Former U. S. Navy officer Patrick O'Neal has the job of salvaging the incriminating letter about China that an American official has sent to the Kremlin. The Soviet Union, in the person of Richard Boone, would also like to retrieve the letter. From here on the participants include George Sanders as a drag queen in San Francisco, Orson Welles as a key Soviet official in New York to address the United Nations, and Bibi Andersson as a prostitute married to a narcotics dealer. The characters have names and code names. There are agents and counteragents and it is difficult to follow just who is doing what to whom.

Huston said the picture was about "the tasteless amorality and senseless violence in our world today" and friends and critics tried to measure how low he—and the world, had sunk since *The Maltese Falcon* and *The Treasure of the Sierra Madre*. Sam Spade turns in Brigid at the end because she has caused the death of his partner, and the ill-begotten gold sand blows to the wind over Old Howard's Homeric laughter. In *The Kremlin Letter* the spies on the side of America the Beautiful have to torture, rape, and murder to prove it.

John was uncomfortable with the cynicism and, in Rome, revealed the extent of his desperation to visiting newsmen: "The depravity has to show through. You look at the wild scenes and you have to laugh or else you'll shoot yourself or something."

When the conversation turned to current events, he was still his moral self and an American. Vietnam was now Nixon's War, expanded and intensified and spilling over into Laos and Cambodia. When Huston was asked what he thought of the war, he sighed and said he feared the worst—that Americans wouldn't learn anything from the tragedy. "What's needed in Vietnam is a moral statement. We have no business there. If we *slip* into peace, we'll be missing the whole point."

Appropriately perhaps, he spent his off hours in Rome deep underground. He was as interested in Etruscan art now as he had been in Mexico in pre-Columbian art and he spent days visiting newly discovered tombs being plundered for "hot pot" archaeological artifacts. He bought some of these bootleg pieces himself, arguing that there were two sides to the moral issue of private acquisition of artifacts from the dawn of civilization. Yes, the archaeological art belonged to the state, to museums, but also a little to those who rescued it.

Portrait of the Artist as a Young Man was the project closest to his heart as he rested up in St. Clerans after completing *The Kremlin Letter*. He had admired James Joyce's autobiographical novel for years, had lined up Max Rosenberg to produce the picture in Ireland, and was toying with the idea of having Maurice Roeves repeat his Stephen Dedalus portrayal from the *Ulysses* that Joseph Strick had directed. *Portrait of the Artist as a Young Man* wouldn't be made any more than *The Holy Week*, the story of the events of the Dublin Easter Uprising of 1916. Huston talked a good line when it came to Irish filmmaking, but his projects required vast American financing. He talked of using actors from the Abbey Players in

The Holy Week, but the picture he envisaged was beyond the resources of his three-million-population adopted country.

Bullet Park fell through, but in December 1970, Huston was in Marbella, Spain, as the replacement director of Carter De Haven's MGM production, *The Last Run.* The film starred George C. Scott as an over-the-hill hood making a last-ditch attempt at staying relevant. Alan Sharp's script was tiresomely explicit and John Boorman had walked off the picture over script differences. Scott had forgotten all about the Ava Gardner episodes on *The Bible.* He wanted John because the part reminded him of an old Bogey picture. In late January 1971, however, Huston quit when he realized Scott was in total artistic control, and was replaced by Richard Fleischer. Six months later John was in California filming a piece of his own youth that was to be the masterpiece of his maturity.

Fat City was a dream. It was drawn from the Leonard Gardner novel and from John's own meanderings among small-time boxers, drifters, and losers. It was a happy reunion with Ray Stark. John hadn't made a picture in the States since *The Misfits,* and *Fat City* turned out to be what those Irish no-go pictures should have been—a modest-budget tonic. It was a sentimental voyage down memory lane in the company of a fresh generation of beautiful actors and technicians. Stacy Keach was Billy Tully, the has-been boxer who has rebelled against the ring but can't stay away; Jeff Bridges was Ernie, the young, innocent fighter setting out on the same doomed path, and Susan Tyrell, her voice all maudlin rasp, as Tully's hard-luck lush of a girl friend. Conrad Hall was on camera, filming a fifties B-picture feel in delicate faded colors; Kris Kristofferson added a wistful song to Marvin Hamlisch's score.

Fat City was shot in its natural habitat—Stockton, in central California. The thirty-seven-year-old Gardner did the script from his own lean, 183-page novel, crying at each scene Huston added. John directed in jeans and army shirt, puffing on cigars and, between setups, reading George Axelrod's autobiography. He staged some gritty fight scenes in which Tully and Ernie get their heads smashed in for a few hundred bucks in airplane hangars, half filled with people with nothing else to do. He gave it all the edge and smell of sweat, fear, and failure and the metallic taste of somebody's last dime. What surprised him was the persistence of the boxing subculture. It was all there, the clammy-walled dressing rooms, the bookers and managers, and the rituals of the gyms, as it had been in 1925. He even found a beautifully battered ring relic, Bob Dixon, a gap-toothed ex-fighter with long scars and rheumy eyes, and put him in the picture. The rest of the supporting cast was recruited from memory, raw Mexican kids, and a black (Curtis Cokes) who keeps insisting that the determination to win "is the sine qua non" even if it doesn't seem to do him much good.

While Margaret Booth supervised the editing, Huston went directly into *The Life and Times of Judge Roy Bean*, "a lark of a picture" packaged around Paul Newman. Together with John Foreman, his balding personal producer, Newman thought he had found another *Butch Cassidy and the Sundance Kid* in this retelling of the story of the stocky, whiskey-sodden native of Mason County, Kentucky, who drifted into western Texas after the Civil War and, in a railroad tent, managed to get himself appointed justice of the peace in 1882, followed the rails west to Langtry, a whistlestop on the Southern Pacific, where, with the Revised Statutes of Texas, he set himself up in business and dispensed justice until he died in his bed in 1903. Wyler had told the story in *The Westerner* in 1940, with Walter Brennan as the judge and Cary Grant as a fictitious stranger accused of horse thieving and sentenced to hang by Bean, then paroled because he claims to be an acquaintance of Lily Langtry, the English actress the judge worshiped but only saw once in his life. The historical actress actually made a trip to Langtry eight months after Bean had died and the towns-people gave her the late judge's pet bear. Not knowing the lady, the bear ran away and the townsfolk made her a present of Bean's revolver, which she took home to England with her.

The Life and Times of Judge Roy Bean had been written by John Milius, a University of Southern California film school dropout, hot-shot screenwriter, and would-be director, who was as stunned as anybody when Newman and Foreman paid him $300,000 for his script. At twenty-eight, Milius was an unregenerate hawk, gun freak, champion surfer, and rewriter of *Dirty Harry* and *Evel Knievel*. He had sold his original screenplay *Jeremiah Johnson* to Newman's *Butch Cassidy* costar, Robert Redford, and more than anything he wanted to direct *Roy Bean*. He offered to come down $150,000, but Newman and Foreman wanted his script, not his untested directorial talent.

The rest of *Roy Bean* didn't come cheap either. Langtry was built near Tucson, Arizona, and burned at the end of the picture to the tune of one million dollars and the final cost of the First Artsts production was four million. But everybody had a good time—except Milius, who thought they were all ruining his script. Mexican actress Victoria Principal played the town girl who saves Judge Bean, Stacy Keach was an albino gunslinger, Roddy McDowell a free-enterprise oil capitalist moving in on the aging Bean's territory, Jacqueline Bisset was Bean's bastard daughter, and, in a wistful epilogue, Ava Gardner was Lily Langtry. Richard Moore, who had photographed *Myra Breckinridge*, was on camera and Huston cast himself as Grizzly Adams, an eccentric desert recluse. A bear named Bruno was the judge's pet.

"You've got to meet the bear," Huston would tell visitors. "He gave a marvelous performance." John would walk the visitor to the cage made from an antique brass bed, take a piece of candy from his pocket, and tell Bruno to shake hands. When a muddy, yellow-clawed paw reached out and shook his hand, John would say, "Kiss, give Uncle John a kiss." Bruno had bad breath and John squirmed as the bear kissed him. "He'll sell his soul for a Tootsie Roll." Newman thought Bruno stole every scene in which they appeared together.

Old buddies were there—Billy Pearson, among others, and John immediately put the former jockey in the picture—and John's new ladyfriend. Celeste was a tall, slim divorcée with doe eyes, nervous manners, and a fast, with-it patter. She was the daughter of a Beverly Hills car rental executive and had ambitions as an actress and social lioness. Everybody called her Cece. John had met her just before shooting start at the Foremans' and made her his production secretary.

Friends of friends were added to the cast—Tab Hunter, Anthony Perkins, Anthony Zerbe, who had starred in Wyler's last picture, *The Liberation of L. B. Jones*. Newman was nervous about his screen persona and his portrayal of the raunchy old bastard judge (it was the first time he had grown a grizzly beard). To the chagrin of Milius, the moral ugliness of a number of scenes were toned down.

"Judge Roy Bean has been turned into a Beverly Hills western," lamented Milius. "Roy Bean is an obsessed man. He's like Lawrence of Arabia. He sits out there in the desert and he's got this great vision of law and order and civilization and he kills people and does anything in the name of progress. I love those kinds of people. That's the American spirit! And they said, 'What you've created is a reprehensible man. We've got to make him much more cute!' So they changed it from a western that was about royalty and greed and power to a western where Andy Williams sings a song in the middle of the movie and the judge and his girl and his pet bear go off on a picnic. It's incredible! He goes on a picnic and sits on a teeter-totter. It's a movie about Beverly Hills people, about John Foreman and John Huston and Paul Newman."

While Hugh Fowler edited *The Life and Times of Judge Roy Bean*, Huston was in New York for the August 1972 première of *Fat City* with his two eldest children and his new fiancée. Father and son were dressed alike in crisp seersucker jackets and rakish ties (Tony was now a strapping six-foot-six) and Anjelica was, according to *The New Yorker*, "a knockout in a white chiffon shimmery gown and pearls." A week later, Cece became the fifth Mrs. John Huston in a cermony held in a judge's chamber in Santa Monica, California. The bride was thirty-one, the groom had just celebrated his sixty-sixth birthday. Following a wedding reception at the home of the bride's parents, the newlyweds flew to St. Clerans.

Cece was many things to John—carnal surprise, social tonic, contemporary flutter, and even a lover of fast horses— but the marriage was also an attempt at giving a semblance of normality to two little half orphans. Allegra was seven and Cece's son, Collin, was six. Allegra had been with Maricela Hernandez, a twenty-one-year-old Mexican governess since

Ricki's death. Cece's concern for Collin, who suffered cerebral palsy, touched John, and he felt they could live like a famly in Puerto Vallarta, which was comfortably out of reach of the IRS yet close enough to the Los Angeles specialists Cece constantly sought for her son.

Anjelica approved of her stepmother. Now a Bob Richardson and Richard Avedon model, she told New York gossip columnists, "My father just got married and I'm truly thrilled. She's really a lovely lady and I hope she changes his life."

The first change was to put St. Clerans up for sale. Cece hated the Druid rains and the left-behind inferiority complexes of the rural Irish. John told friends he had bought the estate when Tony and Anjelica were little. They were grown now and, he added, the upkeep was too much—something that had never bothered him before. He would put the art collection in storage and, when he wasn't working, he and Cece would live in Puerto Vallarta. The asking price for St. Clerans was $320,000.

While they were honeymooning and, together with the ever-efficient Gladys Hill, trying to decide what to keep and what to get rid of, Foreman flew in with new offers. Newman had been happy working with Huston and the corporate Newman-Foreman entity offered John to direct Paul in one or several pictures. *The Life and Times of Judge Roy Bean* had not been the *Butch Cassidy and the Sundance Kid* success everybody had hoped, grossing only five million dollars in its first year in U.S.-Canadian release. John gave Foreman a tour of St. Clarens, and together they happened on Stephen Grimes's original sketches for *The Man Who Would Be King*. They talked way into the night, Huston telling the producer how the Kipling story had started as a vehicle for his father, then for Clark Gable and Humphrey Bogart, then after Bogey's death how Frank Sinatra had entered the realm of probability, and still later how it had become a Richard Burton–Peter O'Toole project. Foreman sent a copy of the script to Newman, who read it and said it was perfect, but not for him. Next, Foreman sent it to Sean Connery and Michael Caine.

In the meantime, *The Mackintosh Man* was rolling in London. The Warner Brothers release starred Paul Newman, Dominique Sanda, James Mason, Harry Andrews, Michael Hordern, and a cast of good English actors. Ossie Morris was on camera and John directed exteriors in the raw, pale November sun wearing a crumpled ginger suit, overcoat with cape, and a kind of tweedy deerstalker. Cece was not with him. Collin's paralysis was worsening in Europe and British doctors told her he would receive better treatment in Los Angeles.

Adapted from Desmond Bagley's tricky cold war whodunit, *The Freedom Trap*, the Walter Hill screenplay was still not finished two weeks into shooting. Nobody really liked the original book, but as Huston told visitors, "Novels that are something less than first class have often been made into excellent films." Newman plays Rearden, an agent who appears to be an international jewel thief betrayed by his employer Mackintosh (Andrews) and the latter's mysterious secretary (Sanda). He is arrested and sent to prison for twenty years, but arranges to buy into a jailbreak, masterminded by imprisoned English traitor Ian Bannen. From here on the plot is sent sprawling and the way the movie picks up the strands and weaves them back together is neither as interesting nor as artfully done as the opening setup.

As Huston wrapped the filming at Pinewood studios, his stepmother died quietly in California. Nan Sunderland had lived in retirement since Walter's death twenty-two years earlier. In December, John was in Los Angeles with Cece and, to pick up some play money to gamble on Friday nights with Paul Kohner and the boys, played a gorilla sage in *Battle for the Planet of the Apes*. Fellow apes included composer Paul Williams and Claude Akins and Natalie Trundy. Even dressed as an ape Huston looked like Huston—not facially, but in his long, gangling stride.

John didn't inherit anything from his stepmother. In her will, Nan established a Walter Huston scholarship for University of California drama students.

23

KEEPING TRUCKIN'

John Milius got his revenge with *The Wind and the Lion*. With *Dillinger*, Milius had become a director and he now *cast* Huston as Secretary of State John Hay in his long, noisy, and less than factual retelling of a 1904 diplomatic incident involving an American widow and her two children in Morocco. Candice Bergen was the widow, Brian Keith was President Theodore Roosevelt, and Sean Connery the Berber desert chieftain kidnaping widow and children. Milius drove his Secretary Hay actor hard on the locations in southern Spain, but between setups Huston could sit in a canvas chair next to Connery and talk *The Man Who Would Be King*.

Acting was becoming something more than an occasional pastime for Huston. More and more younger directors sought the handsomely crinkled face, the distinctive go-to-hell stride, and the mellifluous voice to convey literacy, dignity, and presence when not subdued evil or glib and puckish authority. After *The Wind and the Lion*, John played Faye Dunaway's rotten millionaire father in Roman Polanski's suffocatingly compelling *Chinatown* and Charles Bronson's grandfather in Tom Gries's less satisfying thriller *Breakout*.

"I'm not an actor," he kept insisting. When Gries asked him

if he wasn't sometimes tempted to give advice, he tactfully said he put on blinkers.

"But you can't do that, and you know it," Gries smiled.

"Ah well. There were one or two times on *Chinatown* I was tempted to say something to Polanski. But Roman was doing it his style, different from mine but it worked for him. We'd had one encounter before shooting and I'd arrived with some misgivings, but they were quickly dispelled. He's a powerful little guy, lots of drive. He gets what he wants." Anjelica was interested in her father's costar, Jack Nicholson, and had him introduce her. Two years later she and Jack were living together in the Hollywood hills.

For Orson Welles, Huston played the lead in *The Other Side of the Wind*, an unfinished mystery of a movie that Peter Bogdanovich and a lot of bright young cinema enthusiasts helped put together. John plays Jake Hannaford, an aging director who comes back to Hollywood to make a modish low-budget film full of nudity, symbolism, and radical-chic violence but winds up killing himself in a suicidal car crash. Filming began in 1970 and was still going on eight years later, with John's scenes shot a little everywhere—in Los Angeles, Paris, London, as Welles tried to stay ahead of creditors, union, and the IRS. The film was Welles's 8½, a meditation on the art and business of moviemaking but also pathological obsession, something that he couldn't finish.

To Huston, filmmaking was mostly hard work now and his career was losing focus. Few things had an enduring value for him and to direct movies in the "new" Hollywood meant that problems were coming at him faster and getting bigger all the time. "I like making pictures, mind you," he liked to say. "I will continue to do so as long as I'm asked." Usually, he added that to act in a picture only carried one responsibility— to know his lines. "Acting is a cinch and they pay you damned near as much as you make directing."

In the larger perspective of life, the early 1970s were a curiously vacant time for him. More than ever he needed distractions. "I like highly seasoned things, both foods and people," he said a few months after Ricki's death. "I need the agility of mind in people because that means they have a fresh outlook. Life itself fascinates me, each moment as it comes along." Among the dislikes he was in the habit of enumerating were people, movies, and writing that strain too hard for effect, mawkish popular songs, and the sound of automobile metal in collision. When asked what besides high seasoned foods and people were his likes, he said, "The long, long twilights of Ireland, which are a small eternity, any music by Bach, the sound of hounds in full cry, primitive sculpture, good vodka, rogues and stimulating minds. I don't know that I have a philosophy, but I never do anything that doesn't entertain me. That way a man can't be bored."

It was hard to remain passionate about films because it was difficult to "grow" with a medium that liked to recycle itself. Perhaps he, too, should remake a few of his own films which had seemed full of promise but had never quite worked. "Couple of mine, I could imagine doing over," he told the Los Angeles *Times*'s Charles Champlin a few weeks before the opening of *The Kremlin Letter*. "*Moulin Rouge* got mixed reviews and was successful at the box office, but I didn't like it. It was kind of interesting physically. It just wasn't Toulouse-Lautrec, that's all. You could put him on the screen today; couldn't then. He was sentimentalized. Actually, he was a clinically cold little realist, with the courage to look life in the teeth. He was sardonic, not bitter. There's never been another like him."

"*The Roots of Heaven* might be worth another go. Could've been fine; wasn't. Problems of foolish haste, rushing slapdash into production before it was ready. There were depths to the story that were never touched."

He liked the unstructured new mood of movies, films that explored themselves, let contradictions happen, and had a way of nipping their audiences in surprising ways, although it wasn't the kind of films he could make. He called these "wayward films" and said he meant pictures that were loosely scripted if scripted at all, pictures that stopped when they wanted to. His own films were organized so that everything had significance. "My school, my script, have to be cohesive; it's a matter of habits and perception. But it's different from the wayward kind as the Old Masters are from the new guy who draws on a walk."

A cherished old project suddenly fell into place, not only allowing him to focus the mind and to escape boredom but to direct a big film that managed to be both engrossing with conflict, suspense, and allure and to be sensitive and modern in pitch and resonance. In January 1975, *The Man Who Would Be King* was rolling, an eight-million-dollar John Foreman production for Allied Artists, with Sean Connery and Michael Caine as the two former soldiers who set out to find an undiscovered country where a man might be king.

"It's a great adventure story," he hummed contentedly between takes at Tagdirt-el-Bour high in the Atlas Mountains in eastern Morocco. "It has excitement, color, spectacle and humor, drawn from character. There is also a moral meaning with contemporary significance and it is a splendid tale of two tough and likable rogues who are loyal to each other and to their ideals such as they are."

He added that on a deeper level *The Man Who Would Be King* appealed to the child in him, "the adventure of going into strange latitudes where reckoning ceases to count, the embarking on a voyage where you can't see the end." He had read Kipling as a boy, he said, telling visiting newsmen of the time he had been confined to the sanatorium with both heart and kidney ailments. It was there, when as a twelve-year-old he had dunked himself in primal ice cold water that he had developed a thirst for exotic, distant worlds. "I read so much Kipling, it's in my unconscious. You start a verse, I'll finish it. I didn't commit things to memory. It was simply my poring over things. Kipling writes about a world of the past, a world gone, a geography gone. It's the world of adventure, high honor, mystery."

"I wonder with a bit of envy now about those people who only do one thing all their lives. Maybe there are advantages I've missed. Well, I knew from the beginning that a picturemaker's life is fragmented. And I used to feel very sad when a film was over, when I realized this particular experience would never happen again, these people would never come together again."

The Man Who Would Be King owed a lot to *Butch Cassidy and the Sundance Kid*. As Caine noted wryly, Kipling never saw *Butch Cassidy* but would have reason to be grateful to it, on the grounds that the profitability of palship, which *Butch Cassidy* first confirmed, helped make Huston's quarter-century project bankable. The easy and evident comradeship between Connery's Daniel Dravot and Caine's Peachy Carnehan is the life-sustaining heart of the picture.

"More than chance has been at work here," says the crowned king Dravot, as he enumerated to his sidekick the incredible succession of incidents which helped him on his road to kingship and Carnehan to generalship in the far-flung corner of the world called Kafiristan, a country untouched by western hand since Alexander the Great's in the fourth century B.C. An avalanche brought about by their Homeric laughter helped them over an uncrossable crevasse; during a key battle in their campaign, an arrow hit Dravot's masonic medallion, enabling him to fight on unharmed—for the Kafirs, a clear demonstration of his godhood; the medal was then discovered to bear the mark of a mysterious sign on a temple stone—for the priests, a clear demonstration. "You call it luck," Dravot tells Carnehan, "I call it destiny."

The screenplay was by John and Gladys finally, with elements from the many earlier versions. What was new was replacing Kipling's fictitious storyteller with Kipling himself (Christopher Plummer in Kiplingesque glasses and a baby walrus mustache) and, thanks to the fashion of truculent male twosomes, scaling down the exotic princess leading lady, played by Shakira Caine. "In one script both men were in love with the girl and their quarrels were over her," said Huston. "I felt that was wrong but in those days you had to have a boy-girl romance in it."

With Ossie Morris, Huston filled his screen. The "bitter cold mountainous parts" of Kipling become beautiful landscapes of snow so desolate that the audience half expects Dravot and Carnehan to stumble on the smiling lamas of Shangri-La. As they struggle on toward Kafiristan there is mystery and magic— as when they come upon two scarecrows, designed to scare off people rather than birds looming like giant wood soldiers in the mist. The land, once reached, is at first a sorry Shangri-La, a primitive assortment of warring cities.

But there is a sacred city crowning a mountain above the others and piled high with treasure, awaiting a latter-day Alexander to claim his inheritance. By the luck of the masonic medallion, it might even be Dravot. Amid the fun and adventure, Huston preserves the text of Kipling's message. The pals who would be kings are also the advance scouts of an exploitative society invading an older and more primitive culture with no wish to stay, understand, or share, only to grab and run. Kingship and its trappings are stripped from them, with the contents of a treasure chest cascading down the hillside, echoing the fate of the *Sierra Madre* gold. And Carnehan returns to his starting point, withered, wrapped in rags, clutching the shrunken head of his pal.

Connery, in turban and muttonchops, told the visiting press, "There is something wild here, but also a good deal of sense. Dravot is obsessed with the idea of power, and overdoes it once he gets it." Caine, wearing a jaunty Afghan cap and commanding a dozen soldier extras, said, "I am his buddy who is sort of the voice of reason, the man who says, Let's take the money and run. It's a marvelous role for me, humor, a good change of pace, a real gift."

The location company was big, comprising over a hundred vehicles, 150 actors, and some 500 extras from the local population. The production design was not by Stephen Grimes, but by that other great designer Alexander Trauner. Said Caine, "We're enjoying ourselves here because this is a movie movie. None of this small-screen stuff for TV."

John's delight was Karroum Ben Bouih, a Moroccan who played the chieftain of the Kafirs. Over a hundred years old, Bouih had never seen a film until John showed him the rushes. After watching himself on the screen and conferring with two other elders also in the picture, Bouih said, "We will never die now."

Cece was in Morocco, but before John and she could get to Puerto Vallarta to rest up, he was in Philadelphia directing a twenty-eight-minute film called *Independence* for the National Park Service. Eli Wallach was Benjamin Franklin, Pat Hingle was John Adams, Ken Howard played Thomas Jefferson, Patrick O'Neal was George Washington, and Owen Roisman, the cameraman of *The French Connection*, filmed them and Independence Hall with loving reverence.

"All films are created equal," John said about his half-hour epic for the upcoming bicentennial year celebrations. "I don't think there is such a thing as a small film. We're not pulling any punches here. Scene for scene, everything is being done to the best of our abilities. Each scene as we make it is the best scene I've ever made—in my imagination. I didn't know Owen before, but I have nothing but the highest admiration for his artistry. He's a beautiful, beautiful photographer."

Huston had been approached by Lloyd Ritter, who wrote the script together with his wife on behalf of the National Park Service. "He told me of the spirit in which they were entering this enterprise. I thoroughly approved and saw it as a way to make my obeisance to the progeniture of Uncle Sam." Huston and Roisman filmed exquisite setups: John Adams under a tree reading a letter from Abigail, Washington standing with a group of delegates, and, inside, Franklin reading the final lines of the Declaration while walking down the Independence Hall staircase. *Independence* played in a theater across from the historic site every half hour throughout 1976.

St. Clerans was sold—for $300,000. To have a pied à terre in Ireland, John bought a cottage by the sea in Lettermullen, Connemara northwest of Galway. With Allegra and Collin, Cece and John spent a short month there, but by July 1975 the three-year marriage was on the rocks and Cece filed for divorce in Los Angeles.

Friends had seen it coming and called John and Cece congenitally incompatible; he distracted, aloof, and never easy to live with; she on the make in the business, using and abusing the "Mrs. Huston" which opened doors. The divorce petition estimated his yearly income at one million dollars and sought alimony and division of community property that included a home in Pacific Palisades, a Mexican silver mine, stables and stocks, plus residuals from eight movies he directed or acted in during the marriage.

With Allegra, John moved to Puerto Vallarta and into a rented home situated midway between the new Holiday Inn beach and the Hotel Las Palmas. The spectacular living area was an open, circular room so vast tourists occasionally mistook it for a verandah and walked right through on their way to the beach. They rarely recognized the occupant sitting reading or writing at a huge, round table. Allegra's nanny, Maricela Hernandez, was with him and in July the Los Angeles *Herald-Examiner* reported that Huston was not so disillusioned with marriage that he wasn't ready to marry Maricela, forty-seven years his junior. Rumors would persist that he had made her his sixth wife in 1976.

The Man Who Would Be King was a surprise success. "More than chance has been at work here," critics paraphrased Sean Connery's line as they considered the destiny that had led Huston to film Kipling's early (1888) short story and the two authors' kindred fascination for the wayward ways of men in action and their parallel instinct for plot twists and eccentric characterizations. Huston told the screen story in a straight-forward manner and gave it exotic grandeur, teeming populations, muscular dash, larger-than-life bravura, and managed to say something about the white man's burden and imperialism. New York critics, from Vincent Canby to Pauline Kael and John Simon, were virtually unanimous in their praise, Simon calling it "John Huston's best film in twenty-three years, or since *The African Queen*." In February 1976, Huston and Hill were nominated for Academy Awards for their script, Trauner for the art direction, and Russell Lloyd for the editing. The New York *Times* dispatched a reporter to Puerto Vallarta where he found John and Gladys in the huge circular living room together with a resident American woman artist. "We never talk movies around here," Gladys informed the *Times*-man who watched Huston purchase two small water colors from Kathy Jacobs and express his taste in abstract works with a "Pollock *no*, Rothko *si*." When it came to movies, Huston said he had only made three good films during the past ten years—*Reflections in a Golden Eye, Fat City,* and now *The Man Who Would Be King.*

John liked Puerto Vallarta and found more private quarters by renting Elizabeth Taylor's Casa Kimberly and, when she was in town, the guest house, attached by an over-the-street bridge. The Gringo Gulch, as self-deprecating American residents called the fast-growing condominium strip, was not secluded and a year later, John made a deal with Indians south of Mismaloya to rent one of the small deserted bays and to have a small "compound" built at the water's edge.

"I've leased the land from the Indians for ten years," he said in 1978 when the construction was completed. "If I want, there's an option for another ten. Then they get it all back. So I told the architect to build something that won't last too long, something that will disappear back into the land when I'm finished with it."

The tropical paradise seemed torn from the pages of Conrad or early Malraux. With the jungle reaching the edge of the sea, it was out of the question to bulldoze a road in and John was more than happy that his beach could be reached by boat only. The compound consisted of six elaborate huts, designed by John and built with local labor. There was one for himself, one for Maricela and Allegra, one for Gladys, one for the Indians working for him, and one for guests. The sixth structure was a more imposing, glass-enclosed living and eating area. The only contact with Puerto Vallarta was by shortwave radio and John's forty-five-foot cruiser, riding at anchor in the bay when he was in residence.

Like stepson Pablo fifteen years earlier, Maricela had a keen eye and took up photography. When W published a layout on the cove, the color photos of John, in white peon pajamas, were signed Maricela Hernandez.

If there were no horses to ride, there was fish to catch. The bay and the offshore rocks where John liked to paddle were an aquarium teeming with huge needlefish, with parrot and angel fish and all manner of bright water life. Inevitably perhaps when he sat on his boat and watched Maricela on the beach, his thoughts turned to that other old man at the sea with whom he had gone fishing in a Cuban cove nearly thirty years earlier. *Across the River and into the Trees* was a story about holding off death and about the challenge of a too young woman. Like *Red Badge*, *Moby Dick*, and *The Man Who Would Be King*, it was a project he had lived with a long time. He had been there at La Finca when Hemingway finished the novel. He knew the story behind the story, Papa's self-exposure, his dejection at the book's reception. To keep the compound abuilding and to keep himself distracted while he found someone to bankroll the Hemingway elegy, it was back to acting. Kohner found him three undemanding but quick-shooting parts in a Canadian picture called *Angela*, a French-Mexican coproduction of *The Bermuda Triangle*, and in Ingmar Bergman's *The Serpent's Egg* (conflicting schedules forced Bergman to replace him with James Whitmore). Kohner also got literary superagent Irving "Swifty" Lazar to sell Huston's contemplated autobiography to Alfred A. Knopf for a reported $200,000.

The selling of the memoirs meant a quick sweep through midtown Manhattan publishing houses. "Swiftly and I would go see a publisher or we'd go to lunch with one, and he would sort of intimate all the good stories I had, and I would sort of nod, and Swifty would rub his hands in the taxicab," John told W's G. Y. Dryansky two years later.

Huston celebrated his seventieth birthday at the compound with Allegra, Maricela, and Gladys and received telephoned good wishes from Tony, Anjelica, and Paul Kohner. Six months later, Anjelica got mixed up in the tawdry troubles of Roman Polanski, accused of raping a thirteen-year-old "aspiring actress." The alleged rape, child molestation, oral copulation, sodomy, and providing drugs to a minor took place at the Mulholland Drive home of Polanski's friend Jack Nicholson. Although Nicholson was away skiing in Colorado at the time, his live-in girlfriend, Anjelica, was there along with the housekeeper of neighbor Marlon Brando. While dark inside rumor had it that John had introduced Roman to the thirte-year-old, Anjelica was booked for possession of cocaine and, in a complicated plea bargain, agreed to turn state witness. When

Polanski fled to France to avoid sentencing, Anjelica was back with former boyfriend Ryan O'Neal.

In the summer of 1977, *Love and Bullets, Charlie* was set as John's next. The Lew Grade-ITC Entertainment production was an all-Kohner package. Huston was now Paul's oldest active client and Charles Bronson and his wife, Jill Ireland, Kohner's top-grossing clients. To keep it even more in the family, *Love and Bullets, Charlie* was produced by Pancho Kohner, Paul's son.

Stephen Grimes was the production designer, but Gladys wasn't on the script this time. The screenplay was by Wendell Mayes, the scripter of *The Bank Shot* and *Death Wish* for Bronson. The elaborate chase picture was to be the most far-flung of Huston's far-flung career, with locations in Zermatt, Zürich, Amsterdam, Paris, London, Rio de Janeiro, Dallas, Washington, and Chicago.

Production start was postponed by illness. John suffered what his father had died from—aneurism, and on October 6 underwent open-heart vascular surgery at the Cedars-Sinai Medical Center in Los Angeles. The aneurism—a localized, abnormal dilation of an artery—was in the aorta and the surgical intervention was complicated by anesthesiologists' fears that John's "smoker's lungs" might malfunction after the operation.

John was indestructible. "They tested my lungs to see if I could sustain eight hours of surgery and the results were terrible—they couldn't sustain me for a half hour," he said six months later. "They said, 'It's quite extraordinary those lungs are sustaining you right now.' So they worked on my lungs for ten days with a breathing machine and they beat my lungs, and I came through the operation all right. But you know, it's a terrible thing; they put your intestines on a tray and there they lie smoking and writhing while your aorta is being worked on. I developed adhesions—when they're touched, something happens to your insides—so I had to be operated on for that for another four hours. Well, then the gall bladder started up, and the doctors said if we have to operate on that, that's it. Fortunately, I didn't need the operation."

After the difficult recovery, he was up and about. Willy

Wyler visited at the hospital and found his old friend loping around hallways and nursing stations. Two months later, Huston was back in Puerto Vallarta, where, according to Tony, he was going to live "indefinitely." *Love and Bullets, Charlie* was directed by Stuart Rosenberg.

To pay the hospital bills and to get circulation back in mind and bones, he signed to write and direct another bigger-than-life epic in the *Man Who Would Be King* vein—*Saud*. Ibn Saud Abd al-'Aziz (1887–1953) was the desert king who in 1928 conquered the Saudi province of Hejaz and with it, Mecca, unified four-fifths of the Arabian Peninsula and, three years later, proclaimed himself king of Saudi Arabia. The tentative price tag was twelve million dollars and the big picture would be complicated, and passably multinational. The money was Saudi and the three producers were Eugene Frenke, John's producer on *Heaven Knows, Mr. Allison* and *The Barbarian and the Geisha*, Henri Gebrier of Paris, and Sadik Adlai of Riyadh. Locations were scouted in Morocco, Tunisia, Jordan, and Saudi Arabia, and Frenke was approaching Marlon Brando (with an open checkbook) to star. Principal photography was set for early 1979. To pick up some money in the meantime, he did four weeks' acting in a pair of easy flicks—Giuglio Paradisi's first American film, *The Visitor*, shooting in Atlanta; and Ernest Pintoff's *Jaguar Lives*, filming in Spain, Germany, Italy, Hong Kong, and Japan.

And there was the autobiography. Lazar had said it would be easy, that all John had to do was to sit down with a tape recorder and tell all those wonderful stories to Gladys. But the tape made him self-conscious and there was something silly in sitting stone cold across from someone he had known for thirty years to retell yarns she sometimes knew better than he. "I was just about to give up and hand back the advance when I ran into an ex-Navy diver in town. I found out he loved my stories. So I switched on the tape again and started talking to him. And I got the book done." The memoirs, he cautioned visitors, would make no saucy revelations about his private life. As for a title for the biography, he toyed with the idea of using Long

Shadow, the name the Paiute Indians had given him during the filming of *The Misfits*.

As in Tarzana, a menagerie of less-than-tame animals kept growing at the edge of the jungle. A pet macaw was added to a funny, ant-eating animal on a string locally known as a tejon, two pet boa constrictors and a half-wild ocelot. The boas—one seven feet long, the other four feet—either slept in John's hut or in a special area outside. The fierce little ocelot wouldn't let him out of sight. Maricela snapped pictures when the bony patriarch played with his pets.

Friends showed up, including Richard Burton, who bought his new wife, Susan, a house in Gringo Gulch just down the road from his ex-wife's Casa Kimberly; the Bronsons; and Lew Grade, who wanted to turn *Moulin Rouge* into a miniseries starring Jill Ireland and Omar Sharif. Neighbors, too, crossed the cove. "I know many people, both in town and further along the coast," John told his visitors. "All good people. People who come to live in places like this tend to be interesting. I'm constantly occupied. I wake before dawn and see the miracle occur. Then there's fishing, or swimming or my writing. It's just exactly what I wanted. A place that will see me out."

24

FADING INTO LEGEND

"The next one will be *Across the River and into the Trees*," he said while preparing *Saud*. "I just concentrate on what's going on at the time. I don't look back, unless someone rubs my nose in my past, and I don't look too far ahead, not much past the next picture."

If working and spending it all were the secrets of his longevity, as he liked to say, he was, with Luis Buñuel, the oldest director still at it in the late 1970s. The shoulders were bonier, the slouch stiffer, but the deeply honed face was striking. God, somebody wrote in 1972, must look like John Huston. Wispy hair and a patriarchal beard added to the metaphor. The rich, gentle authority of someone who has experienced most of what he wished in life, was there, heightened by a craggy mellowness and a wheeze with each draw of breath. The puffs under the eyes were enormous but the opaque reddish stare was as stabbing as ever, or, at times, as curiously empty of feelings. In his seventies, John was a very private man.

Life had never been just movies and in the new house in Puerto Vallarta—as in Tarzana, St. Clerans, and Casa Kimberly—filmmaking was not a central obsession. Art and artists were, in quiet impassioned discussions over Jack Daniel's and—until the operation—Don Diegos. Dressed in his billowing robes, his caftans or bush jackets, he liked to wander afield, more in the mind than in the flesh now, to talk about African elephants he had known, about Portuguese wines and the sense of space in pre-Columbian and post-Cezanne art. If Hemingway had had an influence on him, it was not a literary one but in the sense painters express space: giving emotions not by what is said but by what is left out. Pensive, at times almost brooding, he had retained the full-bodied laugh and the ability to make practical jokes, sometimes of dubious taste. He continued to be incredibly well read, and in his new hut, to do his reading sitting on the floor.

His place in history remained uncertain and critics were as reluctant as ever to grant him a place among America's great directors. His persona was in the grain of the biggest of them but in the long view, expatriation was no doubt a mistake, a concession to the picturesque that made him marginal. Hollywood never trusted originality, but it allowed sharpness and it craved relevance. After Ireland, Huston found himself in the ironic position of entertaining—no longer alarming—the bourgeoisie. Yet his charm, his directness, his generosity and his ability to make moviemaking look as if he enjoyed it, was the very stuff of filmic excitement—images of life as fulfillment. Critics remained bewildered, however, by what seemed a lack of focus. His form remained elusive, his themes effusive, and it was hard to tell whether he had declined or matured, gone commercial or refined himself into something deeply personal. He was accused of dwelling on surface excitements at the expense of the spiritual undertows of his material, but his confident style was also seen as the best legacy of a receding golden age of American filmdom.

Personally, he backed into history with bemused detachment. Most of his glories were behind him; some of his recent work had been unremarkable and he had earned his in-between pocket money as a character actor, often in films less distinguished than his own. And he had learned to handle probing young cinemaniacs, to *say* he devoted little time to assessing his work, to seeking hidden meanings and unifying themes. If anything, he would claim, his longevity was all due to his interest in other things, "in jumping around in life and in films." In 1976 he said *Reflections in a Golden Eye, Fat City,* and *The Man Who Would Be King* were the only good pictures of the last decade. Two years later, he thought *Moby Dick* was his most important work—not only the *Moby Dick* up there on the screen but the *experience* of making it—and a general truth seemed to emerge. The circumstances of the making of his films were often as memorable as the movies themselves.

In a business where talent tends to blossom early and relevance is a matter of staying power, he had endured, progressing from the golden age when movies were daydreams peopled with stars bred like prime rib cattle to filmmaking with totally different power base and resonance. In the 1970s, he was a man with a long shadow, a nifty Don Quixote of Hollywood's emotional windmills, the prototypical middle-period director with a kind of rapt affection for pirates and princesses and a low cunning for big, romantic screen fantasies which are, of necessity, a movie staple. Through four decades he retained his creative authority, his means of getting his effects, coaxing his stars to perform for him and holding off intruders.

"You haven't asked me how I like directing my father and daughter," he likes to say. "You must ask me that because I like answering it . . . My father was one of the finest actors ever born—a real gentleman who never disagreed with anyone, let alone his director. My daughter will be good some day. She's young and she has a tendency to ask questions, but then that is a womanly trait and I'm proud of her."

Success in the movies has always been open-ended, tentative, and perishable. What films have to say and how they say it keeps changing as do the new economics, the shifting tastes and general fracturing of the arts. What is almost unique in Huston's case is that in his seventies he can still charm the moneymen into betting on his talents.

"Where I live they know I go away and do movies and they're embarrassed for my sake," he said when he lived in Ireland. "They think movies are an escapade as far as I'm concerned, a sort of distant and unfamiliar sin, and they forgive me." The squire of St. Clerans had given way to the old man by the sea in Puerto Vallarta, living with a growing child and a pair of devoted women, but he is still ready to go away and do movies.

For how long? he was asked one evening during preparations for *Love and Bullets, Charlie.* While he pondered that question, someone reminded him that when he had turned fifty, he had been widely quoted as saying he would live to be a hundred.

"Well," he smiled, "that isn't that long now."

A little later, after somebody else had replenished his Jack Daniel's, he said he thought he knew what was interesting about movies. When he had everybody's attention he said it was their magic. "What you try to become is a bringer of magic," he reflected. "For magic and truth are closely allied and movies are sheer magic. When they are misused of course it's a debasement of magic. But when they work, it's—well, it's glorious."

FILMS DIRECTED BY JOHN HUSTON

THE MALTESE FALCON
Warner Brothers, released October 1941 (100 minutes). Produced by Hal B. Wallis. Screenplay: John Huston from the novel by Dashiell Hammett. Cinematography Arthur Edeson, editor Thomas Richards, music Adolph Deutsch. Cast: Humphrey Bogart, Mary Astor, Sydney Greenstreet, Peter Lorre, Elisha Cook.

IN THIS OUR LIFE
Warner Brothers, released May 1942 (97 minutes). Produced by Hal B. Wallis. Screenplay: Howard Koch from the novel by Ellen Glasgow. Cinematography Ernest Haller, editor William Holmes, music Max Steiner. Cast: Bette Davis, Olivia de Havilland, George Brent, Dennis Morgan, Charles Coburn.

ACROSS THE PACIFIC
Warner Brothers, released September 1942 (97 minutes). Produced by Jerry Wald and Jack Saper. Screenplay: Richard Macaulay from *Aloha Means Goodbye* by Robert Carson. Cinematography Arthur Edeson, editor Frank Magee, music Adolph Deutsch. Cast: Humphrey Bogart, Mary Astor, Sydney Greenstreet.

REPORT FROM THE ALEUTIANS
U. S. Signal Corps, released August 1943 (47 minutes). Written and directed by Captain John Huston. Narration spoken by Walter Huston.

SAN PIETRO (also THE BATTLE OF SAN PIETRO)
U. S. Army Pictorial Service, released April 1945 (32 minutes).
Written and directed by Major John Huston. Camera crew
Jules Buck. Narration spoken by Major John Huston.

LET THERE BE LIGHT
U. S. Army Pictorial Service, made 1945, restricted release (60
minutes). Screenplay: Captain Charles Kaufman. Cinematography Stanley Cortez, technical adviser Lt. Col. Benjamin
Simon. Narration spoken by Walter Huston (*No screen credits
are given in the film itself*).

THE TREASURE OF THE SIERRA MADRE
Warner Brothers, released January 1948 (126 minutes). Pro-
duced by Henry Blanke. Screenplay: John Huston from the
novel by B. Traven. Cinematography Ted McCord, editor
Owen Marks, music Max Steiner. Cast: Humphrey Bogart,
Walter Huston, Tim Holt, Alfonso Bedoya, Bruce Bennett,
A. Soto Rangel, Manuel Donde.

KEY LARGO
Warner Brothers, released July 1948 (101 minutes). Produced
by Jerry Wald. Screenplay: John Huston and Richard Brooks
from the play by Maxwell Anderson. Cinematography Karl
Freund, editor Rudi Fehr, music Max Steiner. Cast: Humphrey
Bogart, Lauren Bacall, Edward G. Robinson, Lionel Barrymore,
Claire Trevor.

WE WERE STRANGERS
Horizon-Columbia Pictures, released May 1949 (106 minutes).
Produced by Sam Spiegel. Screenplay: John Huston and Peter
Viertel from a segment in *Rough Sketch* by Robert Sylvester.
Cinematography Russell Metty, editor Al Clark. Cast: John
Garfield, Jennifer Jones, Gilbert Roland, Pedro Armendariz.

THE ASPHALT JUNGLE
MGM, released June 1950 (112 minutes). Produced by Arthur
Hornblow, Jr. Screenplay: John Huston and Ben Maddow

from the novel by W. R. Burnett. Cinematography Harold Rosson, editor George Boemler. Cast: Sterling Hayden, Jean Hagen, Louis Calhern, Sam Jaffe, Marilyn Monroe.

THE RED BADGE OF COURAGE
MGM, released September 1951 (69 minutes). Produced by Gottfried Reinhardt. Screenplay: John Huston from the novel by Stephen Crane. Cinematography Harold Rosson, editor Ben Lewis. Cast: Audie Murphy, Bill Mauldin, John Dierkes, Royal Dabo, Arthur Hunnicutt, Andy Devine.

THE AFRICAN QUEEN
Horizon–Romulus–United Artists, released January 1952 (106 minutes). Produced by Sam Spiegel. Screenplay: John Huston and James Agee from the novel by C. S. Forester. Cinematography Jack Cardiff, editor Ralph Kemplen, music Alan Gray. Cast: Humphrey Bogart, Katharine Hepburn, Robert Morley.

MOULIN ROUGE
Romulus–United Artists, released January 1953 (123 minutes). Produced by John Huston. Screenplay: Anthony Veiller from the novel by Pierre LaMure. Cinematography Oswald Morris, music Georges Auric. Cast: Jose Ferrer, Colette Marchand, Zsa Zsa Gabor, Suzanne Flon.

BEAT THE DEVIL
Santana–Romulus–United Artists, released March 1954 (92 minutes). Produced by John Huston in association with Humphrey Bogart. Screenplay: John Huston and Truman Capote from the novel by James Helvick. Cinematography Oswald Morris, editor Ralph Kemplen, music Franco Mannino. Cast: Humphrey Bogart, Jennifer Jones, Gina Lollobrigida, Robert Morley, Peter Lorre.

MOBY DICK
Warner Brothers, released June 1956 (116 minutes). Produced by John Huston. Screenplay: John Huston and Ray Bradbury

from the novel by Herman Melville. Cinematography Oswald Morris, editor Russell Lloyd, music Philip Stainton. Cast: Gregory Peck, Richard Baseheart, Leon Genn, Orson Welles.

HEAVEN KNOWS, MR. ALLISON

Twentieth Century Fox, released March 1957 (107 minutes). Produced by Buddy Adler and John Eugene Frenke. Screenplay: John Huston and Lee Mahin from the novel by Charles Shaw. Cinematography Oswald Morris, music Georges Auric. Cast: Robert Mitchum, Deborah Kerr.

THE BARBARIAN AND THE GEISHA

Twentieth Century Fox, released October 1958 (105 minutes). Produced by Eugene Frenke. Screenplay: Charles Grayson from *The Harris Townsend Story* by Ellis St. Joseph. Cinematography Charles G. Clarke, editor Stuart Gilmore, music Hugo Friedhofer. Cast: John Wayne, Sam Jaffe, Eiko Ando, So Yamamura.

THE ROOTS OF HEAVEN

Twentieth Century Fox, released October 1958 (131 minutes). Produced by Darryl F. Zanuck. Screenplay: Romain Gary and Patrick Leigh Fermor from the novel by Romain Gary. Cinematography Oswald Morris, editor Russell Lloyd, music Malcolm Arnold. Cast: Errol Flynn, Trevor Howard, Juliette Greco, Eddie Albert, Paul Lukas, Orson Welles.

THE UNFORGIVEN

United Artists, released April 1960 (125 minutes). Produced by James Hill. Screenplay: Ben Maddow from a novel by Alan LeMay. Cinematography Franz Planer, editor Russell Lloyd, music Dimitri Tiomkin. Cast: Burt Lancaster, Audrey Hepburn, Audie Murphy, Charles Bickford, Lillian Gish, John Saxon, Joseph Wiseman.

THE MISFITS

United Artists, released February 1961 (124 minutes). Produced by Frank Taylor. Screenplay: Arthur Miller from his short story. Cinematography Russell Metty, editor George Tomasini, music Alex North. Cast: Clark Gable, Marilyn Monroe, Montgomery Clift, Thelma Ritter, Eli Wallach.

FREUD (also THE SECRET PASSION)
Universal, released December 1962 (139 minutes). Produced by Wolfgang Reinhardt. Screenplay: Charles Kaufman and Wolfgang Reinhardt. Cinematography Douglas Slocombe, editor Ralph Kemplen, music Jerry Goldsmith; electronic music sequences Henk Badings. Cast: Montgomery Clift, Susannah York, Larry Parks, Susan Kohner.

THE LIST OF ADRIAN MESSENGER
Universal, released May 1963 (98 minutes). Produced by Edward Lewis. Screenplay: Anthony Veiller from the novel by Philip MacDonald. Cinematography Joseph MacDonald, editors Terry Morse and Hugh Fowler, music Jerry Goldsmith. Cast: Kirk Douglas, George C. Scott, Dana Wynter, Herbert Marshall, with cameo appearance of Tony Curtis, Robert Mitchum, Frank Sinatra.

THE NIGHT OF THE IGUANA
Seven Arts–MGM, released July 1964 (118 minutes). Produced by Ray Stark. Screenplay: John Huston and Anthony Veiller from the play by Tennessee Williams. Cinematography Gabriel Figueroa, editor Ralph Kemplen, music Benjamin Frankel. Cast: Richard Burton, Ava Gardner, Deborah Kerr, Sue Lyon, Grayson Hall.

THE BIBLE
Dino de Laurentiis—Twentieth Century Fox, released September 1966 (174 minutes). Produced by Dino de Laurentiis. Screenplay: Christopher Fry. Cinematography Giuseppe Rotunno, editor Ralph Kemplen, music Toshiro Mayazumi. Cast: Peter O'Toole, George C. Scott, Richard Harris, Ava Gardner, Stephen Boyd, John Huston.

CASINO ROYALE

Columbia Pictures, released April 1967 (130 minutes). Produced by Charles K. Feldman. Screenplay: Wolf Mankowitz, John Law, Michael Sayers suggested by Ian Fleming novel. Cinematography Jack Hildyard, additional photography John Wilcox, Nicholas Roeg. Cast: David Niven, Peter Sellers, Woody Allen, Ursula Andress, Orson Welles, Joanna Pettet, Daliah Levi, Deborah Kerr, William Holden, Charles Boyer, Jean-Paul Belmondo, George Raft. Other segments directed by Ken Hughes, Val Guest, Robert Parrish, and Joe McGarth.

REFLECTIONS IN A GOLDEN EYE

Warner Brothers, released October 1967 (109 minutes). Produced by Ray Stark. Screenplay: John Huston, Gladys Hill, Chapman Mortimer from the short story by Carson McCullers. Cinematography Aldo Tonti, editor Russell Lloyd, music Toshiro Mayazumi. Cast: Elizabeth Taylor, Marlon Brando, Brian Keith, Julie Harris, Zorro David, Robert Forster.

SINFUL DAVEY

United Artists, released March 1969 (95 minutes). Produced by William N. Graf for Mirisch Corp. Screenplay: James R. Webb from *The Life of David Haggart* by Haggart. Cinematography Freddie Young, Edward Seaife, editor Russell Lloyd, music Ken Thorpe. Cast: John Hurt, Pamela Franklin, Nigel Davenport, Ronald Fraser, Robert Morley, Fidelma Murphy.

A WALK WITH LOVE AND DEATH

Twentieth Century Fox, released October 1969 (90 minutes). Produced by Carter De Haven. Screenplay: Dale Wasserman from the novel by Hans Koningsberger. Cinematography Edward Seaife, editor Russell Lloyd, music Georges Delerue, English lyrics Gladys Hill. Cast: Anjelica Huston, Assaf Dayan, Anthony Corlan, John Hallam, Robert Lang, Guy Deghy, Michael Gough, George Murcell.

THE KREMLIN LETTER

Twentieth Century Fox, released January 1970 (116 minutes).

Produced by Carter De Haven and Sam Wiesenthal. Screenplay: John Huston and Gladys Hill. Cinematography Edward Seaife, editor Russell Lloyd, music Robert Drasnin. Cast: Bibi Andersson, Richard Boone, Nigel Greeb, Dean Jagger, Lila Kedrova, Patrick O'Neal, Barbara Parkins, George Sanders, Max von Sydow.

FAT CITY

Columbia Pictures, released November 1972 (96 minutes). Produced by Ray Stark. Screenplay: Leonard Gardner from his own novel. Cinematography Conrad Hall. Cast: Stacy Keach, Jeff Bridges, Susan Tyrrell, Candy Clark, Curtis Cokes, Nicolas Colasanto.

THE LIFE AND TIMES OF JUDGE ROY BEAN

National General Pictures release of First Artists Production, released December 1972 (120 minutes). Produced by John Foreman. Screenplay: John Milius. Cinematography Richard Moore, editor Hugh S. Fowler, music Maurice Jarre. Cast: Paul Newman, Victoria Principal, Anthony Perkins, Ned Beatty, Jim Burk, Jacqueline Bisset, Tab Hunter.

THE MACKINTOSH MAN

Warner Brothers, released July 1973 (105 minutes). Produced by John Foreman. Screenplay: Walter Hill from the novel by Desmond Bagley. Cinematography Oswald Morris, editor Russell Lloyd, music Maurice Jarre. Cast: Paul Newman, Dominique Sanda, James Mason, Harry Andrews, Ian Bannen, Michael Hordern.

INDEPENDENCE

National Park Service/Twentieth Century Fox, released 1976 (28 minutes). Screenplay: Lloyd Ritter. Cinematography Owen Roisman. Cast: Eli Wallach, Ken Howard, Patrick O'Neal, Pat Hingle, William Anderson.

THE MAN WHO WOULD BE KING

Allied Artists, released December 1975 (129 minutes). Produced by John Foreman. Screenplay: John Huston and Gladys Hill from the story by Rudyard Kipling. Cinematography Oswald Morris. Cast: Sean Connery, Michael Caine, Christopher Plummer, Saeed Jaffrey, Karroum Ben Bouih, Jack May, Shakira Caine, Doghmi Larbi.

BIBLIOGRAPHY

Agee, James, *Agee on Film*. New York: McDowell, Obolensky, 1960.

Baxter, John, *Hollywood in the Thirties*. New York: Paperback Library, 1970.

Carr, Virginia Spencer, *The Lonely Hunter, A Biography of Carson McCullers*. Garden City: Doubleday, 1975.

Crowther, Bosley, *Hollywood Rajah, The Life and Times of Louis B. Mayer*. New York: Holt, Rinehart & Winston, 1960.

Donaldson, Scott, *By Force of Will, The Life and Art of Ernest Hemingway*. New York: Viking, 1977.

Flamini, Robert, *Scarlett, Rhett*. New York: Macmillan, 1975.

Flynn, Errol, *My Wicked, Wicked Ways*. New York: G. P. Putnam's Sons, 1959.

Goode, James, *The Story of "The Misfits."* New York: Bobbs-Merrill, 1963.

Hamblett, Charles, *Paul Newman*. Chicago: Henry Regnery, 1975.

Higham, Charles, *Kate, The Life of Katharine Hepburn*. New York: Norton, 1974.

———— *Warner Brothers, A History of the Studio*. New York: Scribner, 1976.

Hyams, Joe, *Bogie, The Biography of Humphrey Bogart*. New York: New American Library, 1966.

Kael, Pauline, *Kiss Kiss Bang Bang*. Boston: Little, Brown, 1968.

———— *Deeper Into Movies*. Boston: Little, Brown, 1973.

Kaminsky, Stuart, *John Huston, Maker of Magic*. Boston: Houghton Mifflin, 1978.

Kanfer, Stefan, *A Journal of the Plague Years*. New York: Atheneum, 1973.

Kauffman, Stanley, *A World on Film*. New York: Harper & Row, 1967.

Keyes, Evelyn, *Scarlett O'Hara's Younger Sister*. Secaucus, N.J.: Lyle Stuart, 1977.

Lourcelles, Jacques, *Otto Preminger*. Paris: Seghers, 1965.

Macdonald, Dwight, *On Movies*. Englewood Cliffs, N.J.: Prentice-Hall, 1969.

Mailer, Norman, *Marilyn*. New York: Grosset & Dunlap, 1973.

Maugham, W. Somerset, *Ten Novels and Their Authors*. London: Penguin, 1969.

Morley, Robert, and Stokes, Sewell, *Robert Morley*. New York: Simon & Schuster, 1967.

Nichtenhauser, Adolf, *Films in Psychology and Mental Health*. New York: Health Education Council, 1953.

Niven, David, *Bring on the Empty Horses*. G. P. Putnam's Sons, 1975.

Nolan, William, *John Huston, King Rebel*. Los Angeles: Sherbourne Press, 1965.

Power-Waters, Alma. *John Barrymore*. New York: Julian Messner, 1941.

Preminger, Otto, *An Autobiography*. Garden City: Doubleday, 1977.

Rivkin, Allen and Kerr, Laura, *Hello Hollywood*. Garden City: Doubleday, 1962.

Ross, Lillian, *Reporting*. New York: Simon & Schuster, 1961.

Ruddy, Jonah, and Hill, Jonathan, *Bogey, The Man, the Actor, the Legend*. London: Souvenir Press, 1965.

Sarris, Andrew, *Confessions of a Cultist*. New York: Simon & Schuster, 1971.

Shaeffer, Louis, *O'Neill, Son and Artist*. Boston: Little, Brown, 1973.

Thomas, Bob, *Selznick*. Garden City: Doubleday, 1970.

Tomkies, Mike, *The Robert Mitchum Story*. Chicago: Henry Regnery, 1972.

Tozzi, Romano, *John Huston, A Picture Treasury of his Films*. New York: Falcon Enterprises, 1971.

Tornabene, Lynn, *Long Live the King, a Biography of Clark Gable*. New York: G. P. Putnam's Sons, 1976.

Tynan, Kenneth, *Tynan, Right and Left*. New York: Atheneum, 1967.

Viertel, Peter, *White Hunter Black Heart*. Garden City: Doubleday, 1953.

Viertel, Salka, *The Kindness of Strangers*. New York: Holt, Rinehart & Winston, 1969.

Warner, Jack, *My First Hundred Years in Hollywood* (with Dean Jennings) New York: Random House, 1965.

Zolotov, Maurice, *Shooting Star, a Biography of John Wayne*. New York: Simon & Schuster, 1974.

INDEX

268

273

276

277

Rogers, Ginger, 91
Roisman, Owen, 247
Roland, Gilbert, 93, 94, 108
Rolla, Primula, 70
Roman Holiday, 126
Romulus Films, 125
Roosevelt, Franklin D., 31, 48, 55, 56, 60, 62
Roots of Heaven, The, 8, 173–79, 198, 243, 261
Rosenberg, Max, 234
Rosenberg, Stuart, 252
Ross, Lillian, 105, 109ff.
Rossen, Robert, 74
Rosson, Harold, 100, 106
Rothschild, Philippe de, 77
Rough Sketch, 89
Roulien, Raoul, 33
Roulien, Tosca, 33
Ryan, Nin, 70, 71
Ryan, Tom, 217
Ryman, Lucille, 98

Sacramento River, 106
Sahl, Mort, 186
St. Clerans, 153–55, 156, 161, 167, 174, 179, 185, 190, 191–93, 197, 198–99, 209, 216, 218, 221–22, 225, 226, 229, 234, 238; for sale, 239; sold, 247
St. Joseph, Ellis, 46
Sallis, Zoe, 201, 210
Sanda, Dominique, 240
Sanders, George, 233
San Pietro, 64–65
San Pietro, 65–66, 67, 259
Santana Productions, 88–89, 112, 113
Sarne, Michael, 232
Sarris, Andrew, 197–98
Sartre, Jean-Paul, 6, 130, 164, 165, 172, 179, 187, 190, 191, 193; and *No Exit*, 76, 77
Satan Met a Lady, 47
Saud, 3, 172, 252, 254
Saxon, John, 180, 182
Scaife, Ted, 117
Schary, Dore, 92, 97, 101, 102, 104ff., 109, 110
Schayer, Richard, 38
Schenck, Nicholas, 97, 105, 110
Schlossberg, Colonel, 58, 59

Scott, George C., 196, 197, 210, 213, 214, 235
Sellers, Peter, 219
Selznick, David, 44, 67, 73, 74, 93, 95, 160ff., 166; and *Beat the Devil*, 136, 138–39
Selznick (Thomas), 67
Sergeant York, 47, 48, 49
Serpent's Egg, The, 250
Seven Arts, 184, 185, 196, 208, 223
Seventh Heaven, 42
Seventh Seal, The, 165
Seven Year Itch, 99
Sharif, Omar, 253
Sharp, Alan, 235
Shaw Artie, 215
Shaw, Charles, 157
Shaw, Irwin, (the Shaws), 127
Shaw, Tom, 207
Sherman, Vincent, 60
Sherwood, Robert, 41, 42
Shumlin, Herman, 46
Sienkiewicz, Henryk, 97
Signac, Paul, 124
Sign of the Cross, The, 15
Simon, John, 248
Sinatra, Frank, (the Sinatras), 159, 196, 217
Sinclair, Upton, 32, 33
Sinful Davey, 135, 224, 225–26, 263
Singleton, Wilfred, 122
Siodmak, Robert, 61
Sirocco, 112, 113
Skouras, Spyros, 92, 157, 163, 172, 184, 190
Slocombe, Douglas, 194
Smith, Oliver, 77
Snake Pit, The, 89
So Little Time, 125
Soma, Enrica, *See* Hutson, Enrica
Some Like It Hot, 99
Song of Russia, 91
Sorel, Guy, 53
Sound of Music, The, 179
Southern, Terry, 219
Sperling, Milton, 151
Spiegel, Sam, 87ff., 93, 102, 107, 109, 113, 115, 122, 123, 159, 192
Staël, Nicholas de, 199

278

279